How to Buy and Manage your own Hotel

Fourth edition

Miles Quest FIH

Peter Nannestad FIH

(G) Goodfellow Publishers Ltd

 Published by Goodfellow Publishers Limited,
Wolvercote, Oxford, OX3 8PS
http://www.goodfellowpublishers.com

British Library Cataloguing in Publication Data: a catalogue record for this title is available from the British Library.
Library of Congress Catalog Card Number: on file.

First published by Northwood Publications in association with Brodie Marshall 1979
Second edition by Hutchinson 1984
In association with Brodie Marshall
Third edition by Brodie Marshall in association with Wordsmith and Company, 1996

This edition first published 2015
ISBN: 978-1-910158-22-7
Copyright © Miles Quest 1979, 1984, 1996, Miles Quest and Peter Nannestad, 2015

 Design and typesetting by P.K. McBride, www.macbride.org.uk

Cover design by Cylinder

Printed by Marston Book Services, www.marston.co.uk

Contents

What is a customer?

"A customer is the most important visitor to our premises.

He is not dependent on us –

We are dependent on him.

He is not an interruption to our work –

He is the purpose of it.

He is not an outsider to our business –

He is part of it.

We are not doing him a favour by serving him –

He is doing us a favour by giving us an opportunity to do so."

- Mahatma Gandhi

Introduction

Many people have a dream of owning their own hotel. This is a book about bringing that dream to reality.

Since the first edition appeared in 1979 there have been two further editions – in 1984 and 1996. Many of the general comments made in the previous editions still hold good today but the hospitality industry has changed significantly even since the last edition was published and there have been many new developments which are covered in this edition – the growth of franchising, the development of the budget hotel sector, the introduction of the internet and social media – the new economic power – are just four. They provide new challenges and opportunities for anyone wishing to buy and manage their own hotel.

Yet the principles of buying a hotel are constant. The difficulty of raising finance for all but the most promising purchase only re-emphasises the importance of accurately assessing the worth of a business and its potential earnings; this makes a sound business plan essential. Without a business plan, the dream will remain just that.

The book aims to take the reader step by step from the time of his initial interest in buying a hotel to the day he takes over – and beyond. The later chapters outline some of the most important challenges that a new owner will face.

Incidentally, throughout the book, we have referred to hoteliers in the masculine but this is only for reasons of literary convenience. Few industries offer so many opportunities to women entrepreneurs and there are many examples of hotels and restaurants which they own and operate very successfully. Long may this last.

After reading this book, some readers may be put off by the thought of buying their own hotel. Others may become more enthusiastic. In either case, the book will have achieved its purpose. Hotelkeeping is an arduous profession requiring considerable technical, managerial, marketing and economic expertise as well as total commitment. It is not for the slothful, the faint-hearted, the impatient or the unenthusiastic. If, after reading it, you still want to buy your own hotel – welcome!

But you have been warned.

Miles Quest

Peter Nannestad

June 2015

Acknowledgements

After over 40 years' experience of the hospitality industry, it is impossible to thank all those who have consciously or unconsciously provided us with the information that has been used in this fourth edition, which has been very largely rewritten and expanded because of the economic and social changes and developments in the industry in the last 20 years.

While we need to thank all those who helped make the previous editions so informative, some specific acknowledgments for this fourth edition are required: Peter Hancock, chief executive of Pride of Britain, for permission to reproduce his article – *Why Become a Hotelier?*; Melvin Gold, hotel industry consultant, for his chapter on franchising and branding (Chapter 3), Adam Lansdown FRICS for his chapter on using the business agent (Chapter 6); and Caroline Murdoch, of Redworks PR, for the chapter on social media and Jeffrey Epstein who made some valuable additions to this chapter – Caroline's top ten PR tips will help guide many a budding hotelier through their press relationships. We must also thank Kumar Muthalagappan, proprietor of the Colwick Hall Hotel, Nottingham for his help and advice in Chapter 7 and for his invaluable Acquisition Check List. Martin Couchman, deputy chief executive, British Hospitality Association, offered much valued advice on legal issues and Barry Fogarty, of Fogarty and Co, advised us on Chapter 12. Bob Cotton, formerly chief executive of the British Hospitality Association, gave timely support.

We are particularly grateful to the leading hoteliers who have provided their own pieces of advice to first-time buyers – James Bowie, Beppo Buchanan-Smith, Bob Cotton OBE, Gavin Ellis, Jeffrey Epstein, Adam Fox-Edwards, Melvin Gold, Graham Grose, Peter Hancock, Tim Hassell, Jonathan Langston, Stephen Mannock, Harry Murray MBE, John Pattin, Tim Rumney and Richard Whitehouse. Their words of wisdom will be found throughout the book.

We also gratefully acknowledge tables and other statistical information from the Best Practice Forum, VisitBritain, The Resource Solution/ VisitEngland, and HotStats. Thanks, also, to Angela MacAusland for drawing the bar charts and other illustrations.

Needless to say, while the contributions generously made for this and previous editions have made the book a far more worthwhile project than would otherwise have been possible, any errors or omissions are entirely of our own making.

1 Hospitality – what's it all about?

Owning a hotel is more than a job or a business – it's a way of life. It means total commitment. You'll need patience and a sense of humour. Be prepared for long and unsocial hours, hard work and ungrateful guests. But the rewards are there for the successful owner.

The hospitality industry

The hospitality industry veers from periods of great prosperity and confidence to periods of recession and gloom - swings which are largely caused by factors outside its control. In 2001, for example, the foot and mouth outbreak led to a severe decline in UK tourism, driving away many overseas visitors while discouraging domestic visitors from staying in the UK for their holidays. To a lesser extent, poor weather can have an impact which is almost as negative, affecting a hotel's chances of picking up chance bookings; a sudden cancellation of a particular event on which local businesses may depend, such as Badminton Horse Trials for example, can destroy local trade for the year in question.

Hoteliers have to recognize that they are frequently at the mercy of external events and influences . . .

. . . the most important being the impact of the general economy on discretionary spend. Unless the traveller is on business (and even here, conference calls and the internet may provide viable alternatives) few overnight stays in a hotel are obligatory. People largely stay in a hotel for leisure purposes and their spend on leisure is usually discretionary.

True, taking holidays and eating-out have become life-style choices so people regularly now expect to take a holiday and to eat out but, especially in times of recession, the consumer is generally wary of spending his money. So if he does take a holiday, he might move from a four star hotel to a three star hotel or perhaps to a budget property; when he eats out, he might have two courses rather than three; lunch-time special offers are now frequently offered by even the most expensive establishments. That all-important factor, consumer confidence, is key to the success of the hospitality industry. When it is missing, trading becomes infinitely more challenging.

It is curious, therefore, that in the period 2002-2014 the hotel industry has undergone the greatest expansion in its history, with over 148,000 new rooms added to UK room stock (although over 40,000 hotel rooms have closed in the same period.)

Table 1.1: Number of new hotel rooms built in the UK, 2002-2014

Type	Number
Budget hotel rooms	87,859
Other hotel rooms	60,305

This would appear to show that the hotel industry can survive a recession remarkably well; indeed, in the case of London, this is certainly true. London room occupancy has averaged over 80 per cent in the five years to 2014 with average achieved room rate at an all-time high in 2012 – Olympic Games Year.

The picture in the provinces is less satisfactory and, as the bulk of the hotel industry is located outside the capital and as this is where most people will buy their own hotel, it's important to recognise that the profitability of provincial hotels is much less than that of their London counterparts.

Average annual occupancy in the provinces usually runs ten points behind that of London . . .

. . . with much higher payroll costs as a percentage of turnover. This is because London hotels, being generally bigger, benefit from the sheer scale of their bedroom operation; their food and beverage departments (which are the most labour intensive) also generally generate a lower proportion of revenue and are comparatively less costly to run than F&B departments in a full service hotel in the provinces where food revenue can be twice as high as a percentage of turnover than in a London property. Most London hotels earn over 70 per cent of their revenue from their rooms whereas the figure for a provincial hotel is between 50-60 per cent.

Of course, some London hotels have major banqueting departments which will hugely increase their revenue from their food and beverage sales but these are exceptions rather than the rule and generally only apply to very large or unique properties.

Table 1.1 also points to another development that has taken place largely in the last decade: the growth of the budget hotel sector. The fact that far more budget hotel rooms have been built in the last decade compared with other hotels should be borne in mind by the potential purchaser.

"If you're looking to buy a hotel, research, research, research. Research your market, research your operational capability and research your finances. And then search your soul to make sure it's the lifestyle you want.

"The hotel industry is renowned for being fragmented, having low barriers to entry (in terms of qualifications to own and manage a hotel) and for being littered with people who set out with the best of intentions only to fail.

"On the positive side there has never been more information available about owning and operating a hotel than there is today. Review sites and online travel portals make it easy to research who's doing well and why, and what they are charging. The industry is full of people who love to talk about their business and share their knowledge and experience. And there is no shortage of well qualified advisors whose experience you can call on to help achieve your goals.

"And, if you do the job well, your guests will spread the word, endorse your position and reinforce your success."

Jonathan Langston
Senior Director, CBRE Hotels, London

Developers clearly believe that there is a bigger market for cheaper, no frills accommodation than for more luxurious full-service properties. This has put pressure on the average three star hotel which retails rooms at £100-£175 per night. Although they hopefully provide a higher standard of service and comfort, many consumers will forego these benefits for a lower price.

The budget sector has even encroached on the corporate market. Businesses and corporations, mindful of cutting expenses in recessionary times, have begun to direct their staff to overnight stays in budget properties as a less expensive alternative to full service hotels, thus chipping away at the traditional market for three and four star hotels.

The influx of over 148,000 new hotel rooms is good as it encourages existing hotels to re-invest, refurbish and expand to meet the challenge of new-built properties. However, unless these new hotels can create a new market for themselves the rooms they bring into play will grab a share of the existing market. This is one of the reasons why provincial occupancy levels are little changed from what they were ten years ago whereas London occupancy levels are so high. The London hotel market is expanding, principally through rising numbers of overseas visitors.

In the fight for business in the provinces, occupancy levels and, even more important, the rate at which the rooms are sold can be severely damaged. When occupancy is weak, hotels will always reduce tariffs to fight off the competition and encourage more business. We have only to look at advertisements for hotel offers in the national dailies to see how groups strategically reduce prices to boost demand at certain times of the year, in certain locations and for specific periods of the week. Of course, reducing room prices means that the revenue per available room (REVpar – the sum of money which every bedroom earns per night – an all important factor) declines. This hits profitability.

Because of a hotel's high fixed costs, a decline in occupancy can lead quickly to a drop in profitability and eventually into loss. Much of a hotel's revenue goes towards covering its high fixed costs. It is only when occupancy reaches breakeven point, which would normally be around 50 per cent (much higher in high cost, luxury properties) that the hotel begins to make a profit.

Hotels are thus always vulnerable to even a small dip in occupancy. Even a drop from 60 per cent to 50 per cent is vastly more serious than it might appear because the loss of income is almost entirely off the bottom line; if a hotel can raise its income above the breakeven point then almost all the additional income goes to profit. Raising revenue, maintaining tariff levels and controlling costs are thus the three key economic elements in managing a hotel successfully.

> **Raising revenue, maintaining tariff levels and controlling costs are thus the three key economic elements in successfully managing a hotel.**

Anyone considering buying a hotel also needs to bear in mind that one of the most significant changes that has affected the potential purchaser is the much tougher lending criteria that banks and other funding institutions now demand.

Gone are the days when banks were willing to lend, reinforced by the thought that capital appreciation would cover any trading problems. Funding, more than ever, is based on the amount of investment that a purchaser can put into the acquisition, the projected turnover and profit, and the means of achieving it and maintaining it. Banks are not interested in equity ownership. Funding now largely depends on the level of the purchaser's own investment. More on this in Chapter 7.

A business – and a lifestyle

When buying a hotel, you are buying a business but a hotel is not for those looking for a comfortable way of life.

On the other hand, few industries provide such an attraction for those who want to own their own business. Owning a hotel has about it a certain glamour and holds out the promise of considerable personal and financial satisfaction.

What's your aim?

Why do people invest in the hotel industry?

Here are five main scenarios.

1   It is a lifestyle decision - you are seeking a change of career and believe that owning and managing a hotel yourself (or with your partner) will provide you with a personally satisfying and profitable business which you can develop into the future under your own management and leadership. You are not looking for an exit strategy.

2   You expect that it will give you long-term security. You are attracted to the idea of managing a hotel yourself and to dealing with guests and you are not looking for a quick exit strategy as you see the purchase as a medium to long-term acquisition. You believe a freehold property should appreciate in value over the term of your ownership.

3   You have been to hotel school and have experience of working in the hotel industry and see the opportunity of owning and managing your own hotel as a natural career progression. You believe that your experience will stand you in good stead for ownership and you are already familiar with the issues involved in managing a hotel. This is a medium to long-term commitment which you see as completing your career in the industry so you are not seeking a short-term exit strategy.

4   You are looking for a self-employment opportunity with the promise of a much higher income than you can achieve in employment, and you believe that buying a hotel will enable you to achieve this with a good return on the capital invested. You see a hotel purchase as a business opportunity. You have funding and an exit strategy in place and, although you will take a keen interest in the operation and development of the hotel, you intend to install a manager to run it on a day-to-day basis. You will consider franchising the property and you aim to build up business for an exit within five years.

5   This is an investment decision. You have funds to invest in the purchase of a hotel but you are more concerned with the hotel as a long-term business opportunity than as a lifestyle activity. If the opportunity arose, you would consider buying another property. The hotel's success must match any other investment decision you might make. You will consider franchising the property.

The glamour certainly exists. There is something intensely theatrical about operating a hotel. New and often surprising events occur every day bringing the owner into contact with people, some of them famous, from many different walks of life. There are many examples of businessmen who have come into the industry by buying their own hotel and secured for themselves a happy and prosperous second or third career. However, the glamour can certainly wear off.

Are you a leader or a manager?

Operating a hotel is primarily a management job – you have to manage people and circumstances. *In other words, you have to get job done effectively through other people.*

But it's also about leadership – you may have to change the direction of the hotel and lead it into new markets. The difference between management and leadership is frequently discussed but they are part of the same function: a manager can lead and a leader can manage.

Leadership can be transformational. It's more about vision and innovation; charting a new direction and spearheading new avenues of endeavour and ensuring that they are reached. Management is more about the control and direction of systems and processes that have already been established through the staff employed. A good manager can maintain direction but only the best manager will be able to change it.

In buying your hotel you have to recognise the two roles because no business depends more on the staff it employs. Leading your people to follow you will be the ultimate key to your success. That implies both qualities of leadership, and management skills.

The 21 Indispensable Qualities of a Leader by John C Maxwell (Thomas Nelson) is a first-rate guide.

Operating a hotel can mean long hours and hard work; it also means dealing with people.

If you have never dealt with people face-to-face regularly before, be prepared: they can be critical, irritating, mean-spirited and thanklessly demanding. Your guests will rarely consider your feelings and comfort so don't expect them to respect your privacy and leisure time, either. They will not want to leave the bar at midnight even though you might be dropping off to sleep, nor will they want to know that you have to get up at 6.00 am the next morning maybe to cook and serve breakfast because the chef is ill. One hotelier, leaving a jug of iced water in the room for her American guests, was rung up in the early hours to be asked if it was drinkable. You may well consider yourself mine host – some of your guests will regard you as

1

their servant. At the end of their stay some of them may try to walk off with your towels, your bathrobes, even your toilet rolls, and then write a disobliging piece on TripAdvisor.

Too gloomy? Talk to any hotelier and he will be able to tell you stories far worse than these few examples. To be able to cope with the pressures and aggravation that operating a hotel generates you need to have a powerful sense of humour and a deep conviction that this is a job for you. You won't be able to please everyone all the time, but at least you must want to try.

And beware: if this is your first venture into the hotel industry, be realistic.

It's a common failing for newcomers to underestimate the start-up and purchase costs of a hotel, and the returns that are available on your investment. Owning a hotel is rarely a fast-track to wealth creation. And owning your own business carries its own responsibilities – to your lending institution, your family, your staff and your guests.

However, if you can come to terms with the unpredictable nature of the business as well as the often unreasonable demands of the public then the hospitality industry can offer a life that is highly enjoyable and enormously satisfying. Hotelkeeping is an intensely personal activity in which the hotelier expresses his own personality through his hotel and through the way he operates it. And because he is in constant touch with his guests, unlike the manufacturer of nuts and bolts who never sees his customers, he is able to build up a relationship with them that satisfies some basic human instinct.

And it is, of course, about making money.

This can only be achieved if the hotel attracts certain markets; it must continue to do so or attract profitable new markets if it is to survive. If the hotel loses out it becomes just another building and there are plenty of hotels which are just that – buildings that have been converted to apartments, residential accommodation, care homes or have just been demolished,

A hotel's success comes from people wanting to stay with you. How do you ensure that they do? More about this in later chapters.

Why become a hotelier?

This article, which appeared in Hotel Owner *magazine, is written by Peter Hancock, an experienced hotelier who is chief executive of Pride of Britain, a consortium of some 30-plus privately owned, luxury four and five star hotels.*

What is it that compels a sane, intelligent person with a variety of useful skills to want to own a hotel? Let's face it, there are easier ways to make a living as we all know. Having observed good and bad hoteliers at close quarters throughout my working life, I continue to be surprised by this strange career choice, given the endless pitfalls it offers to all but the most successful.

For some the die is cast before they are out of nappies. Inheriting a family-owned hotel accounts for a large number of today's operators and a few of them have gone on to develop their businesses with even greater aplomb than their forebears. Hotel-keeping is in their blood. It's what they were destined to do and they infect everyone who works for them with their passion for delivering great hospitality.

The majority of hotel owners, however, have come into the business for other reasons, many having acquired the necessary capital through success in a completely unrelated field. What possesses them to risk all when they could opt for a quiet life playing the stock market or growing orchids?

One possible answer is the prospect of asset appreciation which, in good times, puts a safety blanket under any hotel enterprise that makes some profit or sits on a desirable plot. Bricks and mortar have long been seen as a safe investment, with a profitable business the icing on the cake. That must have been the view of banks who lent to von Essen* during the late 1990s, the error of which has now come back to haunt them.

Owning a hotel offers the prospect of a degree of freedom denied to those of us who work as employees. The freedom to arrange things in one's own way, to express one's personality in the décor, to create a menu like no other and, best of all, to have no boss

---

*The von Essen group comprising some 35 mainly country house hotels, went into administration in 2011 with debts of £300m.

1

to answer to (husband and wife partnerships may dispute that last bit). The point is this: an owner is master of his or her destiny in a way that no company executive could hope to be.

A third category is perhaps represented by those who genuinely believe that operating a hotel is an absolute doddle and will be far more relaxing than the work they have done hitherto. That such people exist is a tribute to good hoteliers everywhere who manage to make it look so easy. My friend Harry Murray, now chairman of Lucknam Park in Wiltshire, told me that as GM at The Imperial, Torquay during its golden years, he was frequently accosted by guests who wanted their sons to emulate him and run large hotels themselves.

All they had witnessed, of course, was Harry in his dinner suit calmly gliding around the place smiling and chatting with guests. What they had not seen was the intense work and stress behind the scenes. The unreliable staff who had to be sacked, the broken boiler that had to be replaced pronto, the cancelled group booking leaving a hole in the finances, the stroppy chef refusing to accede to a bride's eccentric choice of food, a local competitor dropping its rates unexpectedly, a mad dash to complete some refurbishment or repairs before the rooms are occupied and endless similar challenges.

In this respect I believe the hotel trade is akin to the world of show-business. What the customer sees, if the 'performance' is done well, masks a whole lot of stress off stage from casting to rehearsals, with plenty of tears along the way. It looks easy enough to fool the thousands who audition for the X-Factor into thinking they can sing or dance their way to stardom too. As we know, most can't.

If there is one quality that great hoteliers share, it is the ability to see the big picture, to get out and notice what others are doing, to be engaged with the wider industry and thereby to keep their own business evolving. Those who make themselves indispensable in the office or kitchen or behind the bar tend to stagnate – they wear themselves out and do not see opportunities to improve their business. This can happen very easily, especially when trying to keep the payroll down, to the point when the owner hasn't time to plan ahead, let alone to go out and find new inspiration. Remember, it was as a customer that the concept of becoming a hotelier was first formed, so it follows that the next good idea might also be gleaned while staying as a customer elsewhere.

By far the best reason for owning or indeed working in a hotel is to do with one's personality. Liking people and wanting to please them comes naturally to some. You can see it in their expressions when greeting guests – they actually take pleasure from providing hospitality and delight in hearing positive comments, rather as a performer delights in hearing applause. Almost no other industry provides this.

There now follows a confession. I am often asked by friends and associates whether I would ever aspire to own a hotel myself. After all, years as both a manager and marketing man would seem to be the ideal preparation for such a move and I have been lucky enough to watch some of the best in the business, so know a fair amount about what it takes to succeed. The truth is that I lack the entrepreneurial fearlessness required, quite apart from the small difficulty of persuading my wife we should borrow a seven figure sum. The willingness to take risks is ultimately what separates owners from the rest of us and always will.

Before making your decision, remember. . . .

1 Holidays and eating-out have become lifestyle choices for many, but the hospitality industry is at the mercy of many external influences, particularly economic.

2 Over 148,000 new rooms have been added to the UK hotel industry since 2000 – and all are competitors. Over 60 per cent of these are budget hotels.

3 The continuing increase in the budget hotel sector poses a real threat to middle-market independent hotels.

4 London has the highest average room occupancy – hotels in the provinces are some ten percentage points lower.

5 Bank lending into the hospitality industry has become much more difficult to arrange – it'll be your biggest challenge.

6 Be clear about *why* you want to buy a hotel.

7 A hotel is both a business and a total commitment – don't ignore the latter!

8 Are you sure you can lead any necessary transformation of the business?

9 Can you cope with the public?

10 Can you cope with the industry's unreasonably long and unsocial hours?

"When I first joined the family business I remember my father telling me that I had to find an interest or hobby outside of the hotel. What with a young family and the 24/7 nature of the hotel business I thought there wasn't much time for recreation. As usual he was right. Unless you make a point of taking time off to do something you really enjoy, the hotel will suck you dry. I tried a few things until I discovered horse riding and hunting to hounds on Dartmoor. Most Tuesdays in the winter I go hunting. One thing is for certain: you can't be thinking about work problems when you're charging over the moor risking life and limb!"

Graham Grose
Managing Director, Thurlestone Hotel, Devon

2 Some basic facts

"Remember - not everyone likes Marmite!

"Taking your first steps into being a hotelier is exciting. Many will have started with research, stayed in many hotels and will be brimming over with ideas and enthusiasm, But guard against your enthusiasm carrying you off down the wrong road.

"The most successful owners are the ones who have sought great advice from other hoteliers, professional consultants or management companies. This advice will aid you to set your vision and will help you separate personal preferences from professional decisions.

"That vision should have a splash of your personality in it - that's your USP - but it should not be dominated by it. You are creating a unique product that your guests will seek out, book, stay in, judge and then, when they have consumed it, pay for it. Not every guest will be 100 per cent happy but as long as your vision has been built on solid foundations of market research and feasibility then stick to your vision. This is because - as we know - not everyone likes Marmite!"

Stephen Mannock
General Manager, The King's Head, Cirencester

This is a chapter of facts and figures. Don't be deterred. It's important to know something about the hospitality industry and some key facts about managing a hotel before you begin your search and this chapter aims to provide a general picture of the industry's size, its structure and some of the key operating hotel data.

The size of the hospitality industry is impressive. Depending on which source you use, it employs over 2m people in all the various sectors – hotels, restaurants, pubs, retail and leisure services, contract catering, catering in schools, hospitals and business and industry. The hotel sector (which includes bed and breakfasts and guest houses) is, in fact, one of the smallest sectors with just over 300,000 employees whereas the restaurant sector (restaurants, takeaway food shops, pubs, clubs and bars) employs over 1.2m and other catering outlets employ a further 750,000.

How many hotels?

There is no all-inclusive register of serviced accommodation in the UK so the total number of rooms and beds in the country is difficult to calculate because of the lack of definition and clear statistics. Table 2.1 is compiled by Melvin Gold Consulting and combines the number of hotels with guest houses, B&Bs and youth hostels but excludes university accommodation, all types of self-catering and most residential training centres and serviced apartments.

The definition of a hotel also varies according to the source used and the difference between a hotel, private hotel, guest house and bed and breakfast establishment has become blurred (but see Chapter 4).

Table 2.1: Serviced accommodation by region, end-2013. Source: Melvin Gold Consulting

Region	Bedrooms
North East	20,166
North West	94,788
Yorkshire/Humberside	47,122
East Midlands	36,190
West Midlands	47,394
East of England	43,707
Greater London	131,056
South East	92,034
South West	85,076
ENGLAND	597,532
SCOTLAND	84,711
WALES	36,353
NORTHERN IRELAND	11,662
	730,258

London has by far the greatest number of bedrooms and taking all rooms into account the average size of hotel in the UK is in the region of 16 rooms, although the average size budget property is nearer 80 rooms; this is because most budget hotels have been built in the last decade and are branded or franchised properties which demand a greater number of rooms to be economically viable. In Table 2.2 we present an estimate of the sector in 2013 by size of property.

The industry is clearly dominated by small hotels and guest houses; 60 per cent of all establishments have under 10 rooms – a figure which rises to nearly 90 per cent if hotels under 25 rooms are included. The hotel industry is truly a small unit industry.

It is estimated that 53 per cent of the total number of hotels in the UK remain in independent hands, but this figure is reducing as almost all new-build hotels are company-owned and operated and many are franchised. The competition which these branded units provide is having a profound effect on the independent sector, forcing it to refurbish and modernise and to be more aggressive in its promotional activities and pricing policies. The independent hotel, competing against the branded property with world-wide web-based marketing and sales programmes and online booking facilities, cannot afford to relax.

Table 2.2: Hotels by number of rooms, 2013. Source: Melvin Gold Consulting

Establishment	Size (rooms)	Number	Bedrooms	Average no. of rooms
Hotel	200+	339	106,734	315
Hotel	101-200	1,141	156,943	138
Hotel	51-100	1,892	135,525	72
Hotel	26-50	2,357	86,395	37
Hotel	11-25	6,300	100,000	16
Other – small hotels, guest houses, B&B, etc. (estimated)	Typically up to 10	32,971	144,661	4
TOTAL		**45,000**	**730,258**	**16**

One particular economic fact about the state of the hospitality industry is the growth of group-owned hotels since the 1990s, when the industry's 30 largest companies accounted for less than 15 per cent of room capacity; in 2013, the ten largest companies accounted for over 240,448 rooms or 33 per cent. Admittedly, not all these rooms are actually operated by the companies concerned. Almost every Holiday Inn, for example, is run by a franchisee of InterContinental Hotels (IHG) but the branding effectively makes all 130+ Holiday Inns in the UK one company in the eyes of the public. The level of investment in branded hotels such as Premier Inn, Travelodge, various brands of Holiday Inn including Holiday Inn Express, Days Inn and others is an even greater influence on the industry than their share of the market would imply. They set the pace for the rest of the industry to follow.

Table 2.1 also shows that many hotels and guest houses in the UK are located in coastal regions or holiday areas such as the South West, South East and North West, and it is in these regions that many first-time buyers will seek to find their hotel.

However, many of these areas of the country face the toughest trading conditions, particularly in relation to seasonality, and will probably continue to do so. Some resorts have invested and the strongest, such as Brighton, Bournemouth and Torquay, have recognised the opportunities presented by conference business; even so, it is noticeable that the major political parties hold as many conferences in cities such as Manchester and Birmingham as in resorts which were traditionally the most popular venues. The reason for this may well be because of aggressive pricing on the part of city centre hotels, keen to fill their rooms, but it is also true that these cities now have many more large, new-build hotels than resorts and their hotels can offer a more consistent, up-to-date product, with every delegate being offered the same size room – an important consideration for many conference organisers.

Manchester, for example has opened over 26 new hotels in the last decade but Bournemouth only three. City centre hotels can also offer a much greater choice of restaurants and other attractions.

What people spend on holiday and on business in the UK

The success of most independent hotels will depend on their ability to grow the domestic market - but this is at a time when overseas holiday destinations have stolen a major portion of the UK long-stay holiday market. Although the one- or two-week domestic holiday market is still important to the UK hotel industry, the short holiday market (1-3 nights) is growing and is now just as big while the domestic long holiday market has been declining for the last 30 years in tandem with the growth in the overseas holiday market. In fact, far more money is spent on holidays and business visits overseas than in the UK, highlighting the difficulty faced by those hotels that used to depend on the domestic week or fortnight holiday; an increasing number of these holidays are now taken overseas.

However, the short break market, while growing, is as vulnerable to economic pressure as long holidays.

People might well decide that they cannot afford a long holiday but they might also sacrifice a second or third short holiday when times are tough. This highlights the industry's dependence on discretionary spending. Cutbacks affect choice; they affect hotels and those areas of the country depending on domestic holidays are particularly vulnerable. This is especially so as most overseas visitors tend to visit (and stay in) London rather than venture too far away from the well-trodden tourist trail of London-Stratford-York-Edinburgh. Tourist agencies are spending considerable sums of money trying to encourage overseas visitors away from London, but the fact remains that over 50 per cent of overseas visitor spend is in London, which is in sharp contrast to the South West, where it is only five per cent.

In growing overseas demand London will always be the main attraction, so it follows that the success of any hotel purchased outside the capital will be more dependent on attracting domestic visitors than those from overseas. This is not to deny that some parts of the country are more successful than others in attracting overseas visitors, but most UK provincial hotels will depend on the domestic market for the bulk of their business.

The critical importance of the domestic market is highlighted by the barely 10 per cent share which London enjoys. London is popular with British people for a short – mainly weekend stay – which is worth some £2bn to the capital's hotels, but they spend over £4.29bn in the South West, a further £2.46bn in the North West and £1.79bn in Yorkshire and Humberside (Figure 1).

The shift away from long holidays in the UK towards short holidays means that hoteliers have to work that much harder to maintain profitability. This explains the heavy short-break promotional advertising in the national dailies by major brands – a development that emphasises just how crowded and competitive the domestic market has become. The tendency to book later, often within a week of arrival, has also led to the leisure market becoming far less predictable than it was while the weather influences late booking patterns.

The corporate market

If leisure is a key sector of the UK market, a sector that cannot be overlooked is the business or corporate market. The corporate market comprises expenditure by business people travelling around the country as well as corporate meetings, conferences and events held in hotels. The business guest spends approximately £105 per night,while the short-stay holiday guest spends only £62 (2013 figures). A hotel's mix of business is therefore critically important. The business market is clearly higher spend and more profitable but it is more difficult to attract because every new hotel is also aiming for that market. Unsurprisingly, this market can be as badly hit by an economic recession as the leisure sector. Overnight stays are either abandoned in favour of conference calls or staff are instructed to downgrade from four and three star hotels (many of which are in the independent sector) to group-owned budget hotels.

It's no coincidence that the major budget groups have made a play for the corporate market – and both Travelodge and Premier Inn have corporate credit cards and business accounts which aim to boost their share of the corporate market. This is a trend which is increasingly likely to impact on the independent hotelier.

The business traveller represents the main source of revenue for many city and town centre hotels from Monday to Thursday night, leaving the hotel potentially empty at weekends – hence the emphasis on reduced tariff weekend leisure breaks. However, during the week, demand may not be so great that the hotel is able to charge the price it wants and some price cutting may be necessary even then – bulk bookers of rooms, such as conference organisers, can hold a particularly strong hand.

Responding to a downturn in business with tariff cuts is certainly one way to boost trade and is widely practised, but it needs to be handled with great care and demands a precise knowledge of costs.

Part of the corporate market, and a further important source of revenue to many hotels, is the seminar, meetings and conference market. Surveys suggest that there are over 1.3m conferences/meetings every year with more than 60 per cent spent in hotels. However, conference organisers are now as aggressive in their negotiations as other corporate buyers and price/value is now the key consideration for the buyer, followed by location and access (car parking) with increasing importance – independents should note – being placed on the brand. Very often, the cheapest quote is accepted by clients.

The future of the conference and events markets is inextricably linked to the level of business activity in the general economy. Here, the small independent hotel with fewer than 15 rooms, unless it is well located or has a unique advantage in terms of style or ambience, will gain little from this sector of the market.

Conference buyers tend to go towards larger hotels with more facilities, including separate meeting rooms and maybe leisure facilities. However, those organising smaller meetings of a more exclusive nature might well opt for an exclusive deal with an independent hotel providing it has sufficient rooms and can offer good food and other facilities.

Don't forget, over half of all meetings and conferences are made up of fewer than 25 delegates.

Expensive to introduce, spas tend to act more as a marketing tool to buyers than as an essential facility for guests. Attractive as they are to corporate buyers, experience shows that few conference delegates actually take advantage of a health spa. For many guests, a spa will act as an attractive amenity but not as a key element in the decision to book at that hotel. The cost of introducing it will typically need to be covered by an individual membership scheme for local users and the investment and space required for these facilities is generally beyond that of most independent owners of small properties.

A niche market for some independent hotels, particularly country house properties, is the creation of a thriving restaurant and bar trade – examined more closely in Chapter 17.

But which market are you in?

It's important that the independent hotelier knows which market (or markets) he is aiming at and focuses on it, so that he optimises his chances of success. In truth, most hotels target a number of different markets at the same time, aiming at both the leisure and corporate market; others target the corporate and weddings market; yet others see themselves primarily as a conference and meetings hotel.

> **It's important that the independent hotelier knows which market (or markets) he is aiming at and focuses on it, so that he optimises his chances of success.**

Some of the markets, however, do not easily sit side-by-side with each other.

Most weddings, for example, usually take place on a Saturday and even in a bigger hotel, other guests are not usually best pleased to find that a wedding party has taken over the hotel's main restaurant and other public facilities for the evening. Trying to accommodate both markets at the same time can lead to friction and customer dissatisfaction even if it is carefully handled.

2

In the final analysis, the choice of which market is most appropriate for a hotel depends on its location, its facilities, its standard - and its owner.

Knowing a hotel's precise market is a key to its success because that influences – indeed, should dictate – the facilities provided, the training the staff is given, the investment made in the facilities and the standards set. Budget hotels, for example, are successful precisely because they know which market they are in.

Adding value, such as free wif fi for example, can thus be an important marketing development but it needs to be carefully handled. The cost of introducing the new facility must be balanced against the resulting gain in additional custom, greater customer satisfaction and larger resulting market share. As always, it is a question of keeping up with customer needs. The hotelier who does not keep pace with his customers' needs is on the slippery slope to insolvency.

As always, it is a question of keeping up with customer needs. The hotelier who does not keep pace with his customers' needs is on the slippery slope to insolvency.

The need to keep up with customer needs is highlighted by a report published by HVS, an international hotel consultancy, which emphasised how dangerous it is for hotels to fail to adapt to new guest demands, which are entirely different to those of previous generations.

"It seems that many hotels have barely changed over the last decades, still consisting of the same in-room amenities, the same heavy curtains, the same check-in process, and the same small desk. This is no longer a place where the modern-day traveller feels at home.

"This new segment of traveller is no longer looking for white-linen service, bellboys to carry their luggage up to their room or a concierge. When the current generation of young travellers enters a hotel, they want to feel completely at home, connected and to be in a setting where they can be part of an experience.

"They are much more satisfied with a hotel lobby they can sit in and drink coffee surrounded by other people, than having a coffee machine in their room.

"Lobbies, for example, are becoming larger, more open social hubs and gathering spaces, with a mix of comfortable couches, communal workstations and meeting spaces. Formal divisions between the lobby, restaurant and bars are also disappearing with guests able to sit where they like or help themselves to what they want.

"Rooms are changing too, with many lifestyle hotels having smaller rooms as guests spend more time in social places.

"Hotel service is becoming more intuitive and casual, albeit with the same level of respect. Some hotels are abandoning uniforms and the days of scripting responses to guests are over.

"Guests are looking for a home-away-from-home."

Not all these changing trends can be implemented by every hotel nor, indeed, would that be desirable but it is the wise hotelier who recognises how subtly customer tastes are changing and the impact they make on his product and services. The independent hotelier cannot ignore the changes in consumer needs that eventually might engulf him.

How international tourism is growing

Despite its cyclical nature, the number of international arrivals has risen consistently in the last 30 years and breached 1bn in 2012, worth over US$1trillion. The annual forecast growth to 2030 is 3.3 per cent per year with Europe attracting over half of all tourist arrivals. This implies 43m additional international travellers in Europe every year of which the UK should be able to attract its fair share.

There is no doubt that tourism and hospitality remains one of the most important growth industries in the world and will remain so.

In international terms, leisure tourism has grown dramatically. By 2014, the number of visitors to Britain (34.8m) had overtaken the 2007 peak of 32.8m. However, as we have seen, the regions do not benefit as significantly as London and UK tourism cannot be complacent.

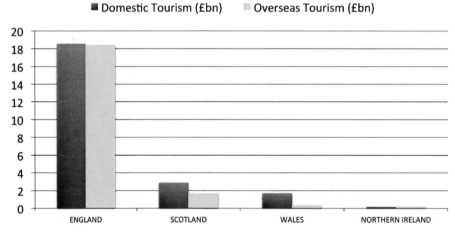

Figure 2.1: What the UK earns from domestic and overseas tourism (2013). England clearly is the most popular destination for both overseas and domestic tourism. Source GBTS/NITB

Hotels and guest houses are just one segment of the accommodation market. In the domestic business market, competition comes from conference centres, training centres and similar institutions. In the leisure market, visiting friends and relations, self catering, caravanning and camping and boating provide the greatest competition.

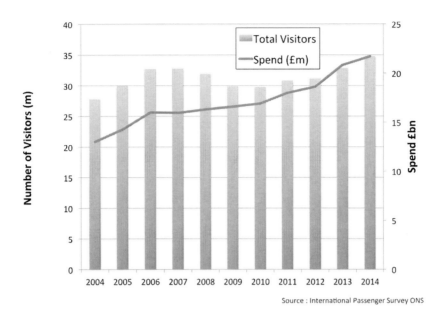

Source : International Passenger Survey ONS

Figure 2.2: Overseas visitors numbers and spend, UK (2004-2014). The impact of the 2008-12 recession is shown in the bars (overseas visitor arrivals) though spend, which is not discounted for inflation (the graph line), continued upwards.

But not everyone stays in a hotel!

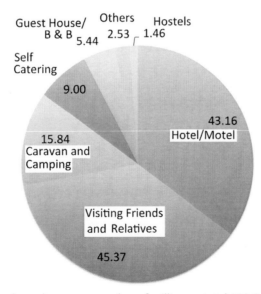

Numbers shown are number of millions – total 122.8m trips

Figure 2.3: Where British people spend their holidays in Great Britain – by total number of trips, 2013 (m). Source: VisitBritain

The business market is largely concentrated in the hotel sector, whereas hotels have much more competition in the leisure market. Hotels must therefore, either expand the leisure market to grow their share or take a share away from other, mainly self-catering, sectors. As these figures have not changed significantly in the last four decades, except for the growth of short holidays at the expense of longer holidays, the independent hotelier has to recognise that his competition comes not only from other hotels but other forms of holiday-taking and, indeed, other forms of consumer spend.

Which are the most popular regions?

London is by far the most popular destination for overseas visitors (Table 2.4); this picture is reversed for the domestic market (Table 2.3). For the domestic market London is thus very much a short stay destination of 2.4 nights whereas overseas visitors spend nearly six nights per visit in the capital.

The South West is the most popular destination for British residents, reflecting the region's popularity as a domestic holiday destination with Scotland, the North West (mainly Cumbria) and the South East also rated highly. The South East is the second most popular region for overseas visitors with Scotland third. London is by far the UK's most profitable hotel market. However, even London comprises a number of different markets, for example the West End and Mayfair, Knightsbridge and Kensington, the City and east London, outer London; not all of them react in the same way to market conditions.

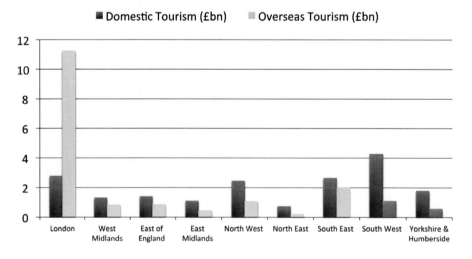

Figure 2.4: What the regions earn from domestic and overseas tourism (2013). The chart highlights the dominance of overseas tourism to London (actual figures appear in Table 2.3) while the South West is the most important region for domestic tourism.
Source: GBTS/International Passenger Survey

Table 2.3: The most popular regions for domestic holidays, 2013. Source: GBTS/NITB

	Trips (m)	Nights (m)	Spend £bn)
	2013	**2013**	**2013**
ENGLAND			
London	12.31	27.29	2.79
West Midlands	9.02	20.71	1.32
East of England	8.96	27.29	1.41
East Midlands	7.89	20.91	1.10
North West	13.98	35.82	2.46
North East	3.90	10.96	.749
South East	17.93	49.77	2.65
South West	19.40	74.28	4.29
Yorkshire & Humberside	10.01	27.83	1.79
ENGLAND	**103.40**	**294.86**	**18.56**
SCOTLAND	**12.12**	**42.73**	**2.89**
WALES	**9.9**	**33.70**	**1.70**
NORTHERN IRELAND	**2.0**	**4.60**	**.19**
TOTAL	**127.42**	**375.89**	**23.34**

Note: Sums may not add up to totals due to rounding up.

Table 2.4: The most popular regions for overseas visitors, 2013. Sources: VisitBritain/IPS

	Trips (m)	Nights (m)	Spend (£bn)
	2013	**2013**	**2013**
ENGLAND			
London	16.784	97.439	11.256
West Midlands	1.869	14.796	.844
East of England	2.006	14.289	.873
East Midlands	1.077	9.160	.459
North West	2.415	17.100	1.076
North East	.431	3.398	.208
South East	4.587	31.820	2.000
South West	2.230	18.577	1.097
Yorkshire & Humberside	1.220	10.391	.584
ENGLAND	**32.619**	**216.975**	**18.397**
SCOTLAND	**2.443**	**19.361**	**1.680**
WALES	**.884**	**5.932**	**.353**
NORTHERN IRELAND	**.366**	**2.133**	**.208**
TOTAL	**36.312**	**244.401**	**20.638**

Note: Sums may not add up to totals due to rounding up.

Room occupancy

One of the most significant ratios in the hotel industry is room occupancy

– the number of nights a hotel's rooms are occupied expressed as a percentage of the total number of rooms. It is noticeable (Table 2.5) that although London's average occupancy has risen by nearly seven percentage points since 2003, that of England has risen only marginally; Scotland, too, has done well as has Wales, though by only two percentage points.

Table 2.5: Annual average room occupancy, 2003-2013. Source: HotStats

	2003	2004	2005	2006	2007	2008	2009	2010	2011	2012	2013
London	74.3	77.8	76.7	82.5	81.0	79.8	79.3	82.1	81.4	81.1	81.7
English regions	68.9	70.3	69.3	69.5	69.2	67.5	65.3	67.9	68.9	69.5	70.6
Scotland	69.1	72.0	72.5	73.6	74.3	73.3	72.1	73.4	73.6	73.8	76.0
Wales	72.2	71.2	71.2	73.7	74.2	71.7	71.3	69.2	69.1	71.4	74.2

Using a different sample of hotels, not only does occupancy vary according to region (Table 2.6), and by location (Table 2.7), it also varies according to property size (Table 2.8), by property type (Table 2.9) and by period of the week (Table 2.10).

Table 2.6: Room occupancy by English regions (%), 2010-2014. Source: The Research Solution on behalf of VisitEngland

	2010	2011	2012	2013	2014
East Midlands	56	67	63	65	64
Yorkshire	55	60	60	64	67
London	79	82	80	82	82
North West	56	56	58	61	61
East of England	57	61	61	64	67
West Midlands	58	63	63	65	68
South West	56	63	65	68	64
South East	56	63	65	68	70
North East	51	65	56	58	59
ENGLAND	**62**	**66**	**66**	**68**	**69**

Table 2.7: Room occupancy by location, England (%), 2010-2014. Source: The Research Solution on behalf of VisitEngland

	2010	2011	2012	2013	2014
Seaside	54	56	57	60	61
City/large town	70	73	73	77	78
Small town	55	61	63	65	65
Countryside	53	57	55	59	58

Table 2.8 highlights the much higher occupancy rates of larger hotels, explained partly by the fact that most large hotels have increasingly sophisticated and successful marketing and sales promotion programmes; in addition, most are based in London or other major cities where occupancy is higher (Table 2.5).

Generally speaking smaller hotels, guest houses and B&Bs (Tables 2.8 and 2.9), which are almost always independently owned, have to work much harder than hotels to fill their rooms.

Occupancy is also lower in the winter months in most parts of the UK, dropping to 40-50 per cent in January and February – even less in some resort hotels many of which, indeed, might close during the winter.

Table 2.8: Room occupancy by property size, England (%), 2010-2014 . Source: The Research Solution on behalf of VisitEngland

	2010	2011	2012	2013	2014
1-3 rooms	41	41	40	41	43
4-10 rooms	49	49	48	50	51
11-25 rooms	56	57	56	59	61
26-50 rooms	64	62	65	69	69
51-100 rooms	69	69	70	69	66
100+ rooms	68	75	74	76	78

Table 2.9: Room occupancy by property type, England (%), 2010-2014. Source: The Research Solution on behalf of VisitEngland

	2010	2011	2012	2013	2014
Hotel	64	68	69	72	73
Guest House	52	54	54	54	55
B&B	47	49	48	49	51

Table 2.10: Room occupancy by period of week, England (%), 2010-2014. Source: The Research Solution on behalf of VisitEngland

	2010	2011	2012	2013	2014
Weekday	61	68	67	70	71
Weekend	59	63	63	65	66

The inevitable conclusion is that smaller hotels and guest houses have greater difficulty in filling their rooms and those in the seaside and countryside have the greatest difficulty of all. When forecasting income for a hotel, it's important that the hotelier is realistic and recognises these average occupancy figures. No potential purchaser should ever assume he will be 100 per cent full all the time.

Occupancy rates do not tell the whole story and should be treated with some caution.

An equally important statistic is the rate at which the occupied rooms have been sold (Average Room Rate - ARR); the combination of the two is reflected in Revenue per

Available Room (REVPar). However, it is true to say that the lower the occupancy, the lower the REVPar is likely to be and vice versa.

ARR is calculated by dividing the net room revenue (exclusive of breakfast + VAT + other inclusive items such as dinner) by the number of rooms let; REVpar is calculated by dividing the room revenue by the number of rooms available for sale. ARR provides the average income per let room – a key trend figure which shows annual growth in room revenues. REVpar shows the average annual room revenue if all the hotel's rooms are let, not the number of occupied rooms. Why is this important? Because it indicates the success of the hotel in filling rooms at all times of the year – in the low season when tariffs are low and in the peak season when demand and tariffs are higher.

Both of these figures are important but for the independent hotelier, the ARR which gives the average amount of money earned per room per sale is critically important. The figure will undoubtedly be below the 'rack' or published tariff because even a small hotel will have to discount the room charges on occasions due to competition, commission and seasonal factors. The rack rate represents the most optimistic level of revenue; the ARR shows the reality and should always be used when it comes to budgeting. It should be noted that many major London and city centre hotels now operate computer-based yield management systems which automatically adjust the price of rooms according to demand.

In preparing cash flow forecasts and budgets, hoteliers should not forget the impact on total revenues of the cost of commission on credit card sales as well as more serious payments to commissionable internet sales agents (commission on rooms is a direct cost, while commission on credit card is viewed as an indirect cost.) Chapters 6 and 9 explain this in more detail.

Table 2.11: Average Achieved Room Rate (£), 2004-2013. Source: HotStats

	2004	2005	2006	2007	2008	2009	2010	2011	2012	2013
London	96.16	102.53	113.43	127.78	129.24	122.70	123.32	133.51	146.04	145.24
England	57.90	60.30	63.10	65.82	65.76	62.66	66.75	67.79	67.51	68.36
Scotland	58.20	65.30	68.40	72.68	72.71	69.91	74.34	76.61	81.63	86.21
Wales	60.66	60.30	63.10	67.76	67.22	66.02	67.78	69.17	68.21	68.45

Table 2.12: Revenue per Available Room (REVPar) (£), 2004 -2013. Source: HotStats

	2004	2005	2006	2007	2008	2009	2010	2011	2012	2013
London	74.77	78.64	93.58	103.54	103.10	97.32	101.20	108.66	117.03	118.58
England	40.72	41.82	44.49	45.52	44.33	40.92	45.32	46.72	46.41	48.29
Scotland	42.31	48.26	51.56	54.02	53.28	50.44	54.53	56.37	59.73	65.54
Wales	43.19	43.10	45.01	50.26	48.23	46.94	46.90	47.79	48.54	50.82

What other key figures?

Table 2.13 gives the distribution of average revenue and expenses compiled by HotStats from a sample of over 500 full service hotels.

Table 2.13: Percentage distribution of revenue and expenses, 2013. Source: HotStats

	London 2013	England 2013	Scotland 2013	Wales 2013
REVENUE				
Rental and other income	2.6	2.5	2.6	3.3
Other departments	5.4	12.0	11.1	18.9
Beverage	6.5	10.4	9.9	11.7
Food	13.5	22.1	20.6	24.4
Rooms	72.0	53.0	55.7	41.7
EXPENSES				
Energy	2.9	5.4	4.7	5.8
Property operations and maintenance	2.7	2.9	2.7	2.5
Sales and marketing	2.8	3.7	3.7	3.2
Beverage	1.4	2.6	2.5	3.0
Administration and general	4.4	6.1	5.5	4.5
Food	3.6	6.5	6.0	6.9
Departmental expenses	10.5	11.6	11.0	11.7
Minor department cost of sales	1.0	1.7	2.0	3.4
Payroll and related expenses	24.2	32.1	31.4	35.9
Gross operating profit	**45.8**	**27.4**	**30.5**	**23.0**

Many hotels in the capital are basically 'rooming factories', providing a room and breakfast but little else for guests who will seek food and other entertainment elsewhere in the city. As a result, payroll costs as a percentage in London are lower than for England, Scotland or Wales where they take up almost one third of all income generated and in individual cases may be much higher.

Because of all these advantages, Gross Operating Profit is almost 20 percentage points higher in London which is, of course, reflected in the much higher price of London hotels when they come up for sale. The table also gives the average cost of other operating areas (but see Chapter 6 and 9 for a more detailed breakdown of hotel costs).

Hotelstats produce on subscription a monthly analysis of hotel operating statistics www.hotstats.com; more comprehensive figures of regional occupancy and domestic and overseas visitor trends can be obtained from VisitBritain (www.visitbritain.org), VisitEngland (www.visitengland.org), VisitScotland (www.visitscotland.org) and VisitWales (www.visitwales.org)

Growth of hotel supply – does it threaten the independent?

The simple answer is yes. This has been the biggest expansion in the industry's history and its impact on the independent hotelier has yet to be fully felt.

Whereas many towns and cities have always had one or two hotels that have traditionally been the centre of their social life, new hotels opening up not only inside the town but outside mean that competition for trade is far greater than ever it was. Unless the independent can match the standards of the new hotels, and surpass them in many aspects, trade will drift to the new properties. But there are clear examples where the traditional hotel has succeeded in maintaining and even exceeding the standards of new-build properties. The criticism of many new-build properties is that they are too impersonal, often run by a faceless manager; for many customers, it's difficult to tell the difference between one hotel and another (indeed, they can change brand with alarming frequency.) An independent hotel may not be grand but it can most definitely be personally run by an owner who appears front-of-house on a regular basis so that guests can talk to him.

The independent hotelier can still succeed if he recognises that it will be largely his personality, his expertise and his welcome that attracts people to his hotel in the first place, and encourages them back for a return visit. That is the independent's Unique Selling Point (USP).

> **An independent hotel may not be grand but it can most definitely be personally run by an owner who appears front of house on a regular basis so that guests can talk to him.**

Of course, price is also a factor. Whether the budget hotel is stealing business from the independent sector or whether it is creating new business of its own is a moot point. There will be guests who move down market because of the budget sector's lower prices; but those lower prices also encourage people who may never have stayed in a hotel before to book into a hotel as a new experience, as a result of which the budget sector is actually expanding the market.

Whatever the outcome, the budget hotel market is here to stay and will grow bigger. Its very existence in a town will act as competition to the small independent. It will always act as a brake on the independent's pricing policy unless there are clear differences in style, service, product quality and amenities between the competing hotels.

Franchising

The advantage of franchising, as the next chapter points out, is that the hotel has a familiar name, familiar signage, and the use of a worldwide reservations network that expands its market on a global scale. A high profile brand name is a valuable asset. Hilton's *'Take me to the Hilton'* advertising some years ago, indicating it was the only hotel in town, still lives in the memory

On the other hand, franchising is about uniformity. Brand standards mean that one hotel in a brand will be of a similar standard to any other hotel in the same brand. This can be an advantage: the customer understands what to expect. But it can also act as a deterrent if customers don't like the brand for whatever reason. Franchising can also be expensive. There are fees to pay to the franchisor for the use of the brand name and for all the services that the franchise company provides. Initially, there might also be some investment required to bring a property up to the expected brand standard; in some cases, this cost might be quite considerable. On the other hand, being able to use a brand name, and relying on it to attract customers because of it, is part of the franchise hotel's marketing strategy. Using a franchise brand's worldwide reservations network could open up markets that an independent hotel could never hope to attract, which might enable it to dispense with some sales staff or other sales activities. Joining a franchise brand can be a key part of a hotel's marketing strategy and its cost (and benefits) would be seen as part of the cost (and income) of marketing the hotel.

What is certain is that franchising is here to stay and new franchise brands are being introduced every year. From the first-time buyer's point of view, however, his purchase will rarely be attractive to a franchise company as most franchised hotels are new-build and specifically designed to brand specifications though this does not prevent owners swopping brands. Accor's Mercure brand belies this format as it consists of many of the former Trust House heritage inns and hotels which were built in the nineteenth century or earlier, with very little common ground except that they are quite small, traditional English properties. The fact that they have all been branded with a French name, Mercure, creates a certain marketing dissonance.

It is unlikely that a first-time buyer would be acquiring a property of sufficient size and suitable character to merit becoming a franchisee which, by doing so, would mean he would lose his independence More likely, he would consider joining a consortium (see page 184).

Even here, however, there are disadvantages. Some years ago, Best Western, which was founded in the United States and is still led from there, insisted that all member hotels in the consortium throughout the world should use the Best Western name in the hotel title. As a result, what might have been the Crown Inn in a town became the Best Western Crown Inn. There were significant other requirements promoting the Best Western name on stationery, telephone enquiries, signs and other public announcements. The reason for this is obvious: the consortium wanted to raise the profile of its name to the general public and giving the brand name to every member would lead to every member hotel being identified as part of a global group. If Holiday Inn could be synonymous with a certain type of hotel, so could Best Western, went the reasoning. Clearly, the more the Best Western name is identified with a certain kind of hotel, the stronger is the brand.

Impeccable marketing logic, however, did not take account of some owners' feelings. The Crown Hotel would be publicly viewed as a consortium hotel not as an independent hotel which was part of a consortium – not the same thing at all. So strong was their opposition to the new edict that a number of UK hoteliers came out of membership.

Franchising poses a similar problem. The advantages of taking on a successful franchise are many but what the hotelier loses is the one thing that is most precious to so many: independence. Although he remains in ownership a franchisee does not operate an independent hotel. He has to conform to brand standards, charge (more or less) brand prices and operate as a branded outlet. There are huge benefits to this providing the franchise is successful (not all of them are) but any franchise chain or consortium is only as strong as its weakest link.

How people book now – the vital importance of internet bookings and TripAdvisor

Perhaps the most significant trend so far in the hospitality industry is the growing importance of internet bookings, the social media generally and TripAdvisor. No hotel can now survive without a website, many of which have the ability for people to book directly through it. Well over half of the people booking a hotel room (either directly through the website or by other means) consult TripAdvisor beforehand.

In the UK, about 50 per cent of all hotel bookings are made through the internet and the ability of people to access hotel websites through mobile devices such as tablets and smart phones ensures that this number will continue to increase; this is particularly so for hotels that rely on visitors from overseas, where internet bookings will become even more prevalent. There are costs involved in creating a hotel website which has the ability to book rooms and some hotels may be just too small to offer this facility, but prospective hoteliers must be aware that the trend is sharply towards more automation in booking procedures as well as in gathering information about hotel facilities and services (and their quality).

Comments on TripAdvisor and those on other social websites have gained in importance as more and more potential guests seek previous guests' opinions about quality and standards; for the hotelier, good reviews should always be encouraged and poor reviews should never be ignored. The ability of guests to use social media, such as Facebook, Twitter, Instagram and others means that comments about a guest's stay in a hotel can be instantly circulated to a wide circle of friends and contacts in a way that was impossible even a decade ago. Hoteliers have to be more than ever aware of what is being said about their property on a daily basis.

For a full discussion on this, see Chapter 16.

For your search – ten points to remember

1 The average size UK hotel is in the region of 16 rooms; London has by far the most rooms but by no means the most hotels.

2 Just over half of the total number of hotels in the UK remain in independent hands . . . . .

3 . . . . but the growth of branded hotels, and the development of franchising (see next chapter) is setting the pace for the rest of the industry to follow . . . . .

4 . . . . and thus poses a real threat to the independent sector.

5 The market for short (1-3 nights) holidays is bigger than that of long holidays.

6 London attracts over half of all overseas visitor spend but the South West attracts the biggest domestic visitor spend.

7 Outside London, the domestic leisure and business market is critical to the success of any hotel.

8 Clearly define your market sectors – focus on developing them.

9 People are now booking more and more on-line – and are hugely influenced by social media.

10 The independent hotelier's USP is his personality and his personal attention to the hotel's guests and its activities.

"Whether you buy a B&B, country house hotel, city hotel, a one star or five red star hotel, your prime objective should be to aim for excellence and to be the very best at what you do. But to achieve excellence you need a clear vision, a clear strategy and a highly motivated and engaged team which is totally focused on building sound customer relationships and consistently delivering the promise.

"Good hospitality is based on traditional values and some simple but effective basic skills: a warm greeting, a smile, eye contact, listening carefully to what the customer wants (not assuming anything) and being immediately reactive to adverse comments. You have to inspire every member of the team to do the same. Most important of all – inculcate that rare ability to make every guest feel that he or she is the hotel's most important customer."

Harry Murray MBE
Chairman, Lucknam Park, Wiltshire

3 Franchising and branding: where the challenge lies

by Melvin Gold FIH, Hotel Industry Consultant

Brand names hang over the door of an increasingly significant proportion of UK hotels. Their number will grow and the independent operator needs to be aware of the challenge they face. In fact, franchising is not new to the UK hotel market though it has undergone recent rapid growth and its structure is changing.

In global terms five of the top six of the world's largest hotel companies – InterContinental Hotels Group (IHG), Wyndham, Hilton Hotels, Accor and Choice Hotels International - are active in the UK market through franchising. The exception is Marriott International. Indeed, at present Wyndham and Choice are only active through franchising whereas the others are also active through other business models including management agreements, leases and (in limited cases) through development and ownership. Wyndham has stated that it will consider management agreements in the future.

The UK's two largest budget hotel chains, Premier Inn and Travelodge, have shied away from the franchising model despite having products which would apparently lend themselves to it. The only company in the UK budget hotel market that started up as a pure franchising operation is easyhotel; in this case the company is leveraging the 'easy' brand rather than initially having the brand presence in the hotel sector.

It is significant that the largest of the companies, IHG, franchises almost 4,096 of its hotels worldwide, manages 735 and owns just nine (IHG website, March 2015).

Why is franchising so important to brand holders when the business model offers them relatively little control of customer-facing activities – this, in an industry where customer-facing skills are so important?

The big companies are attracted by the limited capital investment required, most having embraced the asset-light model. Reduced capital and the ability to work through a broad-based franchisee network enables more rapid network growth and better local knowledge (many franchisees are 'local' to a particular operating area).

Return on capital for the franchisor is typically strong, not least because capital expenditure is low, and a steady stream of fee income from an expanding network is an attractive proposition. This, however, depends on size and growth; for the franchisee, who now has a choice of brands to choose from, brand strength is key. The brand has to produce business. That depends on brand strength and marketing and a strong reservations system and online presence.

Table 3.1: Franchisor hotel companies and brands available for franchise in the UK (2015). Source: Melvin Gold Consulting research

	Full Service	Mid-market (standardised)	Mid-market (variable design)	Budget (standardised)	Budget (variable design)	Lifestyle
InterContinental Hotels	Crowne Plaza		Holiday Inn	Holiday Inn Express		Indigo
Wyndham Hotel Group			Ramada	Ramada Encore,	Days Inn	
Hilton Hotels & Resorts	Doubletree	Hilton Garden Inn		Hampton by Hilton		
Accor	MGallery	Novotel	Mercure	ibis, ibis Budget	ibis Styles	
Choice Hotels International			Clarion, Quality Inn		Comfort Inn	
easyhotel					easyhotel	

Major brands bring marketing muscle to hotel owners, including powerful global reservations systems, sales organisations, and customer databases.

Often these are supported by loyalty schemes and consumer advertising. Normally these factors are on a scale that is simply beyond the reach of the independent hotelier.

One of the key factors in franchising is for the customer experience to be consistently achieved.

Careful vetting of franchisees and monitoring of their performance is therefore critical. A franchisee operating a poor standard franchise damages the whole brand. In the hotel world the model lends itself most easily to the mid- and budget markets. Not that the upper tier of the market lacks in delivery to the customer but it is more individualistic in style and that makes for a more difficult definition of standards and consistency of delivery.

However, franchising depends on the availability of finance and that has remained difficult to obtain in recent years. Higher equity requirements have further hampered progress. Most franchisees are small or medium sized companies and, given the economic environment, may have financial stress in their existing businesses and have difficulty in raising further capital from the banks.

As a result, the claimed development pipelines of the big brands increasingly depend on the ability of third parties to be able to fund new development or to persuade independent properties to attach a brand to their premises. Even this requires capital – the properties have to be brought to compliance with brand standards.

As well as financing requirements, hotel owners and developers have to consider the cost of the fees payable to the franchisor and the cost of ensuring continued compliance with brand standards. For independent owners this is a huge issue because currently they are their own boss in this regard, able to control capital expenditure to their own timescale and pocket. That luxury departs with a franchise, although undoubtedly compliance with brand standards will be better for customers in ensuring more consistent standards.

Fees are many and various and their quantum varies between the brands. There is normally an initial fee based on the number of bedrooms, a franchise fee based on a percentage of rooms revenue, system and reservation fees per reservation, and marketing fees. Normally there are no additional fees in respect of food and beverage and other revenue. For an existing property owner these costs have to be considered against the incremental revenue and profit that will be generated by a well known brand.

Franchising will no doubt continue its growth in the UK hotel industry in the years to come as the big companies seek to get bigger.

Banks, already showing a preference for a brand name over the door rather than an independent operation, have gravitated even more towards this. With the influence of the internet and third party agents, hoteliers increasingly need to find a viable route to market through these important customer and revenue generating sources.

These factors combine to ensure that the proportion of UK hotels that are branded or part of consortia will continue to grow in the coming years and will pose an increasing challenge to the independent hotel sector. Franchising will become an increasingly prevalent business model in the UK hotel industry and the independent owner operator needs to recognize the threat it poses to his own business.

Melvin Gold FIH is a leading independent hotel industry consultant (www.melvingoldconsulting.com)

Don't forget – franchising is a threat

Franchising is here to stay. It is the most potent threat to the independent hotel because of the strength of individual brands, the sophistication of their pricing policies, the facilities they provide, and their marketing muscle.

4 What kind of hotel will suit me best?

> "Ensure that the hotel is in a location and of a style that you can empathise with and get behind. There is little point buying a hotel in a rural location if you love the city life, nor should you buy a hotel which majors on shooting and fishing if you have no interest in such pursuits. Bear in mind that you will spend almost every hour of every day in the hotel so it will become a huge part of your life. If you are always longing to be elsewhere then things will start to unravel. And remember, if you are not going to live in the hotel grounds, be no more than 10 to 15 minutes' drive away so that when the fire alarms go off at 2.00 am, or the boiler breaks down, it's easier to sort the problem out."
>
> *Tim Hassell*
> *Proprietor, Ilsington Country House Hotel , Devon*

Because there are numerous small hotels and other hospitality businesses available in almost every part of the country, the hospitality industry offers ideal opportunities to the eager and able entrepreneur. The major groups influence the industry greatly but they do not – yet – dominate it. This goes a long way to explaining why so many people find the idea of owning and managing a hotel or catering establishment such an attractive proposition.

One of the most attractive reasons why owning a hotel is so alluring is that the capital involved in purchasing a business can be realistic. Depending on location and size, purchasing a small hotel or a large B&B in a resort may cost little more than a large house in an expensive town or city centre, so bank finance might not be the problem that a larger acquisition would pose. With the added benefit of living in the premises (though the accommodation used will reduce the number of rooms available for letting and thus your revenues) the financial attraction of owning and running your own hotel is obvious. But there are disadvantages.

One derives from the nature of the industry itself. A hotel is defined in the Hotel Proprietors' Act 1956 (and still in force) as 'an establishment held out by the proprietor as offering food, drink and, if so required, sleeping accommodation without special contract to any traveller presenting himself who appears able and willing to pay a reasonable sum for the services provided and who is in a fit state to be received'.

This means that a hotelier who operates within the meaning of the Act and who has a room available cannot legally turn away anyone who arrives, providing he can pay and is in a fit state to be received – for example, he is sober. Within certain limits he also takes on responsibilities for the guest's property but he can retain the guest's baggage and dispose of it to help meet any unpaid account. Hoteliers cannot legally pick and choose their guests though an experienced operator might tactfully refuse a person by saying that he has no accommodation available.

The implication of this is that a hotel is a very public place indeed; a hotel is, most definitely, not at all like running a large home.

However, there is another kind of hotel – what is sometimes called a private hotel (to which we should add guest house and bed & breakfast) – which does not consider itself to be operating within the meaning the Act. Most of these premises are unlicensed but being licensed is not a requirement under the Act.

Any establishment that calls itself 'Such and Such Private Hotel' does not hold itself out to receive 'any traveller presenting himself'. A private hotel can pick and choose its guests making it, as its name implies, a much more private establishment to run. No hotel, however, whether private or not, can refuse to accommodate guests on account of their disability (in certain circumstances), gender, pregnancy, sexual orientation, religion or race. Discrimination includes providing different standards of service, different products, charging different prices or having different terms and conditions.

There are real dangers here. In 2011 a guest house was successfully prosecuted for refusing to allow a gay couple to share a bedroom. In 2013 a major London hotel apologised to a gay couple for the receptionist insisting that they took a family room, ie: a room with separate beds. The Twitter account of this encounter was on the front pages of most national newspapers the next day – a warning that news now travels very fast in today's social media.

If you happen to buy a private hotel you can change it the day you take over by deleting the word private and by displaying the statutory notice of the Hotel Proprietors Act.

A second disadvantage of ownership is that you really are on your own.

This is often viewed as an advantage but increasing government and EU legislation particularly in employment law, VAT regulations, income tax and the difficulty of raising long-term funding and securing overdraft facilities, all conspire to make the life of the independent hotelier increasingly complicated every year. The need to keep up with the demands of the social media adds new challenges.

Many people coming into hospitality have a background in other industries. If you are accustomed to a range of support services, don't forget that, in your establishment, you will need to be your own accounts expert, personnel manager and wages clerk rolled into one unless you have the financial resources to farm out some of these activities (wages, for example) to a specialist provider. Above all, you will have to be the person to persuade your bank to finance your business and to support you through the bad times as well as the good.

4

What are you looking for?

The decision about which type of establishment to buy will depend largely on your own inclinations and resources but you will save travelling time and considerable sums of money if, at the outset, you know what you are looking for.

A resort or town property, in London or in the provinces, in a town or in the countryside? What kind of business attracts you? A steady all-year round trade that most town hotels experience, or the peaks and troughs of a resort hotel? Do you want to cater for the holiday-maker or the business traveller?

There are pros and cons to all these options. A seasonal hotel means hard work for four to six months of the year and a long winter of little or no trade which obviously brings financial pressures. A town hotel may be busy in the week but quiet at the weekend.

You will also need patience in your search – six months to a year is an average time to find the hotel you are seeking; it's not unusual to take longer. You might still have to make expensive journeys to far distant parts of the country but, if you know what you want, these journeys can be cut down and some of the searches can be undertaken on the internet or on the phone with the estate agent.

London hotels

In the capital, the biggest, branded hotels exploit both the corporate and leisure market; many also have a major conference and banqueting trade. Smaller hotels in London, which will be those that the first-time buyer might purchase, are largely focused on the leisure market – both domestic and overseas; few of these hotels will have a significant food and beverage operation, indeed, many will only provide breakfast and snacks during the rest of the day, perhaps with a bar. The bigger hotels dominate the capital but there are many independent properties outside the West End which prosper by providing just bed and breakfast.

Even during a recession, London enjoys higher occupancies than the provinces.

As a result, London property values are so much higher in comparison to the provinces that most first-time buyers will find it difficult, if not well nigh impossible, to consider purchasing a property in the capital unless they have significant self-funding arrangements.

Town House hotels/boutique hotels

A new breed of hotel has emerged in recent years called the town house hotel, or boutique hotel.

These are generally high quality properties of up to 40 or so rooms, designed to a high standard, with their own individual character, frequently with a high quality food and beverage operation and a high standard of personal service. Although pioneered by such groups as Hotel du Vin and Malmaison, there are others which are owned and operated by individuals. By their very nature, these are expensive hotels to create and they form a niche market in major towns and cities (London being a prime example) where high net-worth individuals are looking for a quality product with a degree of privacy that does not have the heavy stamp of a group on it.

This is certainly a market that the well-financed first-time buyer can consider entering, but the principles of good hospitality, good service, a welcoming and stylish ambience and understated luxury are never more important than here. This is not a sector for the cash-strapped buyer who needs to find his feet in an industry of which he has had no previous experience. The boutique hotel needs to understand customer needs more than most, be alive to changing customer demands and be able to satisfy them at all times with a high level of personal service and luxury. Nor is success guaranteed. Operational costs are high with a high staff/guest ratio, and all boutique hotels need a quality restaurant and bar operation. To operate such a property is to operate at the top end of the market where customer demands have to be met more or less without question. Prices may be reassuringly high – but so are the costs.

Provincial town hotels

These hotels can offer the most attractive business opportunity for the first- time buyer but competition from major branded hotels makes the life of the provincial hotel owner that much more difficult.

However, many, long-established, independently owned properties have developed as the social centre for their local community and their F&B operation is an important revenue stream showing that, with a good reputation and providing the right product in the right ambiance, the independent hotel can be a highly successful operation.

The ideal hotel is one in which all three departments – rooms, food and beverage and bar – make a positive contribution to the business.

In the provinces, the mix is generally in the region of 50-60 per cent room sales, the remainder being food and beverage sales. The mix between food and beverage varies according to the type of hotel and, perhaps surprisingly, its location; the further north in the UK the stronger the drink sales, so that while food and beverage might be split 20-30 for food in food-based hotels, the split might reverse towards beverages in hotels that have a strong bar or liquor trade.

The food and beverage operation can be profitable if it is well organised and properly costed (see Chapter 17) but few provincial hotels have built up their reputation on food alone. The emergence of 'gastro pubs' has put additional pressure on local hoteliers. This is partly because hotels are not (now) generally viewed as eating-out destinations in their own right. Diners also have to overcome a reluctance to enter the hotel in the first place in order to reach the restaurant – a subtle deterrent; a stand-alone restaurant has no such barrier.

In many ways, a provincial hotel is one of the most difficult for an inexperienced first-time buyer to take over . . .

. . . because it will have a restaurant that needs to provide at least breakfast and, most likely, dinner (to get an AA rating, all but one star hotels have to provide dinner as well as breakfast; four- and five-star hotels also have to provide lunch). Chapter 17 shows that running any restaurant can be a quick way to lose money. The first-time buyer with little or no catering experience in hotels needs to be aware of the difficulties of buying a hotel with an extensive food and beverage operation; it is often preferable to build up a restaurant operation after you have had some experience of running a hotel.

Country house hotels

These are hotels whose siren songs are often the most alluring.

The first-time buyer should treat them all with the caution that they deserve. From the outside they look irresistible. There is many a potential purchaser who, walking up the drive to meet the vendor, sees himself dispensing hospitality to all as the local landlord-cum-squire-cum-landowner. The rose-coloured spectacles are firmly in place and no negative factor ever enters the purchaser's mind.

Then reality should kick in.

Country house hotels have three things in common: they have built up their reputation over a long period of time (or have lost it over the same period – hence, perhaps, the sale); they are generally in a unique or unusual location, often with extensive grounds; and they have carved a niche in the market for themselves typically by the ambiance of their surroundings and interior design and furnishings and the quality of their restaurant. People go to a country house hotel for good food as much as for good accommodation. So a good kitchen is *de rigeur*.

There are many highly successful country house hotels but there are equally many that have fallen by the wayside.

Reasons for the latter vary: their standards were insufficiently high to attract and, more important, retain their clientele; they might have been unable to recruit the right staff; if they had large grounds, the cost of upkeep might have been prohibitive; above all, their prices might have been too high and thus they provided poor value for money. Word gets around.

Those hotels with the highest standards will generally succeed as they aim at high net worth individuals who are accustomed to staying in expensive hotels and are concerned more about quality than price. In addition, there is the special occasion market – those events, like a birthday or wedding anniversary - which prompt people to splash out on a weekend of indulgence away from home, no matter what the cost. And in any recession, there are people who are able to ride it easily and have money to spend. This market is surprisingly resilient. But it follows that standards of comfort, welcome and food cannot fall if the country house is to continue to be successful. Maintaining these standards provides the most difficult challenge.

By their very nature, hotels in the country are costly to keep up. Typically they are large, old buildings, frequently listed (which makes alterations difficult) and need plenty of expensive maintenance. Their upkeep is much more demanding than that of a modern hotel.

Success in this sector is difficult to predict because there are so many indefinable qualities that make up a good country house hotel. Undoubtedly, the atmosphere of the building, its standard of furnishing, its comfort and the quality of food are key factors - **but the most important is surely the personality of the owner – mine host.** This is true of any hotel but it is in the country house hotel where the owner's personality must shine the strongest because it is usually such a compact, self-contained entity that most resembles a private home in style and ambience.

The country house hotel without the owner, or someone who can be visibly seen to be in charge, is like a ship without a captain.

His stamp must be seen to be on the property and on the way it operates; without it, the hotel will be a soulless place. It is, perhaps, this very quality that makes the purchase of such a property that much more hazardous for the first-time buyer. How loyal are guests to the previous owner and how loyal are they to the hotel itself? How best can you maintain and enhance standards? Do you have funds to invest further in the business? It might be salutary to remember that von Essen, one of the largest operators of country house hotels, went into administration in 2011; its 37-strong portfolio, including such grand properties as Cliveden, was brought down by too much debt and by the need for costly, constant re-investment.

Few hotel groups are now exclusively in the country house hotel market and those that are have tended to create a country resort, with extensive leisure and sporting facilities, rather than offering just a country house hotel.

Resort hotels

These are by far the most numerous. Within this large market there are all types of styles – from grand hotel to B&B, at all levels of quality – but success depends not only on such things as the facilities of the establishment and, indeed, the attraction of the resort itself, but on such variables as the weather.

A resort hotel is more vulnerable to factors outside its control than most other hotels.

As people are booking later and later, resort hotels have become ever more vulnerable to poor English summers which can deter holiday-taking. The short season is also an inhibiting factor.

The small resort hotel is not in the corporate market so it is automatically excluded from a sector worth well over £4bn a year. Some larger resort hotels have introduced conference and meeting rooms or health club and recreational facilities and have thus found new markets for their product; providing the resort itself has sufficient attractions, these hotels will survive profitably but smaller hotels in resorts, which are most likely to be the target of the first-time buyer, need to be aware of the difficulty of trading almost exclusively in one (fickle) market for only six months in every year.

Another factor outside the control of the hotelier is the reputation and success of the resort itself.

The number of seaside resorts that have fallen on hard times is high and hotels in these resorts fare worse than those in resorts that are seen to be attractive and successful. It is difficult for a hotel to attract custom when it is situated in an area which is seen to be falling into decline.

Nevertheless, a small resort hotel can be an excellent introduction to hotelkeeping for the inexperienced couple, though it is unlikely that they will become millionaires as a result of their efforts.

Most of these properties offer bed and breakfast (larger and more sophisticated outlets will also provide dinner) and the majority are small enough for the husband and wife to operate themselves with the help of one or two part-time staff. The demands of these guests are also relatively simple, though becoming increasingly sophisticated and demanding, with private bathrooms, greater comfort and more imaginative food now widely expected in even the most modest establishment.

Resort hotels have another advantage for the newcomer: they are generally less expensive to purchase than other hotels because few professional hoteliers want to enter the resort hotel market.

This is not to deny that there are some highly successful companies with a predominance of resort hotels – Brend Hotels and Richardson Hotels, both significantly based in the South West, are two family-owned companies in this market. Torquay Leisure Resort is another example of a hotel company moving with the times and offering a blend of hotel and self catering accommodation, leisure and entertainment all on one site.

With low values, resort hotels are thus a prime target for the first-time buyer but funding can be a problem precisely because of the low or non-existent income during the winter months. All funding charges have to be met from income during the summer season and, more specifically, from the six weeks from mid July to end August. However, there are many resort hotels on the market for little more (in some cases much less) than the value of a private house and commercial funding might not be an issue.

Your choice

The choice of which sector to enter is personal and will be influenced by the funds you have available and by the availability of properties, but consider:

1. Examine your motives carefully.

If you are thinking of retiring in peace to a hotel, forget it; better to invest your money in National Savings.

Owning and managing a hotel is only for the most energetic and the most committed.

2. If you want to come into the industry because you like meeting people, think very hard about the consequences.

A hotel is a very public place; anyone can use your facilities and unless they are being a nuisance, there is very little you can do to stop them. It's difficult to escape them. They will be demanding. People you do not like will certainly walk in and you will have to deal with them. Will you be able to cope with them? You will need endless patience and a good sense of humour. If you want to come into the industry because you like meeting people, do people like meeting you? The honest answer to that question will largely dictate the success of your business.

3. If you want to buy a hotel 'to get away from it all' be sure you know what you are escaping from and what you are letting yourself in for.

For many, it is a liberating move giving an immense amount of personal satisfaction. For others, it has been a step inside a prison of work in which there is no free time and little opportunity to get away from the premises. Even those who have experienced the excitement of building up a business from scratch have eventually succumbed to a worrying lack of personal freedom, unable to get away from the business for any appreciable length of time.

Working continuously long hours without a break becomes common practice.

4. This problem is compounded by having young children.

Bringing up children in a small hotel is one of the most difficult of achievements and brings tensions to both children and parents. The hours of work demanded mean that parents are frequently torn between the needs of the child and those of the guest. There is little home life in the accepted sense of the word. Some hotelier parents have felt obliged to move out of their hotel because they discovered that their children were giving orders to the staff. It could be argued that living outside is always the best solution anyway as it gives the owner breathing space out of the hothouse atmosphere of the hotel. In a perfect world, this would always be the case but there are few buyers who can afford to buy both a hotel and an accompanying house at the same time. One of the attractions of the hotel industry is that it provides a business and a home on the same premises.

5. Finally, if you want to buy a hotel to 'try something new' you might be reassured that hotelkeeping takes kindly to the inspired amateur who, without any previous experience, can set up a business that exactly fulfils a need in a market.

By offering something new with an approach that is fresh and imaginative, they create a successful business against all the odds. There are numerous examples of people coming into the industry and making a success of it, but it's important to recognise that no-one has succeeded without the commitment and long hours that are always necessary. Of course, apart from embarking on a new career that is hopefully satisfying and fulfilling, the main reason for coming into the industry is to make money.

It is a point that needs emphasising and it is certainly one on which the bank will need considerable reassurance. The rewards can be big but the penalties for slipshod control, poor standards and ineffective marketing are obvious. The need to provide value for money is paramount.

"The American industrialist, Andrew Carnegie, once attributed his great success to having 'the courage to surround myself with people who are smarter than me.' So my advice to the aspirant hotelier is based on that, and my dealings over the years with owners all around the UK, some very successful and others less so, tell me that this applies to any business in which the owner does not personally possess all the practical skills involved in delivering the goods or services that the business needs: hire the expertise of people who know what to do, whether on the payroll or as consultants.

"Of course, these days it is particularly important to have access to good marketing and revenue management people, since the way rooms are sold has become so much more competitive and digitally reliant."

Peter Hancock
Chief Executive, Pride of Britain

Who's in control?

This is an area full of personal pitfalls. Most couples who are thinking of buying their own hotel are in middle age where the husband and perhaps the wife have both worked separately. They hardly know each other in a business environment. Running any sort of business together can put a strain on any partnership and it can kill a marriage through the stress of work. Many couples adjust to this environment and happily prosper; others survive only long enough to talk to the Divorce Court judge. Hotelkeeping has a high divorce rate because the hotel itself is so frequently the marriage partner; there is little time left for any other relationship. Couples who are successful devise their own *modus vivendi* but it is likely that one of them will eventually emerge and be seen as the boss. This is natural but ongoing decisions about the operation of the business and its future need to be taken after consultation and by agreement with the other if the partnership is to prosper and develop.

To aid this, well defined and separate areas of responsibility are recommended. One partner might be responsible for the kitchen, the restaurant and the general upkeep of the building while the other might be responsible for the accounts and front office and general guest comfort. It is vastly preferable that each does not interfere with the other's area of responsibility – people have to make their own mistakes and to learn from them. Of course, if one or the other sees a catastrophe looming then it is obviously to everyone's advantage to point it out but do so when you are rational and sensible and not under pressure at the point of service or before staff or customers. It is here that patience and a sense of humour are so necessary.

Finally . . .

Before you seriously begin to embark in your search for a hotel:

Talk to as many hoteliers as you can beforehand. They are usually happy to give advice and recount the pleasures and pitfalls of ownership.

Work in the industry for at least a month to get the feel of it – longer if possible. **Anyone who has not worked in a hotel should do so before he takes the plunge into ownership. That experience will tell him more about hotelkeeping than any book can possibly explain.**

Face-to-face contact with customers and experiencing the pressures of a busy hotel will be an invaluable introduction to hotel life. Read the trade press. Attend appropriate conferences. Get the feel of the industry.

Commit yourself to the process of buying a business. Try not to be deterred. If you look hard enough and if you are sufficiently determined, your hotel will finally emerge.

Don't equate your personal standards with commercial standards. On your inspection a hotel may not be as clean or as well furnished as your own home but that, of course, might be one reason why the hotel is on the market; the vendors have taken little interest in the business and its upkeep and are keen to quit. Although the state of repair will affect the price somewhat (to your advantage) it also means that you will need to budget for any necessary refurbishments and you must consider whether the poor standards have damaged the reputation of the hotel.

Learn the basic economics of managing a hotel. In Chapters 6 and 9 there are examples of hotels for sale which appear attractive but which, on analysis, need careful consideration before purchase.

Understanding the costs of running a hotel and the necessary margins to be obtained is critical. You must understand how these costs arise and how significant the margins are.

Customers can be very difficult – so keep your cool!

Don't underestimate how difficult customers can be. This is an abridged extract from "Business at the Bear" - a series of real-life articles written by John and Amanda Wilmott, then the proprietors of the Bear Hotel, Wantage, Oxfordshire, for a weekly catering magazine.

"Every hotelier must have had one of those disastrous days when he believes that things cannot possibly become any worse – and then they do.

We had one such day last Saturday. Our problems began in the evening at the commencement of a specially promoted dinner dance that we had organised. A party of 22 had booked in wishing to eat early at 7.30. We had agreed to this and the band was due to begin at 7.30. However, at 7.45, as the party was being served their main course, the band had still not arrived. They eventually turned up at 8.00 and spent the next 40 minutes setting up their equipment and establishing that their amplifier was faulty – it was emitting a high pitched buzzing at regular intervals.

By this time, another large party of 15 people had arrived and things began to hot up.

We suggested to this party that they might like to congregate in the bar and we would take their orders there. Their organizer seemed to assume that we were delaying their dinner for some reason and, having seen the party of 22 already seated in the restaurant, complained that it was unfair that his party should be unable to sit down until other people had left. We assured him that this was not the case and that his table was already prepared.

He accepted this and returned to the bar although, as we later discovered from our bar staff, he omitted to pass on this information to the other members of his party.

Having successfully served the first course to this group, our next big hitch came with the main course. The same gentleman waited until all the dishes had been silver-served and the vegetables passed around and then called us over. Without even picking up his knife and fork to taste the food, he demanded that all the meals should be returned to the kitchen because they were stone cold (some of his party had already begun to eat their dinner and with obvious enjoyment.)

Chaos reigned for the next few minutes as plates of food were hurtled back to the kitchen. The other large party clamoured for more coffee, the band's amplifier buzzed and our 'awkward customer' told everyone in the restaurant that his meal had obviously come straight from the freezer.

In order to make amends to those people who had had their meal whisked away from under their very nose, we provided the party with additional complimentary wine. The meal was re-served and despite a number of sarcastic comments to the members of staff, all 15 people ate it.

Comments continued throughout the service of the sweets although at all stages of the meal no wasted food was returned to the kitchen.

The chain of events was completed by a disastrous mistake over the bill – the complimentary wine was charged for.

Despite our apologies, the atmosphere created by these few unpleasant people permeated the restaurant and the smaller parties were also affected. The 15 left us declaring they would not return – a sentiment of which we heartily approved.

We certainly never wish to relive that night. After a post mortem of the evening's events we agreed that we had learned some valuable lessons about human nature.

We feel sure that none of those 15 people would have behaved in a similar way in a bank, shop or in their own home, but good manners are sometimes not preserved for hoteliers. To make matters worse, when we expressed our dissatisfaction to the band, they refused to accept any responsibility for their faulty equipment and their resulting poor performance. We wish we could deal with complaints in a similar fashion although, if we did we should soon be out of business.

We were delighted when one of the smaller parties present that night returned later in the week for dinner and made a point of telling us how badly behaved they considered the party of 15 had been. We are hoping that other present on that fateful night also thought along those lines!"

The moral?

This piece was written some years ago – but what might have been the consequences of the evening's events today? With the advent of social media, having 15 unhappy customers would be far more serious. With 15 people Tweeting during the meal and the likelihood of unfavourable entries on TripAdvisor afterwards, the impact of reports of the evening's events on the hotel's reputation would be infinitely more damaging now – something that today's hoteliers must recognise.

The moral of this story is to keep your cool in the face of mounting chaos – the customer is always right, even though he can be blatantly wrong. On a busy night, any hotel can be overtaken by events; the only way to deal with them is not to panic and not to argue with the guest in public.

Critical comments on TripAdvisor should never be ignored and should always be answered. The willingness to reply, and perhaps apologise to any critical comments made by guests (which are almost always made after they have left the premises) limits the damage that they might cause. Replies also show that the hotel is on the ball and unafraid of answering criticism.

Before you take the plunge – ten points to consider

1   Never forget: a hotel is very public place – it is not like running a large home.

2   Remember: you are on your own – any help you need has to be brought (and bought) in.

3   Decide, first, on the type of business you want.

4   Decide on the location.

5   Confirm why you want to buy a hotel.

6   Remember, a hotel imposes great restrictions on your domestic and family life.

7   Obtain some experience by working in a hotel for a while.

8   Decide who will be in control – you alone, your partner, your partners?

9   Understand the basic economics of managing a hotel before you begin your search.

10 The search for your dream hotel is likely to be long and frustrating.

"There are simply three requirements for any hotelier:

  Marketing- to get guests into the hotel.

  Accounts - to make sure they pay when they leave.

  Human Resources - to make sure that your team can look after your guests' expectations. This is the biggest challenge.

If you are buying a hotel, I would not recommend one with a bridge for access, nor one with a mile of drive, nor one on its own 350-acre island. But if you do, I would recommend ensuring that all three of these are budgeted for in the initial forecast as my parents forgot to add them all in when they bought our hotel. It has taken the last 40 years to get to where we are now, and will take another 40 years to complete the project!"

Beppo Buchanan-Smith
Isle of Eriska Hotel, Eriska, Scotland

5 Location, location and location

"The most important consideration when buying a hotel is: will it make a reasonable profit? Where's the business plan that shows the profit it'll make in the immediate future and in the longer term? It's very dangerous to buy a property on a whim or a hunch - the figures have to stack up and they must be realistic. The bank will need that and so will you. Of course, location is key here. A good location will make the task easier, a poor location that much harder – but you have to decide yourself whether a location is good or poor. Some hotels in inaccessible places are very profitable, other hotels in what look like a good location can be failing badly. The difference usually lies in how well a hotel is managed At the end of the day, it comes down to your judgement on the location, your ability to manage the costs, your hostmanship and, not least, your commitment to the enterprise. That needs to be total."

Bob Cotton OBE
Consultant, (Chief Executive, British Hospitality Association, 2000-2010)

Conrad Hilton once defined the three most important factors in the success of any hotel, guest house or Bed & Breakfast as 'location, location and location'. This analysis has become the most famous remark in the hotel industry because it provides one of the key reasons for success of any hotelier whether he owns his own business or whether he is the president of an international hotel corporation.

When Hilton made that remark he was being quite insightful. The success of a hotel, he was saying, depends not only on the country in which it is located but the area of the country in which it is located and its precise location in that particular area. All three factors are important and all of them are inter-dependent because the location of the property will tend to define the market in which it has to operate. However, in the last couple of decades the hotel industry has expanded throughout the UK (and indeed the world) so that the importance of location has become somewhat blurred.

Why location matters

In the continuing rush for expansion, hotels have sprung up in the most unlikely places - and new hotels have been built in what are termed secondary or even tertiary locations as the availability of land in primary locations has become increasingly difficult and expensive to find.

New tourist and business destinations are also emerging, so that there is now a concerted rush by major international brands to build hotels in China, for example, which was only beginning to appear on the groups' radar 15 or so years ago. To a much lesser extent, the same has taken place in the UK. In London, for example, the West End and westwards towards Knightsbridge and Kensington have traditionally been the most favoured locations for new hotels but, theoretically, the premium location in London is Park Lane and a few blocks eastwards to take in Mayfair. Here, hotels can charge the highest rate because that is where people most want to stay (ironically, access to Park Lane is limited except by bus and taxi). The advantage of a premium site is that, all things being equal, the hotel can charge a higher rate than hotels in lesser locations. Today, however, new hotels have moved both eastwards and westwards and into almost every London borough, so that London has sites in many different parts of the city, not just in the West End.

Most hoteliers would recognise a city centre as a primary location, though not every site in a city centre would be recognised as primary and some provincial cities and towns, even if the hotel is sited in the centre, would be regarded as secondary locations. Hotel groups have thus expanded and developed into less important towns and secondary locations in order to obtain the necessary geographical spread. This is particularly the case with budget hotels which cannot afford premium price primary locations anyway, even though there are many budget properties in town centres and in the centre of London.

For those thinking of buying a property, the difference between a primary, secondary or tertiary location might be considered a technicality; what is critical is that the location will tend to dictate the type of business that the property is able to attract.

So, location is important if you are purchasing any type of hotel or guest house and it will be a critical factor in its success.

Is the property in or near a busy town? Is it in the town centre or in a side street? Is it near a busy shopping area or in a quiet backwater? Is it in the countryside which depends on people being able to get to it easily by car? Is it in a resort which is quiet in the winter months? All these are factors that affect occupancy. Certain towns are clearly better than others because they are bigger or because they have a thriving commercial and business centre or because they have a particular attraction to brings visitors to the town – Stratford-on-Avon, for example (though many of these visitors come for the day only and do not benefit occupancy levels.)

When building new properties, hotel groups, particularly budget operators, seek to fill any discernable gap in their coverage throughout the country; this often leads them to having more than one hotel in major cities. For example, both Premier Inn and Travelodge have many hotels in central London as well as in cities like Birmingham and Manchester. For them, there is no one right location – there are many right locations depending on the town, the city or the area. So while the location is important for them, the construction of a new hotel is driven more by their wish to be able to offer a complete range of locations in the belief that their customers will follow the brand in the same way that Tesco, for example, expanded to cover almost every shopping opportunity in the UK. So blanket coverage by budget hotel companies aims to satisfy demand for hotel accommodation wherever it arises. Frequently, hotels are now built into the planning of new developments by their developers, not by hoteliers, who are then sought to operate the property.

The significance of this to the individual buying a hotel is that he needs to recognise the predatory nature of budget hotel companies as they encroach on the traditional markets of the independent operator.

Eventually, there will be very few areas of the UK where the independent does not have to face competition from a budget hotel. Bearing this in mind, the potential purchaser must consider where his business is going to come from and how it might be constrained by competition. In this he will need to use every available marketing and sales technique, including extensive use of social media (see Chapters 16–18).

Some parts of Britain are more popular than others, have higher occupancies and enjoy greater demand. It is perfectly possible, however, to run a highly profitable hotel in an area which is not so popular but where your hotel has far less competition. It is important to take regional demand only as a guide. A solo hotel in an out-of-the-way area can do good business just because of its isolation.

Of course, once a purchaser has decided on a hotel there is little that can be done to improve its location; it cannot physically be moved to increase its business.

As a result, many hotels – perhaps the majority – have to ensure that customers find their way to them rather than relying on attracting customers in as they pass by.

A hotel well off the beaten track or up a minor lane will always have more trouble in generating custom than one in a prominent position by the roadside where its location is well known and where it can attract chance trade. As planning authorities strictly control the erection of directional signs it's important to know how easily the hotel's present clientele can find the premises. A hotel might well be able to overcome what appears to be a poor location but it will be more difficult for it to maximise its turnover and it will always be more costly to attract custom, even if it develops, as it will have to, an effective marketing and sales promotion strategy.

The next step is to look more closely at the area and decide whether there are any particular locations you favour. If there are, get to know them. Stay for a few days if you can. Find out their relative prosperity. Walk and drive around the area. Read the local guides to see what competition there is and visit it so that you get to know what's available. Talk to as many people as you can – hoteliers, restaurateurs, locals and council offices. Contact the planning department to see whether there are improvements or development plans in the pipeline. Get to know what makes the area attractive to visitors. What major companies are there and do they have plans to develop? How much business do they bring to hotels in the area? Is the local authority keen to attract new industry? Are new houses being built?

> *"Understand the local plan, and understand what is going on around the property. What other investments are being made? Are other buildings going for conversion or reversion perhaps from offices to hotel or hotels to flats or homes? This is very important. Understanding this can fundamentally change your perspective on whether you invest in the hotel or (possibly more importantly) change the market position of the property to maximise revenue. An abattoir planned 500 meters down the road would be bad news but a new housing estate might offer an opportunity that the vendor does not appreciate."*
>
> **Gavin Ellis**
> **Proprietor, Knockomie Hotel, Forres, Scotland**

In deciding on the significance of the hotel's location, the most important factor is the ease with which the customer can find the establishment.

A city centre hotel may pick up passing pedestrian trade but if it does not have convenient car parking facilities, car owners will be more attracted to the hotel that does offer them, which might well be the out-of-town hotel; an even more important reason for out-of-town locations is the lower land and construction costs and space for car parking. Some new hotels are also located in or near trading estates (an important source of business in their own right.) There are other advantages, too: out-of-town sites can provide space for the future expansion of the hotel.

Location will influence the ultimate success or failure of a hotel, but two nearby hotels in the same town, with similar facilities, can achieve strikingly different profit results. While location is important, it is by no means the only criterion for success in hotel ownership. Three other factors critically affect hotel profitability: the marketing strategy, the cost control of the operation and the commitment and competence of the owner/manager.

In any hotel purchase, you need to consider a number of different factors. Is the current pricing policy of the hotel correct for the market and appropriate in view of the competition? What is the level of occupancy and can this be improved, bearing in mind that even a five cent increase could hugely improve profitability. Is it charging too much for the facilities it offers or can it charge a higher price if standards are improved? What would be the cost of improving standards?

Is the hotel too dependent on one source of business - tourist or holiday maker, coach trade, corporate businessman or conference delegate? If it is trying to obtain a good mix of business, does one market source affect another? A hotel filled with a cheap coach party might have no room for commercial traffic for which a higher tariff can be charged – but will a hotel that fills with holiday traffic be suitable for the corporate market anyway? Different types of clientele tend not to mix socially and one type can deter another: nor will a hotel that aims specifically at the meetings and conference market be likely to succeed in attracting the individual leisure visitor who is looking for cosy comfort and good food.

The ultimate success of any property depends on ensuring that it offers a product that is targeted to its specific market; even more important, that product must be connected to the market through a comprehensive sales and marketing programme. The quality of the product, the quality of the management, and the quality of its connection with the market are the critical qualities in the success of any hotel or guest house. But, of these, the key ingredient of success is the effectiveness of the owner or manager in controlling and leading the enterprise and its staff.

A good owner can develop a hotel in the most unpromising location; an ineffective owner can ruin the best-located hotel. This is seen, time and time again, in the pub and restaurant sector where a previously failing establishment is taken over by a new owner who – largely with the same furnishings and décor – transforms the business into a raging success through his own personality and better or different food.

Business potential

In buying a hotel you not only purchase the building but also its business potential. There are many hotels where the potential is not yet fully realised. To be able to judge the merits and potential of a business is important, which is why it is better to visit as many as you can before making a final decision.

Success in turning a business around will not come quickly or easily and even experienced hoteliers can underestimate the time required to achieve success. But, generally speaking, it is far better to buy a hotel that has unrealised potential, which you can exploit, than to pay dearly for the successful effort already undertaken by the vendor, which may be difficult for you to replicate.

A badly-run hotel merely indicates that the potential is not being fully realised. Such a property gives you an opportunity to grasp.

A hotel with a record of poor results will cost less to purchase than a professionally-run establishment already making handsome profits. Buying a hotel that is maximising its profits leaves little room for growth except through price increases. Of course, purchasing a poorly run hotel will mean that you will have a harder job convincing the bank that you can turn it round, so you are likely to have greater difficulty in raising matching capital if you need it; you are betting on your own abilities to turn it around.

When Buying Your Hotel . . .

1 Falling in love with a hotel is a commonplace experience for any prospective purchaser – but keep your feet firmly on the ground.

2 Stay in the area and get to know it before you put in an offer. Is the local area flourishing? Does it help you in defining your markets?

3 Be firm with your offer. The vendor knows you will offer less than the asking price. But don't be hassled into offering a higher price unless you believe it's really worth it. Higher offers from competitive bids don't always win through.

4 All things being equal, poor trading results can represent a buying opportunity, providing the location is right and you know why the hotel is trading so badly. But, conversely, poor results make raising finance more difficult.

5 Your personal banks might reject your loan application. If at first you don't succeed…

6 Try again.

7 Make sure you employ a good lawyer.

8 Never enter a contract race - if you win, you might regret buying the property in such haste, if you lose you will still have to pay heavy legal fees.

9 Don't underestimate the working capital you will need – you never have enough. There will always be items of unexpected expenditure. Try to give yourself some financial leeway.

10 Your business plan needs to look ahead at least two years, with realistic estimates of turnover and profit. Your lender will be interested in past trading but even more interested in the future.

5

Ask questions!

Having got as far as inspecting a hotel, talk to the vendor to find out the answers to the many key questions. Don't be fobbed off with vague responses. It is absolutely vital that you know the true position of the business and you must be aware of the dangers of cursory inspections of the premises and guarded replies to your questions.

All too often, inspections are made in hastily arranged circumstances and frequently when the owner is anxious that his staff is not made aware that the hotel is being sold. As a result, inspection becomes a quick tour of the premises without the detailed questioning which you need. And even on a second visit, the situation might not be much more satisfactory. By far the best course of action is to stay for a night in the hotel – under a false name if need be – so that you get a better feel of the place. That will tell you more about the hotel than any show-round.

The first question to ask is why the hotel is on the market.

This could be for any number of different reasons: the present owners may be nearing retiring age and are just coasting along; they may have put the business in the hands of a manager who does not care; they may have neglected to maintain the property, thus deterring potential customers; or they might be merely incompetent. Some hoteliers move from hotel to hotel, climbing the ladder by acquiring bigger properties. Conversely, some want to move to a smaller hotel so they have fewer commitments. Some just want to quit the industry. A reasonable time for a proprietor to develop a hotel is three to five years – if your vendor is selling more quickly than this the hotel might not be working out satisfactorily. If the latter, you must judge whether, with your own greater efforts and personal commitment, you could make it work better.

The most important next step is to look at the accounts. Ideally you need access to figures for the last three years in order to judge the true performance of the hotel and to assess its growth and profit record.

Hotelkeeping is cash generative (though less so now when many guests pay by credit card) and not all accounts reflect the true nature of the business. In other words not all the revenue goes through the accounts. HMRC pressure and VAT regulations have made this less of a problem than it was in the 1970s, but the fact remains that the accounts of some small hotels need to be treated with caution. The industry offers such scope for the treatment of particular items of expenditure that every set of accounts must be carefully analysed before you can judge whether the profit is real or imaginary, understated or overemphasised.

---

10 key questions (among many others)

1 Is the location right for the market you want to satisfy?

2 Why is the hotel on the market?

3 What markets does the hotel currently aim at?

4 How successful is it in this?

5 What other markets can you exploit?

6 Is the structure of the building sound?

7 What's the overall business potential of the hotel?

8 Are the accounts readily available?

9 Can you understand them?

10 Is it worth making an offer?

"Understand the competition to the fullest extent possible. Who has the best rooms, restaurant, bar, and service? Especially service. Which ones seem expensive and which ones are cheaply priced, and why? What are the differentiating factors - car parking, technology, views? Where would you choose to stay, or eat, and why?

Stay or eat in the competition, to the extent that time and money allows. When you are established in your hotel they will be your competition and by then you'll be time-constrained to visit. In any case, your business plan will need to address the competitive market. And your business action plan (whether written or just in your head) will need to combat the competitive threat.

Competition is a fact of commercial life so make sure you understand it from the outset. But remember, it's not a sport. You don't have to beat your competitors. You simply have to compete effectively enough to win more than your fair share of the market and keep your customers satisfied and coming back for more."

Melvin Gold
Hotel Industry Consultant

6 Using the business agent

by Adam Lansdown FRICS
Specialist hotel and licensed property agent and valuer since 1982

> Most buyers will find their hotel through a business agent. He is acting for the vendor but he needs a buyer to succeed, so make use of him, explain what you are looking for – and keep in touch with him.

Contrary to popular myth – and of course simple commercial logic – it is essential that buyers of hotels appreciate that they are very important to the hotel agent and will be looked after and cultivated with care and close attention. Just because the agent is being paid by the vendor (in virtually all UK transactions) if he does not have any buyers, then he is not in the market.

At its simplest and crudest, the agent has only two issues to deal with: the vendor and his property, and the buyer and his money. He has also to reconcile two diametrically opposed objectives: the vendor who wants far too much far too quickly and the buyer who wants a bargain entirely on his own terms. In the real world these sentiments are manageable and it really does benefit the buyer to get to know the agents and to share with them his needs and requirements.

A very good example of this attitude and conduct was shown between the agents and the chief executive of a small and successful Scottish hotel company who let it be known to the agents that "I never pay more than five times earnings ..." when buying hotel property for his group. By ingraining this principle into the mind of the main agents he was able to set any conversation or negotiation off in a clear and dependable direction and over the years he accumulated some fine properties and a profitable company.

The point of this story is that here was a buyer whose motives and criteria were very clearly known to the agents and whose conduct and behaviour was reliable and consistent. He was an unashamed bargain hunter who did, in many eyes, miss some very attractive investments. But nonetheless this is an ideal position for the agent who can demonstrate competence, involvement and knowledge of the buyers who they introduce to the vendor's property. The hotel market in the UK is relatively small and the main agents have a strong and respected relationship with buyers like this, as well as with the owners of the hotels that will eventually come onto the market.

Something else that is not always fully appreciated is the objective which an agent aims to achieve. In almost all sales the agent is trying to deliver a safe and proper transaction, satisfactory to both seller and buyer. Of course the agent is doing his best to secure the best terms but it must be stressed that the BEST terms may not necessarily be the HIGHEST price.

However, there should be a word of caution here as there are two types of agent now active in the hotel market. There are those who take a very serious and close interest in the vendor, take a great deal of care in presenting and negotiating individual sales and ensuring that the transaction is properly completed.

On the other hand, there are agencies that operate predominantly as a listing and promotional service, using a range of devices (online web sites, press adverts, For Sale boards . .) where the effort is put into exposure and coverage with a tendency to react to enquiries, as distinct from leading a buyer through an intense negotiating process. Involvement and negotiation are passive and the agent's business model is simply to announce that a hotel is for sale and thereafter to respond to any enquiries and interest as and when it develops.

Guide price is not market value . . .

Here, it is essential that potential purchasers are not misled by the guide price into thinking that it represents the correct market value. The guide price is precisely that – the price that the owner wishes to be seen published and from which negotiations can be developed.

The good agent will discourage the publication of an unrealistic guide price but buyers cannot always see when this has occurred. Guide prices may not always be achievable and in some cases can be some way out of line with the actual level of achieved prices from similar sales.

. . . . but what is value?

What is actually meant by 'value'? With property in general, and hotels in particular, from the purchaser's point of view 'value' is a mixture of two reactions: a strictly objective, calculated and measured amount for which a particular business has 'worth' to him at that time, and the market price which other buyers appear to be willing to tender and which must be bettered if they are to be successful in the purchase. Therefore, if you are to be successful in acquiring a particular premises, you are going to have to offer more than anyone else, which may be perfectly correct as the 'value' to you will exceed its value to others; but it may not be if the 'value' to you (as with our Scottish company) is less than the other offers on the table.

Market value must not be confused with or thought of as being the same as worth. Market value is the level of prices that are being paid by buyers at any given time. Just as with any market, prices for the item can be 'high' or 'low' – relative to the benefits that are being derived from owning the item being traded. It is entirely correct for some buyers to consider a market price to be too high (when compared to their own perception of the worth) and therefore they will not be a buyer; conversely, it is perfectly reasonable for a buyer to perceive that the price demanded is low and therefore he will keenly offer to purchase the item and exploit the benefits that it bestows upon him.

'Worth' on the other hand is the value of an item to the person buying. **The reason why people make slightly different offers for hotels (or any item for that matter) is because they each have slightly different perceptions of 'worth' for that asset or item.** For example, some buyers will reap greater value from a comfortable private house included with the hotel and will pay for that benefit. They are perfectly correct to do so. Equally a buyer who would reap no benefit from that house is correct to avoid paying a 'premium' (from his point of view) for something that is not going to do him any good.

In a booming market, where a large number of transactions are taking place in a relatively short time scale, vendors generally have the initiative and can negotiate an apparently premium price. Conversely in a weak or dull market a steady and considered approach could well achieve an acquisition on relatively favourable terms to the buyer. **Timing is everything.**

The good agent will identify a serious and correctly funded purchaser and do his very best to negotiate the best terms. Occasionally these may not be acceptable to the vendor, in which case a transaction does not occur – but at least everyone has tried.

It is also worth remembering that the main agents are also panel valuers for the principal banks and lending institutions and therefore know the requirements and criteria that have to be met in order for a loan to be secured to assist with a purchase. Whilst wearing his 'agent's hat', the agent will endeavour to anticipate as many of the questions and issues in advance in order to facilitate a relatively smooth transaction and to help the lenders meet their loan requirements, satisfy any internal or external due diligence requirements, and assist the valuers in completing their task. For example, in recent years the Energy Performance Certificate has been a requirement for all commercial sales (with a few exceptions) and at the time of writing there are certain regulations that may introduce additional factors prior to subletting in years to come. These are known to the main agents and are anticipated in their pricing and negotiating strategy.

'Off-market' sales

At the higher end of the market it is relatively common practice for owners to approach an agent seeking a discreet or 'off market' disposal. If you are known and respected by the agents as being an effective, competent and fully-funded purchaser you will be involved with confidential information and invited to consider the hotel in an exclusive and privileged position.

Again, the experienced agent will have a good idea of the requirements of individual and respected purchasers and will be able to place a potential opportunity with the right buyer at the price sought by the vendor without resorting to overt advertising, exhaustive publicity and other sales techniques. Quite often an overt and explicit promotion is uncomfortable for vendors as they wish to avoid alerting staff and clientele to their intentions.

Talking about money

When you talk to the really experienced battle-hardened agents they will generally tell you that the main and overwhelmingly important function that they provide is to overcome that splendidly British resistance to talking about money. The good agent is the intermediary who can do just that.

He will probably have two figures in mind when he offers you a hotel: one is the price that he is asked to publish and to try to achieve and the other is the price that he knows he can sell it for. Quite often these are different and occasionally some way apart.

The good agent also knows the hidden agenda that the vendor is trying to meet. These hidden agendas – that is, the REAL reason for the transaction – are not always broadcast but may include health, financial and personal motives over and above the purely commercial. It used to be said that there are only three reasons why anyone sells a property – the 'three Ds' of estate agency – Divorce, Death and Debt. Recently the residential agents have added a fourth: 'Done the DIY'. Hotels are sold for these and other reasons including company reorganisations, being surplus to requirements, incompatibility, compulsion due to competition – and many others.

The good agent will have primed his vendor that, for all that might otherwise be said, the only real reason that a buyer is looking at his business is to make money.

There are two types of money to be made – regular income and capital gain. Sentiment between these two motives varies over time and sometimes favours capital gain and sometimes favours profit and cash flow.

A certain logic suggests that the two are connected but it is surprising how often purchasers tend to keep the two issues separate. A poorly performing hotel requiring substantial capital investment might well appeal and have considerable value to a purchaser who is looking to make a capital gain, whereas a brand new well-equipped hotel will appeal to a purchaser seeking immediate and regular profit and cash flow.

Make yourself known!

Inevitably, however, human nature creeps in. The best service from the agents tend to go to the buyers who are most conspicuous and make the most noise. If you are a ready and able buyer, make yourself known to the agents. They need you, and they will like you – a lot!

Although it is recognised that it can take months – or sometimes even years – for a buyer to find his hotel, if he is quiet then he risks being swamped by the newer and fresher buyers who are more recently active. So keep in front of the agents on a regular basis.

Collect as much information as possible. Read, listen and walk '… into the market…' to get the flavour and feel for what is available. Agents will provide a wealth of valuable information, summarised in sale particulars, and enlarged in follow-up inspection packs designed to answer as much Due Diligence as possible.

Don't be shy about asking and insisting on this information. Your lender will need it anyway. And if you are a cash buyer, do not forget that you are really lending to yourself so behave as a banker and demand lots of detailed information. If you get it wrong, the costs and consequences can be very severe and expensive. Challenge the vendor's business and all the information provided to prove that it can deliver an adequate return on your investment and be able to service the debt as well as give you the income that you want.

Active agents spend a great deal of time anticipating and responding to a buyer's needs and collating the information needed for him to make a considered and a permanent offer. It is not in the agent's interest to confuse or restrict the information required by a buyer and then have to renegotiate at a later date.

But there will have to be a negotiation. All the maths and science in the world will not get the buyer and the seller to the same figure. A good negotiation is where both parties feel that they have been treated professionally and fairly. The good agent is able to achieve this relationship and is worth his fees from the vendor. He is the one who knows his market, knows his buyers, knows their needs and their expectations – in other words, knows *you* when you are looking for your hotel. Make sure you take advantage of him.

Within normal bounds of discretion and courtesy, be open and honest with the agents as to your needs and resources. Negotiation is a time-consuming process and nothing irritates more than misleading or less than totally accurate statements.

7 Is the business sound?

*"Read this chapter a couple of times. Why? Because you really need to get under the skin of the business you are considering buying. Then remember **caveat emptor** - Let the buyer beware. Lesson one in any purchase is that the vendor has most of the information and it's up to you and your advisors to try and reverse this! Investigate everything.*

With this in mind . . . check the boilers. We backed out of one purchase because the boilers were hopelessly inefficient. Check all substantial equipment. When we purchased Knockomie I failed to check all the kitchen equipment in my enthusiasm to get started. The big number on day one was a new dishwasher as the one on show was exactly that – on show!

Most buyers do not know or understand the legislation that surrounds the kitchen area. Does the current equipment, such as refrigeration and air extraction, meet current legislation standards, never mind an incoming chef who might talk you into the latest induction oven. We recently ran an appraisal over a small inn but the kitchen would have swallowed £25,000 in a heart beat. And remember, if you are new to an establishment the authorities will be around to ensure you are operating legally.

As a surveyor's son, I always look at windows and guttering as a lot can be determined from how they look and how they hang. I carry a damp meter with me on inspections.

How easily will guests find you? Drive to your prospective property from every angle, at different times of the day, including the goods entrance if there is one, and make notes on what you see, what you don't see; what are the traffic flows, is the lighting good, is the signage clear?

Gavin Ellis
Proprietor, Knockomie Hotel, Forres, Scotland

Buying a business, particularly a hotel, presents similar problems to buying a house but they are greatly magnified. Buying a hotel means you not only have to be satisfied that the structure is sound but that the business is on firm foundations, too. Maintaining a hotel is an expensive operation; if you buy a property that needs rewiring, replumbing or a new roof you can incur enormous unbudgeted expense.

Before you discuss the business with the vendor, make sure you are familiar with the hotel's accounts.

Here, it would be wise to hire an accountant to go through them with you **but bear in mind that most accountants know little about the hotel industry.** They might try to advise you against the purchase on the basis of the accounts alone whereas they might mask the true potential of the business.

Initial discussions with the vendor will have established the main facts about the business, particularly on turnover and profits. Either at the first meeting or at a later discussion you need to ask the questions that are covered in this chapter. In an ideal world you should then go away to think about the hotel for a few days. This might make you even more enthusiastic about the property; alternatively, you might begin to lose interest, the drawbacks and disadvantages overcoming an initially favourable view. For those who continue to be non-committal about the hotel it is probably wise not to pursue the purchase. If you are unenthusiastic when you buy it, what chance is there of becoming more committed afterwards?

In any potential hotel, you need to consider a number of questions.

- Is the current pricing policy correct for the market and appropriate in view of the competition?

- What is the level of occupancy and can this be improved?

- Is it charging too much for the facilities it offers or can it charge a higher price if standards are improved?

- What would be the cost of improving standards?

- Is the hotel too dependent on one source of business?

- If it is trying to obtain a good mix of business, and does one market source affect another?

Having got as far as inspecting a hotel, you need to talk to the vendor to find out the answers to the large number of key questions that follow in this chapter.

These can be best divided into four different sectors: land, property, business, stock and contents.

The lists given here are not intended to be completely comprehensive but the questions indicate the areas which you should be probing. Some of the questions are obviously in the province of your surveyor or lawyer. Professional fees can be high but it is better to incur them before you buy the property than to find high unforeseen expenditure afterwards which a professional could have warned you about. Rancorous disputes can also be avoided in this way.

Land

These questions affect your fundamental ownership rights.

1   Is the land leasehold or freehold?

    If leasehold:

2   Who is the landlord?

3   What is the current rent?

4   What is the length of the lease and is it fully repairing and insuring?

5   How many unexpired years remain?

6   Can you use the lease as security for a loan?

7   When and how often is the rent subject to review and on what basis?

8   Does the lease contain restrictive clauses concerning such aspects as entertainment, liquor licence, car and coach parking?

9   Are there any rights of way, rights of parking or access, rights of cropping or grazing?

10 Who is responsible for the maintenance of exits, entrances, boundary walls and fences?

The name of the landlord in the case of a leasehold will, of course, be of interest to you but it will not be critical – don't forget, you are buying the lease only. Most of these questions fall properly within the province of your lawyer. If the hotel agent is doing his job properly, he will know the answers to most of these questions anyway.

There are two schools of thought in the hotel industry on the merits and disadvantages of leasehold property.

One views the hotel industry as a business primarily concerned with maximising the use of a property. The structure itself is viewed as the main asset and, because of this, it is important to own the freehold. In this way, any rise in freehold values through inflation and improvements are reflected in the accounts, thus giving the business an ever more solid asset base. With no rent reviews to be implemented, the cost of purchase of a freehold property becomes historically cheap particularly in times of high inflation. A freehold property is thus (or should be) an appreciating asset which, on sale, should provide a profit.

The other school of thought, which is now gaining much ground particularly among hotel groups, views property primarily as a tool for a business purpose. The ownership of the building is irrelevant and may even be detrimental because it ties up capital in bricks and mortar which cannot earn money until the building is sold. Most of the leading hotel groups take this view and have sold and leased- or managed-back many of their freehold assets.

This is one of the most significant trends in the industry in the last ten years or so, to such an extent that most of the largest hotel groups are now hotel operators rather than owners; some are even brand owners rather than operators.

A leasehold hotel, therefore, should not be rejected out of hand but it needs careful scrutiny because the business has to be made profitable within the period of the lease to enable you to get your investment back with interest.

Property

The next area to look at closely is the property itself.

1   Has a 'suitable and sufficient fire assessment' been carried out?

2   Is the property connected to the main sewers?

3   If the hotel is not connected to the main drainage, how is sewage treated and disposed of and what is the cost, if any, of this operation? Why are main drains not connected? Will pressure be exerted on you by the local authority to connect the mains?

4   Have any verbal or written warnings been issued to the vendor by any of the following:
    (a) Fire officer
    (b) Environmental Health Officer
    (c) Police or local licensing authority over the liquor licence or any other matter
    (d) Landlord
    (e) Neighbours
    (f) Local authority surveyor
    (g) Health and Safety Executive
    (f) Trading Standards Officer

5   Is the site subject to flooding or subsidence?

6   Is the property officially listed as being of outstanding architectural or historic importance or in a conservation area?

7   What planning and other applications have been submitted for future extensions and improvements? What has been the result of these applications?

8   What are the Business Rates? When was the last rates assessment made?

9   Is a new assessment likely because of recent improvements or additions?

10 Is a new review due shortly?

11 Has any work been carried out during the last ten years to remedy structural failures or weaknesses, subsidence or rising damp? Are there any guarantees regarding rising damp or woodworm?

12 How old are the boilers and how are they fired? Are the boilers able to cope satisfactorily with supplying hot water to extra rooms if you want to extend?

13 How long is it since the property was rewired and has the electrical installation been recently tested throughout by a qualified electrician?

14 Is the water hard or soft? Has a softener been installed?

15 How many customer car parking spaces are available and where are the nearest local authority parks? What is their capacity?

16 Are nearby car parks open until midnight, seven days a week?

17 Are main gas services available in the immediate vicinity?

18 What is the hotel's EPC (Energy Performance Certificate) rating?

These questions indicate the main areas of the property that need probing. The hotel agent will have answers to some of them but it is always wise to check either yourself or through your lawyer. The difficulty with leaving questions to anyone other than the lawyer is that a typical contract for the sale of a hotel will include a clause stating that the purchaser acknowledges he is not relying upon anything said to him or information given, except in reply to formal enquiries made by the lawyer. There are exceptions where, for example, there are warranties by the vendor in the contract itself as to the correctness of certain information, e.g. the accounts.

Fire certificate

Under the 1971 Fire Precautions Act, the local fire brigade had to issue a fire certificate to hotels and guests after an inspection. This was revoked in 2005 and the onus is now on owners and managers of hotels to conduct their own fire risk assessment and to keep a record of it. Is the assessment available for inspection and has a proper log book been kept to record the servicing and maintenance of the fire protection measures? Are staff trained in fire drill and are Fire Safety Notices on the back of each bedroom door? To be trading, the hotel will have had to carry out this assessment but it is important to check that it is up-to-date and there are no outstanding issues.

Sewers

Some country hotels are not connected to the main sewer. This need not necessarily be a disadvantage but it is important to know how the sewage is collected and emptied and how much this costs. Get your surveyor to check that the system works properly.

Warnings

Warnings by any of the parties mentioned in the checklist need to be investigated initially through the vendor's agent, though you should always get your lawyer to check if you are in any doubt. The local environmental health officer may have visited the hotel's kitchens (like the fire officer, he has a right of access at all reasonable times) and may have warned the vendor about poor food hygiene practices.

Warnings from the police indicate another possible danger area and complaints from neighbours about noise and other nuisances should also be investigated. A large percentage of a hotel's revenue might come from evening functions or a late night disco. Their continuing success must not be endangered by constant complaints from nearby residents about the noise from the music or from people slamming car doors and talking loudly when they leave. Is the hotel in an area where the local council has imposed (or is about to impose) an Early Morning Restriction Order which restricts the sale of alcohol only to resident guests during certain hours?

Food safety

If you provide food to guests you must comply with the provisions of the food safety and hygiene legislation; the hotel must have undertaken a Hazard Analysis and Critical Control Points (HACCP) assessment and be implementing a food safety management system. Make sure this is still operative and the hotel has a good food hygiene rating; check when the environmental health officer last visited the premises. Make sure, also, that he has not visited the hotel and demanded extensive improvements in kitchen facilities and equipment. **These would become your responsibility if not already implemented when you buy the property.**

Listed building

A listed building may sound an attractive proposition but it can be a hotelier's nightmare. Planning regulations on listed buildings (there are various grades) make it more difficult and sometimes impossible to extend or adapt the property. In a listed building, both internal and external alterations need to be approved by the local planning authority and some hoteliers have had to abandon much-needed improvements because of the difficulty in obtaining planning permission.

The local authority is also responsible for approving all exterior signs. Has permission been refused to erect directional signs?

Planning applications

A key aspect of any hotel is a possible extension either in the form of new bedrooms or by the addition of some other facility such as a conference suite or health and leisure club. If the vendor has already made an application which has been rejected, it is important to know why. A revised application might succeed but in some cases the planning authority will not consider the application under any circumstances.

Structural weaknesses

A new damp course for a large building is expensive; a roof slipping because the beams are rotten and full of woodworm could ruin you. Few professional hoteliers would be prepared to purchase a hotel without a thorough survey. A serious structural defect could make it most unwise to buy a property. There are other key areas, such as subsidence, drainage, electricity and plumbing which should be investigated by specialists before purchase. It is not uncommon to have to rewire a building after

30 – 40 years. One hotelier spent £5,000 on a full survey of a 25-room hotel and found to his alarm that a new roof and a new electrical system were required and that one wall suffered from subsidence. He reckoned the money was well spent and bought another hotel. You must satisfy yourself that the property is structurally sound.

Boilers

A hotel consumes vast amounts of hot water and needs a constant supply of expensive energy. The boiler is the heart of its energy system. If that breaks down, the business collapses. With no hot water for the guests or kitchen and no heating, a hotel can hardly operate. Boilers are expensive and very difficult items of equipment to replace because they are large, bulky and usually sited in inaccessible places. Any boiler and hot water system over thirty years old needs to be inspected carefully, but there are hotels in existence with boilers that are much older and still work well. Wherever possible, it is preferable to have a standby boiler, sometimes also used for central heating, which will prevent the hotel being without hot water if the main boiler fails. There are other points to consider. The heat loss through unlagged pipes in any hotel is enormous. The roof also needs to be insulated and cavity walls filled. Has this been done? And beware – hotels that have been shoddily converted from private houses are likely to have inadequate plumbing and electric circuits to provide for hotel demands.

Once you have purchased the property, it would be wise to engage an energy consultant to advise on obtaining the best tariffs and reducing energy costs by installing energy efficient light bulbs, double glazing in places and other energy-saving measures.

Soft water

Hard water scales hot water pipes and boilers, reduces the pressure and eventually blocks up the system. All hot water, if it is not naturally soft, needs to be softened with a commercial water softener. Is one in place – does it work satisfactorily?

Car parking

Over 85 per cent of the public go on holiday in their car; most business and conference delegates arrive by car; almost all your local customers will use cars. The importance of an adequate car park therefore can hardly be overemphasised. Unfortunately not every hotel has a suitable area and local car parks may have to be used. How convenient are these? Are they closed at night when your evening trade will need them to be open? Are you dependent on street car parking and, if so, is this likely to be restricted in the future?

Mains gas

Oil is an expensive commodity but so is gas and electricity. Mains gas is likely to remain the most cost-effective energy source and gas boilers require less maintenance and gas has another advantage – it demands no ugly storage space or deliveries, unless the hotel uses bottled gas. If you want to change over from oil, is gas available for the hotel and how much would this cost?

The business

The next area that must be investigated is that of the business itself – its accounts, its customers and its staff. The need for the accounts to correspond to industry norms is covered in the next chapter but this is an initial checklist.

Accounts

1   Are properly audited accounts available? If not, why not?

2   Are the sales figures shown inclusive or exclusive of service charge and VAT?

3   Does the owner pay a proper salary and expenses to himself and relatives who help him to run the business?

4   Are adequate sums to cover maintenance and deprecation charged to the accounts?

5   What is the annual sales promotion budget?

6   What is the total value of stock normally held?

7   What is the gross profit on food and liquor? (Gross profit is revenue less cost of food and beverage items used expressed as a percentage of food and beverage sales – see age 72)

8   What is the growth in turnover per annum over the last three years?

9   What forward bookings have been obtained and at what prices?

10 What deposits are held against forward bookings?

Customers

11 Who are the principal customers of the hotel?

12 What is the bedroom and sleeper occupancy over the last three years?

13 When was the room tariff last increased? By how much?

Staff

14 How many staff live in and on what terms and conditions?

15 What are the wage costs, including staff meals, as a percentage of sales?

16 When were the members of staff last given a wage rise, by how much and on what understanding?

17 How many managers have been employed in the last ten years?

18 Have the staff been informed of the decision to sell?

General

19 What service, maintenance and hire contracts exist and can they be cancelled or renegotiated?

20 What brewery ties exist and can they be cancelled or renegotiated?

21 Does it have a premises licence to sell liquor?

22 Does it have a television licence?

23 Does it have a Performing Rights Society licence to play copyright music? This applies even to providing a radio in a guest's bedroom.

24 Does it have a PPL (Phonograph Performance Ltd) licence for playing music in public areas, even from a radio?

25 If the hotel offers a DVD film library, does it have a DVD Concierge Licence?

This may appear a formidable list of questions but the answers are necessary to give you an accurate picture of the business, as the following comments make clear.

> *"Prior to acquiring the property you must prepare a business plan to include a SWOT analysis based on an accurate and detailed assessment of the state of the business. The analysis should include the full financial performance during the previous five (ideally) years, monthly occupancies, average room rates, customer profile, and physical state of the property. It is also important to carry out competitor analyses. The purpose is to establish the strengths, weaknesses, opportunities and threats which the business faces so that you can set a vision and agree a strategy to move it forward. The bank will certainly have requested a business plan to ensure that you are not over-leveraged which, unfortunately, is one of the main reasons why so many hotel businesses fail."*
>
> **Harry Murray MBE**
> **Chairman, Lucknam Park Hotel & Spa, Wiltshire**

Performance and profit

A business should develop logically and steadily. A roller-coaster performance, in which turnover and profits rise and fall in an uneven sequence of events, shows that the business is either out of control or is developing haphazardly. Ideally, what you are looking for is evidence of a steady increase in sales and profit (before owner's salary, interest charges and depreciation) of between 20-25 per cent of revenue over the previous three years, though any recession might blow a hotel off course. The net profit shown on the accounts presented will, however, probably show about 5-10 per cent of revenue after all outgoings, including servicing the capital and depreciating the capital investment. Make sure that the basis of the profit figure is sound and judge whether the accounts understate the true position or whether the business has potential for development – or both. Fully engage your accountant in this.

Owner's salary

This is one way by which the vendor may try to increase the scale of his net profit. An owner operator needs income of two kinds – a regular salary to remunerate him for his work and effort, and a profit on his business activities that pays for the capital he has employed and rewards him for the risk he has taken in developing the enterprise. The two should not be confused but often are.

It is true to say that hoteliers (and their families) do not need to pay themselves what may be regarded as an adequate wage because they are living on the premises and do not need substantial income for personal expenses. Although, theoretically, an owner should pay himself a reasonable salary depending on the nature and size of the business, in practice it may not pay him to do so for tax reasons. If this is the case, an allowance should be made for this in interpreting the accounts. In any case, an allowance should be made for any outgoings such as food and beverages consumed by the owner and his family.

VAT and service charge

Money collected for VAT should not be incorporated in the sales revenue but should be shown separately. If VAT is included, the revenue is being artificially inflated and needs to be reduced by the amount of VAT (see Chapter 8).

The situation with service charge is more complicated. The money raised by a service charge legally belongs to the owner of the business. Although the customer pays in the belief that it goes to the staff in the form of a gratuity, the current legal position is quite clear: the owner can dispose of it as he wishes. He can distribute all of it to his staff or only some of it; he can put it towards staff wages (but not towards the National Minimum Wage) or he can pay it to them in addition to wages. Alternatively, he can keep it all for himself. It follows that a considerable sum of money is involved if a 10-15 per cent service charge is imposed. In studying the accounts it must be clear how the vendor has treated the distribution of the service charge. If all of it goes to the staff, then it should not be included in the revenue because it is not going to be retained in the business.

Maintenance and depreciation

No hard-and-fast rules can be laid down on the annual amount that is needed for repairs and renewals as every hotel is different.

What is certain is that every hotel needs regular maintenance and the industry norm is some five per cent of net turnover though this will not be achieved in every case.

However, the longer this is put off, the more expensive it will eventually become. Has regular maintenance taken place and has the depreciation of plant and equipment been realistic during the past five years? A heavily-used city centre hotel restaurant will need to be refurbished more frequently than a less busy restaurant.

Bedrooms, if occupancy is high, will need attention every three years or so. Your visual inspection will help you form an opinion on whether or not adequate sums have been charged in the accounts for repairs and renewals in the past. If not, then make the necessary adjustments to the figures.

Marketing

Have the marketing activities, if any, been consistent over the years or are they high one year and low the next? Effective sales promotion, whether it is reliant on internet and commissionable sales, advertising, face-to-face sales calls, telephone interviews, mail shots or brochure production, depends on consistency. An inconsistent effort will result in an ineffective response. What you are looking for is regular sales promotion expenditure because this shows that the hotelier has been developing his business consistently. Expenditure for most hotels ranges from three to five per cent of net turnover. If the hotel is a member of a marketing consortium (see page 182) - a sign that it is serious about promotion - the membership fee will be part of the total marketing costs. If no sales promotion is undertaken it may indicate that the hotel is too small to need it or that the hotelier does not care, in which case his occupancy will be low.

Successful marketing is the key to your future prosperity, so it is important that you ask the vendor some key questions:

1 What records has he got that will enable you to judge the hotel's main markets – and how much is each market worth in terms of revenue generated? What other markets can be attracted?

2 How dependent is the hotel on a particular market – or on a particular client – and what is the value of that market/client? How vulnerable is that one market?

3 Check occupancy levels during weeks and days in the previous year – they will tell you the pattern of the hotel's business, its strengths and weaknesses. Can the strengths be enhanced? Can the weaknesses be eliminated? How do they compare with figures in Tables 2.6-2.10?

4 Check previous sales and marketing activity. What methods have been used? How effective have they been? If the hotel was previously group owned, how dependent is it on the group's central reservation bookings system? How easily can it be replaced?

In the answers to these questions, you will be able to consider whether you can increase occupancy and, in doing so, increase the room rates. Ultimately, these must be your two overriding objectives but your initial aim will be just to maintain present levels of occupancy and not lose any custom through the change of ownership. Of course, you might also conclude that you have to implement an immediate refurbishment programme to enable the hotel to compete more effectively with other hotels in the locality.

Turnover

If there has been a rise in turnover in the past three years, is it steady? Is it a genuine increase in excess of inflation? Has the general economic situation made it particularly tough to increase occupancy? It is possible for a business to increase its turnover and profit in money terms but not in volume (e.g. the number of sleepers) by charging a higher tariff but volume is usually the most important factor, whether it is interpreted as the number of customers in a restaurant or the number of rooms occupied during the year. Establishments that rely merely on price increases to yield greater revenue should be suspect. However, if a hotel is operating at near peak occupancy it might only be possible to generate more profit by further price increases, although better in-house selling (i.e. persuading the customer to spend more in your hotel on ancillary goods and services) is another way to boost revenue. In these circumstances, building an extension to accommodate more guests might be the only way to increase turnover.

Forward bookings

Bookings are now made much nearer the time of arrival. How many bookings are there for the next year and how much has been taken in deposits? **All payments in advance (for weddings, for example) should be transferred to you on completion.** Forward bookings used to be a sign of health in resort hotels but lack of them indicates little now and even less in those hotels that rely on chance trade and internet bookings. Changing customer trends mean that resort hotels now have a pattern of forward bookings similar to many provincial hotels and they have to rely much more on chance or late-booking guests. A seaside hotel with no summer bookings in the early part of the season is not necessarily in trouble but it should be viewed with some caution.

Customers

Who are they? The success of every hotel depends on attracting customers but where do they come from and how much are they willing to spend?

These are important questions that need answering. Occupancy figures vary from area to area, city to city and resort to resort. Confusingly, occupancy can vary within hotels in one area because of management and marketing expertise. What matters is how many rooms the hotel has, how often they are occupied and the price obtained for letting them.

Hotel pricing structures are now largely on a per room rather than on a per person basis. Indeed, the current trend is that every room now should be able to offer at least double occupancy. You may have to consider converting small singles into a larger double as rooms (particularly at the luxury end) are getting bigger. **The average size room thirty years ago was around 300 sq ft, but is now nearer 400 sq ft; on the other hand, some rooms are getting smaller – the hub by Premier Inn rooms at 118 sq ft are 45 per cent smaller than the average Premier Inn room.**

Tariffs

The tariff needs to be realistic in relation to the hotel and its services and to the tariffs charged by other hotels in the area. The hotel may have high occupancy at an artificially low and unprofitable rate. In that case, a sudden increase in tariffs without increasing standards would create ill-will which would affect the level of business. All tariff increases have to be judged carefully.

It is worth emphasising here (see also Chapter 8) that the development of on-line booking agencies, and their growing use by the public, means that the commission charged by them, which can be as high as 30 per cent (average 12 per cent) is becoming a significant cost for hotels. Allowance must be made for this cost when preparing budgets.

Stock

There are still some hotels and restaurants that have a wine cellar representing a five-figure investment.

A wine cellar filled with fine wines which are rarely sold may satisfy the proprietor's ego but it does not help his cash flow.

Similarly, over-stocking on food and groceries can lead to spoilage and wastage. On the other hand under-stocking can lead to inefficiencies. Stock includes other items which are frequently used, chiefly table linen and bedlinen. Most hotels now use commercial laundries with daily deliveries, which both eliminates the need for them to hold stock and passes the stock control issues (at a cost) onto the laundries. Stocks of food – generally perishable – should be within three to seven days but anything up to 45 days is appropriate for beverages, including beer, wine and spirits.

Stock and contents

1   Does an accurate inventory exist? When are you entitled to have it?

2   Of all the items of furniture, furnishings, fixtures, fittings – china, glass, cutlery, pictures, antiques – what belongs to the vendor and what is not part of the property for sale?

3   Is cutlery, china and glassware to be treated as contents or as stock to be paid for?

4   Are any motor vehicles included in the sale?

5   Are linen, blankets and duvets in stock or are they hired? What other items are hired or on lease?

6   What items of stock not required for normal day-to-day trading are in hand?

Always ask for a full inventory of fixtures, fittings, furnishings and effects which are to be included in the sale. One hotelier bought a hotel thinking he was purchasing all the excellent paintings that hung in the restaurant and hallway; on taking over, he found they had been stripped out by the vendor. Subsequent investigations revealed that they were the personal property of the owner and were not included in the sale. Detailed questioning at the outset and a close examination of the inventory will prevent such a situation occurring in your purchase.

When you take over you will have a full stock-take and an inventory check (see Chapter 12) but before deciding to purchase it is important to know whether stock in hand is going to cost you £4,000 or £40,000. You must agree a fair figure before-hand and stipulate, if you want, that the stock should not exceed a certain figure on the day of take-over.

A stocktaking firm is essential here. Try to withhold an agreed sum from the purchase price until you are satisfied that all the stock remains.

Gross profit

Gross profit (GP) on food is the price of the meal (food only) less the cost of the food. In most sizeable restaurants, the gross profit is not less than 70 per cent and is as high as 75 per cent in many popular units.

We cover the importance of gross profit in Chapter 8. Increasing the GP and main-taining it is a difficult job for the inexperienced caterer. The natural tendency is to give too high a quality or too large a portion for the prices charged. But many restaurants take too inflexible an approach to their GP, especially with wine sales. Restaurants mark up wine, for example, by 300 per cent or more on their purchase price, but this may be a mistake. There is much to be said for marking it up by less to encourage more sales. It is better to sell two bottles at a profit of £4 each than one at a profit of £6. The relationship between price and volume is critically important; by reducing your gross profit on wine and spirit items (but not food) you might be able to achieve higher sales and profits. It would, however, be very unwise to reduce your GP on food in this way unless you have a particular promotion.

Remember: the restaurant is usually the most difficult area of a hotel to operate and control and is frequently the least profitable (see Chapter 19).

Staff

Payroll

You will see from the accounts what the staff costs (including employers' NI, staff meals and other benefits) are. These tend to vary from region to region (see Chapter 2) but average between 28-35 per cent of turnover. Although a de luxe hotel is gener-ally much more heavily staffed (and will thus have a bigger payroll bill), the payroll ratio should not change much because the hotel's revenue is that much higher. Particularly check here whether the proprietor is costing in his own salary.

The wage percentage of a hotel is partly an indication of the efficiency of the man-agement. Payroll is the largest single expenditure and the management's ability to control it greatly influences the profitability of the enterprise.

Too high a wage percentage may indicate slack control; or it may show that the hotelier is providing a higher standard of personal service than the business warrants; in other words, he is employing more staff than is justified. Less likely, he might be paying them too much. It would be useful for you to know how many members of the staff are on the National Minimum Wage (NMW) and what increases (if any) they have had in the last year or so. Even a three per cent increase on an annual wage bill of £80,000 would cost £2,400 which could dent the profit forecast of any small hotel. You should ask whether any member of staff is on a bonus, how many live in and how long they have been employed. The latter will give you an indication of the hotel's ability to retain staff and whether they have a favourable attitude towards the hotel.

Bear in mind that there is pressure on employers, not only in London, to introduce the so-called London Living Wage, which is over one third higher than the NMW. The pressure on payroll costs is always upward, whether it is through wage increases or through regulatory issues such as the new workplace pension reform.

Previous proprietors or managers

A long procession of proprietors or managers implies an unhappy hotel, troublesome staff and, more than likely, disgruntled guests. To have had only one owner or manager in the previous ten years or so does not necessarily mean the reverse is true but it is likely to be so.

You will have to use your own judgement, but if you do not like what you see and if there is a manager and you do not want him to stay, you will be responsible for redundancy payments since a new employer is required to observe all the terms and conditions of employment which applied before the transfer of ownership under the Transfer of Undertakings (Protection of Employment) Regulations 1981 (TUPE). TUPE regulations preserve employment rights on the transfer of a business for those staff then employed in that business.

However, the buyer of a business might wish to make changes such as bringing in computerisation or changing shift patterns, which means that fewer staff are needed to run the business. If the purchaser is able to show that because of 'economic, technical or organisational reasons' fewer staff are needed to run the business, then dismissal of surplus staff will not be automatically unfair, although the ordinary redundancy and unfair dismissal rules will still apply.

Incidentally, the regulations do not apply where there is a take-over by transfer of shares in a company because, in that situation, there is no change in the identity of the employer, i.e. the employees are employed by the company throughout. Merely because there are new faces in the boardroom is not a fair reason for dismissal. Clearly, the situation is complicated and legal advice is advisable before committing yourself to any particular course of action.

Telling the staff

Most hoteliers are unwilling to reveal that their hotel is on the market. There are two major reasons for this: they believe that customers will be deterred if they know the hotel is about to be sold; they also think that staff will become unsettled and leave. This is particularly so if the hotel is in the hands of the receiver. Unless the personality of the proprietor is such that he acts as a powerful attraction in his own right, the danger of staff leaving is more serious than customers staying away. Staff naturally become worried about a change of ownership and it is much better to ask the vendor to tell staff formally than to allow the news to leak out which will inevitably lead to rumours and counter-rumours – much more unsettling than the plain truth.

General

Contracts

What regular contracts are there to service boilers, the kitchen and electrical equipment and other major items? These are indications that the vendor is looking after the property. The equipment should be in reasonable order. Inspect the kitchen yourself, preferably with someone who knows about catering equipment, and make sure no major pieces need replacing.

Brewery ties

A brewery tie is not necessarily unsatisfactory though few professional hoteliers like them. They restrict the supply of beer, wines and spirits and prevent the proprietor from obtaining supplies elsewhere, possibly at a lower price. But a tie often helps the hotelier. The brewery might be willing to help finance the fitting out of a bar.

All these many questions are designed to help you analyse the state of the business and its potential. With this information, and presuming you have a three-year set of accounts, you will be in a position to assess the past performance of the hotel. With the key ratios in mind which are outlined in Chapter 8 – food cost and staff percentages (and other percentages which you can check against the averages) – you can assess how efficiently the business is being run.

Before you are able to make an offer, however, you must undertake one more exercise: you must produce a business plan for the hotel to show how realistic the asking price is and how profitable you believe you can make the hotel in the future. Chapter 9 explains how the plan should be prepared.

Ten pieces of advice

1 Get answers to all the key questions.

2 Why is the vendor selling?

3 Make sure the structure of the property is sound.

4 Carefully inspect all kitchen equipment, boilers, central heating and electrical systems.

5 Check out the hotel's markets. Are they being fully explored?

6 Has the hotel's business developed haphazardly? If so, check why.

7 Check out the hotel's reputation locally – will you have to live up to it or try to live it down?

8 What are the chances of expanding the business with additional bedrooms?

9 Meet key members of staff as soon as you can.

10 Check the inventory *before* purchase.

7

Acquisition Check List

Here's a brief check list of the most important points in any hotel purchase.

1   **Licences**
Obtain Premises Licence
Application for new DPS (Designated Premises Supervisor)
List of personal licence holders
Prepare company resolution

2   **Fire Certificate**
Date premises were last assessed/inspected
Any alterations made since which could affect certificate?
Where is certificate?

3   **Services**
Notify authorities as follows
  Rates
  Water
  Electricity
  Gas
  Telephone
  Cess pit
  Refuse Removal
 Meters to be read and details of new company sent
 Copies of contract to be obtained

4   **Equipment Hire and Rental**
Schedule of all items on hire or lease
Inform leasing and rental companies

5   **Laundry/Linen Hire**
Arrange stock check on day of takeover
Dirty linen on day of transfer to be listed and charged to vendor
Inform laundry company and obtain full stock details
Obtain copy of agreement

6   **Maintenance Agreements**
List of all agreements in operation
Inform companies of change of ownership
Calculate any prepayments

7   **Advertisements**
Any long term contracts?
Any boarding or adverts on other people's land subject to rents?
Any of the above subject to planning?
Transfer of website
Details of website contract to be obtained
Transfer domain name and Email addresses

8   **Central Heating Boilers**
Gas or oil
Maintenance contracts
Energy Performance Certificate (EPC) to be obtained from landlord
Does a Display Energy Certificate (DEC) need to be displayed?

9   **Suppliers**
Obtain full list of suppliers with:
  Trading terms
  Discounts
  Address and telephone number
 Write to all suppliers advising of change and requesting terms
 Are any suppliers paid weekly?

10   **Inventory**
It is the vendor's responsibility to prepare an inventory to form part of the contract
Agree items that are not to be included
Check inventory on takeover

11   **Stocks**
Arrange stock check on day of handover
 Is fee to be split?
 Is there a time limit to value?
Agree what is to be included
    e.g. cleaning materials, oil, Calor gas
Are stationery stocks included in the agreement?

12   **Value Added Tax**
Rubber stamp all stationery with new number
Obtain copies of bill stationery
Arrange for EPOS machines to be re-programmed

13   **Banking**
Arrange for new PDQ machines
Arrange for new bank paying in books

Arrange for delivery manual Zip Zap credit card machines to be delivered (in the event of having to go manual)
Open new bank account for restaurant
Make arrangements with local bank

14   **Salaries and Wages**
Obtain list of all staff to show:
 Full name
 Date of birth
 Address
 Date started
 NI number

7

Job title
Salary or hourly pay
Overtime rates
Exemption certificates for reduced NI
Full list of holiday pay paid in advance or due
Copies of contracts of Employment
Are staff uniforms supplied?
Do all staff receive food on duty – and what is given?
What is policy with regard to staff drinks?
List staff in staff accommodation
List frequency of payment

15   Trade debtors
Full list of sales ledger balances to be collected on behalf of vendor

16   Cash Floats
Verify on takeover, if any, and include in completion statement
Obtain acceptance signature
Detail all floats held

17   Deposits
Obtain full detailed function list with details of any deposits received
Include details in completion statement
Write to all concerned giving details of new owners and amount of deposit held

18   Billing
Review system and implement any changes
Are weekly statistics prepared?
What is week end day?

19   Accounts
Obtain copies of last three years trading results
Where possible get monthly figures

20   Budget
Obtain budget where possible and F&B statistics
Any special prices e.g. Sunday lunch?

21   EHO
Obtain copies of all recent correspondence
Are there any demands or works outstanding?

8 The importance of occupancy – and interpreting the accounts

"When my father died in 1980 my brother and I decided to ask our cousin to join our Board as non-exec chairman; he worked in the paper industry as overseas director for Wiggins Teape and he established quarterly meetings. We also appointed another non-family non-exec who had had a long and successful career in the hotel business. Every meeting we review our performance and consider the strategic direction of the business. Without this discipline I'm not sure the business would have survived. It makes us work 'on' the business rather than 'in' the business at least some of the time.

"To me this sort of governance is essential, regardless of the size of the enterprise. It doesn't need to be a formal Board but minutes should be taken. Finding the right people is critical but don't be afraid to ask someone you admire and respect (and preferably someone entrepreneurial). In my experience people are very willing to help and it shouldn't cost much either!"

Graham Grose
Managing Director, Thurlestone Hotel, Devon

How critical is occupancy? The answer is: very. In this chapter, we outline the approach to a hotel purchase by examining the trading potential of a hotel and the impact of different levels of occupancy on profitability.

Occupancy is an important indicator of hotel profitability but the key determinant is the ratio between occupancy and the rate per room. A variation in either can have a significant impact. In the example that follows, there is a £22,809 difference in net profit between 60 and 70 per cent occupancy and a further £22,433 improvement if occupancy can reach 80 per cent.

The fictitious Jolly's Resort Hotel is for sale at £1.1m. It has a good reputation, and is open all year round. It has 11 rooms (nine doubles and two singles) and enjoys a light lunchtime and bar trade and a good dinner trade, but has no conference or meeting rooms and cannot accommodate parties except in the restaurant. The hotel has a tariff of £240 per room per night including breakfast; for the accounts, we have allocated £15 as a nominal price for breakfast, thus assuming the room rate is £210 per night for a double let.

The example shows the impact on revenue and profitability of occupancy at 60/70 and 80 per cent; we use industry norms against which any set of hotel accounts can be examined in order to establish the true profitability of the property you are considering purchasing.

To buy the hotel, we are assuming that the buyer is able to invest £700,000 from his own resources and has to borrow £400,000 from the bank. Any likely offer from the bank would be for a 20 year period loan at 4.5 per cent fixed rate of interest which, with capital repayments, would cost £38,000 per year. In addition, we estimate that the owner will need to withdraw £25,000 a year from the business to sustain his family's living quarters which are outside the hotel.

A realistic estimate of revenue and costs must be adopted if any business plan is to be accepted.

For example, not all rooms will be sold at the full rate so the cost of discounts, which includes special offers, can reduce net income from rooms sold by 30 per cent or more. The figures quoted in Tables 2.11 to 2.16 are guides and will differ from hotel to hotel, according to each property's location, facilities and type of trade, but the principles remain the same.

VAT

When calculating any potential revenue stream, it is important to remember that, unless the business is not VAT registered, 20 per cent represents VAT and belongs to HMRC, not to you. So, in the example the rooms which sell at £210 per night (excluding breakfast) are actually yielding only £175 (£210 divided by 1.2)

Discounted rooms and commission

We also make provision in the accounts for the fact that the hotel has to discount its rooms in order to encourage sales. Here, we estimate that 30 per cent of room revenue has to be discounted.

This would be especially true if occupancy is only 60 per cent, which implies that the hotel is struggling for business and would thus be likely to have to offer rooms at a discounted rate to boost occupancy. A further cost, often ignored, is the commission which the credit card company charges. This will vary but it is likely to be in the region of 1.5 per cent. Charge cards, such as American Express and Diners Club, average between 2.5-3 per cent – the reason why many businesses do not accept them. As the majority of people now pay by credit or charge card, this cost must not be ignored. An estimate for this is included in Administration and General costs.

Why discount?

Discounting has become a fact of life in the 21st century hotel industry. One survey showed that one third of travellers would never buy a hotel room unless it had been discounted – a figure that will certainly grow in the future. Discounted rooms are available through various websites such as Booking.com, Laterooms.com, Expedia and Hotwire.com. In effect, the hotel provides the website with a number of rooms at a discounted price which are then sold at a mark-up by the agency. Problems arise when a still discounted price on the agency's site is less than that charged on the hotel's website. Some hotels have tried to regulate the prices at which these discounted rooms are sold so that they match the price charged on the hotel's website, but this practice is currently being challenged by the competition authorities in the UK and is considered against competition rules.

In fact, discounts, special offers and online booking agencies have become necessary for hotels to fill rooms. They are an essential sales tool because the public increasingly expects rooms to be available on these sites. Although they provide a far bigger audience, they not only reduce net income (as we see in the following tables) but they can have a negative impact on a hotel's reputation. If a hotel always has rooms for sale at a discount, there is a danger that its reputation becomes devalued, making it more difficult to sell its rooms at the published price. This is why many hoteliers call these websites a necessary evil. To be an effective management tool, it has to be carefully controlled.

It can, however, be particularly effective in promoting special offers. For larger properties it can be equally important in filling those last vacant rooms by targeting mobile customers – a growing target market for hoteliers in London and busy urban centres. Deeper discounts are offered nearer to the time of arrival with the deepest discounts offered in the last 24 hours.

To avoid the hotel gaining a reputation for constant discounting some use a model called secret hotels or 'opaque' discounting, in which the name of the hotel is not revealed to the customer until payment has been made. This helps a hotel to reach desired levels of occupancy without letting its premium rate customers know that it has rooms available on websites at a discounted rate. Again, this is particularly prevalent in London where protecting the name or brand of the hotel is particularly important.

See Chapter 17: Boosting Your Sales

8

Meals taken

When calculating revenues, be realistic. In this example, we assume that all resident guests have both breakfast and dinner. Indeed, while almost all guests will have breakfast only a proportion will have dinner and in a busy town, with attractive restaurants nearby, the number of overnight guests having dinner may be quite low and in London could be negligible. On the other hand, some hotel restaurants might be able to attract chance diners. We have ignored these variations in our examples.

When breakfast is included in the room rate, the food cost must not be ignored.

Bed and breakfast rates are still widely prevalent but many hotels now prefer to offer room-only rates and charge extra for breakfast, which is how many hotels have been able to disguise a tariff increase. In the examples below, we assume a food cost of £4 per breakfast on a nominal £15 price. For simplicity's sake, we are assuming that the hotel does not impose a service charge on restaurant bills; if it does, the revenue will be allocated to a service charge account for later distribution to staff.

Payroll costs

Payroll, including employer's NI and pension contributions, is the biggest cost factor in every hotel operation . . .

. . . so increasing staff numbers needs careful thought because of mounting employment costs. Most hotels will attempt to cope with any increase in occupancy by paying staff to work longer hours rather than employing more staff. Similarly, it is more effective to reduce hours worked when occupancy falls rather than getting rid of staff because of the cost and aggravation of laying off staff – though redundancies would certainly need to be considered if occupancy consistently falls below 50 per cent. A one or two per cent reduction in payroll costs, if it can be achieved, will go straight to the bottom line whereas an increase will have the opposite effect. However, reducing staffing levels endangers standards and should be undertaken with great caution while over-staffing does not necessarily mean better service; too many staff can mean too little work for too many people – the devil finds work for idle hands.

Care should be taken over calculating payroll costs.

It's true that wage costs average some 30 per cent in the industry but these vary from department to department and from region to region. Wage costs are higher in the F&B area. This implies that wage costs are likely to be higher in a hotel that has a strong F&B revenue stream than in a hotel that is largely a rooming operation, where the staffing cost of servicing the rooms is quite low. In the examples below, we have calculated payroll costs as a percentage for each major operating division, which gives a more accurate percentage.

How to view the accounts?

Tables 8.1 to 8.9 not only illustrate the key ratio between occupancy and room rate but the importance of recognising the variety of costs that are involved in hotel operations. These need to be scrutinised in any purchase. The percentages used in the tables are average figures for the industry.

Industry averages shown can be compared against the actual results of your intended purchase and checked for any variations.

It's quite likely that a vendor about to sell will not have invested five per cent of net revenue into the maintenance of the building in recent years so more than five per cent might be required to bring the hotel up to standard once you've purchased the property. The vendor might also have slimmed down staff numbers to improve the hotel's performance and thus make the hotel look more profitable. Other areas to check are food and beverage costs (are they over the 30 per cent norm?) and the sales and marketing budget; the latter could be too low because the vendor wants to improve the P&L account by reducing his promotional costs prior to the sale of the hotel. However, this reduced investment in sales and marketing might have already damaged its occupancy levels and its profitability.

Jolly' Resort Hotel

11 rooms (nine doubles, two singles)

Nine doubles and two singles means that there are 20 potential sleepers so the sleeper ratio is the number of sleepers divided by the number of rooms:

20 divided by 11 = 1.8.

At 60 % occupancy

Table 8.1: Jolly's Resort Hotel – assuming 60 per cent occupancy

	£

Room revenue

Assuming 60 per cent room occupancy: 11 rooms x 365 days x 60% = 2,409.

Calculation: At £240 per room - £30 revenue per breakfast = £210 x 2,409 = £505,890 – VAT @20% (divide by 1.2) = £421.575 – 30% for discounted rooms (£147,525) = **£295,103**.   295,103

(handwritten: 126·47)

The average room rate is £295,103 ÷ 2,409 = **£122.50**

Food Revenues

Breakfast: Assuming that every sleeper has breakfast.

Calculation: Revenue is 11 rooms x 365 days x 60% x 1.8 (sleeper rate) = 4,336 breakfasts x £15 = £65,040 - VAT at 20% = **£54,200**

54,200

Lunch: Assuming an average of ten lunches a day

Calculation: 10 lunches at £10 each x 365 = 36,500 - VAT at 20% = £30,416

30.416

Dinner: Assuming 2,409 rooms sold with 1.8 sleeper occupancy.

Calculation: 4,336 sleepers x £35 per head = £151,760 – VAT @ 20% = £126,466.   126,466
In this exercise, we assume that every guest will have dinner and ignore any chance dinners the hotel may attract; in fact, not every guest will eat in-house and the hotel would be likely to attract chance diners so, in practice, the numbers would be likely to even out.

Total food revenue: £211,082   211,082

Beverage revenues

Beverage: We are assuming beverage revenue is 40 per cent of food revenue - 40% of £211,082 = **£84,432**   84,432

Total revenue = £590,617   590,617

It is noticeable how different the average room rate is from the published rate (£240 including breakfast) and how misleading it can be to calculate room revenue on published rates, without allowing for VAT and discounting.

Table 8.2: Payroll costs at 60 per cent occupancy

Payroll	£
Rooms: 20% of room revenue (£295,103 x 20%)	59,020
Food: 35% of food revenue (£211,082 x 35%)	73,878
Beverage: 16% of beverage revenue (£84,432 x 16%)	13,509
Management/Admin: 5% of total revenue (£590,617 x 5%)	29,530
TOTAL	175,937

Payroll represents 29.8 per cent of total revenue - slightly under the national average principally because the hotel is achieving a good average room rate (ARR) of £122.50.

Table 8.3: Jolly's Resort Hotel – assuming 60 per cent occupancy

	£	£
REVENUE		
Rooms	295,103	
Food	211,082	
Beverage	84,432	
TOTAL REVENUE	**590,617**	**590,617**
DIRECT COSTS		
Payroll/ NI @ 29.8% of total revenue	175,937	
Food @ 30% of food revenue	63,324	
Beverages @ 30% of revenue	25,329	
Commission @12½% of room revenue	36,887	
Total direct costs	**301,477**	**301,477**
Gross profit (48.9%)		**289,140**
INDIRECT COSTS		
Rates and water rates (est)	40,000	
Energy @ 4% of total revenue	23,624	
Insurance (est)	5,000	
Telephone, broadband, mobile and fixed line (est)	3,000	
Sales and marketing @3 % (inc website costs)	17,718	
Training/recruitment	1,500	
Repairs and Renewals @ 5% of revenue	29,530	
Admin and General @ 4% of revenue (see note)	23,624	
Misc : Rooms @ 5% (see note)	14,755	
Misc: Food @ 5% (see note)	10,554	
Misc: Beverages @ 1% (see note)	844	
Total Indirect Costs	**170,149**	**170,149**
Gross operating profit (EBITDA) @20.3%		**118,991**
Depreciation @ 5% of revenue	29,956	
Interest repayment @ 4.5%	18,000	
Directors' Drawings	25,000	
TOTAL	**72,956**	**72,956**
Net profit/Loss (7.7%)		**46,035**

Note: Miscellaneous costs are incurred in all three key revenue-earning divisions of the hotel – rooms, food and beverage. These are explained after the last table in this series, Table 8.9.

At 70% occupancy

In Table 19, at 70 per cent occupancy, we see a £22,809 improvement in net profit compared with occupancy at 60 per cent.

Table 8.4: Jolly's Resort Hotel – assuming 70% occupancy.

	£
Room revenue Assuming 70 per cent occupancy: 11 rooms x 365 days x 70% = 2,810 rooms sold. **Calculation:** At £240 per room - £30 revenue for both breakfasts = £210 x 2,810 = £590.100 – VAT @20% (divide by 1.2) = £491,750 – 30% for discounted rooms (£147,525) = **£344,225.** The average room rate is £344,225 ÷ 2,810 rooms = £122.50.	344,225
Food Revenues **Breakfast:** Assuming that every sleeper has breakfast. **Calculation:** Revenue is 11 rooms x 365 days x 70% x 1.8 (sleeper rate) = 5,059 breakfasts x £15 = **£75.885** - VAT at 20% (divide by 1.2) = **£63,237**	63,237
Lunch: Assuming an average of ten lunches a day **Calculation:** 10 lunches at £10 each x 365 = £36,500 - VAT at 20% (divide by 1.2) = **£30,416**	30,416
Dinner: Assuming 2,810 rooms sold with 1.8 sleeper occupancy = 5,058 sleepers. Calculation: 5,058 sleepers x £35 per head = £177,030 – VAT @ 20% (divide by 1.2) = **£147,525.** We are again assuming that every guest will have dinner and ignoring any chance dinners the hotel may attract.	147,525
Total food revenue: £241,178	241,178
Beverage: We are assuming beverage revenue is 40 per cent of food revenue - 40% of £241,178 = **£96,471**	96,471
Total revenue = **£681,874**	**£681,874**

Table 8.5: Payroll costs at 70% occupancy

Payroll	£
Rooms: 20% of room revenue (£344,225 x 20%). No night porter	68,845
Food: 35% of food revenue (£241,178 x 35%)	84,412
Beverage: 16% of beverage revenue (£96,471 x 16%)	15,435
Management/Admin: 5% of total revenue (£681,874 x 5%)	34,093
TOTAL	**202,785**

Payroll represents 29.7% of total revenue

Table 8.6: Jolly's Resort Hotel – assuming 70% occupancy.

	£	£
REVENUE		
Rooms	344,225	
Food	241,178	
Beverage	96,471	
TOTAL REVENUE	**681,874**	**681,874**
DIRECT COSTS		
Payroll/ NI @ 29.7% of revenue	202,785	
Food @ 30% of food revenue	72,353	
Beverages @ 30% of revenue	28,941	
Commission @12½% of room revenue	43,028	
Total direct costs	**347,107**	**347,107**
Gross profit (49.1%)		**334,767**
INDIRECT COSTS		
Rates and water rates (est)	40,000	
Energy @ 4% of total revenue	27,274	
Insurance (est)	5,000	
Telephone, broadband, mobile and fixed line (est)	3,000	
Sales and marketing @ 3% (inc website costs))	20,456	
Training/recruitment	1,500	
Repairs and Renewals @ 5% of revenue	34,093	
Admin and General @ 4% of revenue (see note)	27,274	
Misc : Rooms @ 5% (see note)	17,211	
Misc: Food @ 5% (inc breakfast) (see note)	12,058	
Misc: Beverages @ 1% (see note)	964	
Total Indirect Costs	**188,830**	**188,830**
Gross operating profit (EBITDA) @ 23%		**145,937**
Depreciation @ 5% of revenue	34,093	
Interest repayment @ 4.5%	18,000	
Directors' Drawings	25,000	
TOTAL	**77,093**	**77,093**
Net profit/Loss: (10%)		**68,844**

Note: Miscellaneous costs are incurred in all three key revenue-earning divisions of the hotel – rooms, food and beverage. These are explained after the last table in this series, Table 8.9.

At 80% occupancy

In Table 21, we calculate occupancy at 80 per cent and see a further £22,430 improvement in net profit compared with 70 per cent occupancy.

Table 8.7: Jolly's Hotel – assuming 70% occupancy.

	£
Room revenue	
Assuming 80 per cent occupancy: 11 rooms x 365 days x 80% = 3,212 rooms. .	
Calculation: At £240 per room - £30 revenue for both breakfasts = £210 x 3,212 = £674,520 – VAT @20% (divide by 1.2) = £562,100 – 30% for discounted rooms (£168,130) = **£393,470.**	393,470
The average room rate is £393,470 ÷ 3,212 rooms = £122.50 (*at this level of occupancy there would be scope of increasing the room rate.*)	
Food revenue	
Breakfast: Assuming that every sleeper has breakfast.	
Calculation: Revenue is 11 rooms x 365 days x 80% x 1.8 (sleeper rate) = 5,781 breakfasts x £15 = £86,724 - VAT at 20% () = **£72,270**	72,270
Lunch: Assuming an average of ten lunches a day	
Calculation: 10 lunches at £10 each x 365 = £36,500 - VAT at 20% () = **£30,416**	30,416
Dinner: Assuming 3,212 rooms sold with 1.8 sleeper occupancy = 5,781 sleepers.	
Calculation: 5,781 sleepers x £35 per head = £202,335 – VAT @ 20% () = £168,612.	168,612
We are again assuming that every guest will have dinner and ignoring any chance dinners the hotel may attract.	
Total food revenue: £271,298	271,298
Beverage: Assuming beverage revenue is 40 per cent of food revenue - 40% of £271,298 = **£108,519**	108,519
Total revenue is £773,287	773,287

Table 8.8: Payroll costs at 80% occupancy

Payroll	£
Rooms: 20% of room revenue (£393,470 x 20%)	78,694
Food: 35% of food revenue (£271,298 x 35%)	94,954
Beverage16% of beverage revenue (£108,519 x 16%)	17,363
Management/Admin: 5% of total revenue (£773,287 x 5%)	38,664
TOTAL	229,675

Payroll represents 29.7% of total revenue

Table 8.9: Jolly's Hotel – assuming 80% occupancy.

	£	£
REVENUE		
Rooms	393,470	
Food	271,298	
Beverage	108,519	
TOTAL REVENUE	**773,287**	**773,287**
DIRECT COSTS		
Payroll/ NI @ 29.7% of revenue	229,675	
Food @ 30% of food revenue	81,389	
Beverages @ 30% of revenue	32,555	
Commission @ 12½% of room revenue	49,183	
Total direct costs	**392,802**	**392,802**
Gross profit (49.2%)		380,485
INDIRECT COSTS		
Rates and water rates (est)	40,000	
Energy @ 4% of total revenue	30,931	
Insurance (est)	5,000	
Telephone, broadband, mobile and fixed line (est)	3,000	
Sales and marketing @ 3% (inc website costs))	23,198	
Training/recruitment	1,500	
Repairs and Renewals @ 5% of revenue	38,664	
Admin and General @ 4% of revenue (see note)	30,931	
Misc : Rooms @ 5% (see note)	19,673	
Misc: Food @ 5% (see note)	13,565	
Misc: Beverages @ 1% (see note)	1,085	
Total Indirect Costs	**207,547**	**207,547**
Gross operating profit (EBITDA) @ 22.5%		172,938
Depreciation @ 5% of revenue	38,664	
Interest repayment @ 4.5%	18,000	
Directors' Drawings	25,000	
TOTAL	**81,664**	81,664
Net profit (11.7%)		91,274

Note: Miscellaneous costs for the rooms division include the cost of linen and laundry; costs for the food division include linen and laundry and uniforms, while costs for the beverage division include glassware, uniforms and cleaning materials. These are called *departmental expenses* and a full list appears on the following page.

Departmental Expenses

1. Heat, light and power (maximum 4% of total revenue)
Gas, electricity, bottled gas, oil, wood/peat

2. Telephone
Equipment rental/hire,

3. Miscellaneous Food (5% of total revenue)
Guest supplies
Linen supplies
Disposables
Uniforms/cleaning
Cleaning supplies
Staff feeding supplies
Printing of menus etc
Contract cleaning
Laundry costs
Silverware/china
Kitchen supplies
Entertainment
Transport (late staff working)

4. Miscellaneous rooms (5% of room revenue)
Guest supplies
Linen supplies
Uniforms
Uniform cleaning
Cleaning supplies
Printing (directory)
In house movies
Background music
Contract cleaning
Transport (late staff working)
Linen hire
Laundry costs

5. Miscellaneous beverage (1% of beverage revenue)
Guest supplies
Uniforms/cleaning
Cleaning supplies
Printing (price lists)
Contract cleaning
Glassware
Entertainment
Licences
Transport (late staff working)
Contracts
Disposables

6. Training fees (1% of total revenue)

7. Admin and general (4% of total revenue)
Bad debt costs
Management fees
Computer support
Guests travel costs
Postage
Office supplies/first aid
Legal /professional fees
Bank charges (current account)
Bookkeeping fees
Audit fees
Subscriptions
Donations
Consortium fees
Credit card commission
Management expenses
Travel expenses
Motor expenses
Staff recruitment
Office equipment rental
Printing and stationery
Contracts

8. Advertising and promotions (3% of total revenue)
Social media expenses
Website development and promotion costs
E-mail shots
Brochures and other promotional print
Consortium fees
Local events and promotions
Local advertisements
Travel expenses

9. Repairs and maintenance (5% of total revenue)
Building maintenance
Window cleaning
Lift maintenance
Electrical
Fire equipment
Curtains
Carpet and floor cleaning
Plumbing and heating
Grounds and signage
Equipment renewals/hire
Maintenance contracts

10. Rent and rates
Business rates
Water rates
Waste removal
Ground rent

So would Jolly's Resort Hotel be a good purchase?

The hotel is based in an attractive seaside resort that is able to attract visitors on a year-round basis; higher levels of occupancy in the peak months tend to compensate for lower occupancy in the off-season. The hotel cannot expand in any way nor does it have the space to attract meetings and conferences. As all other options are closed, there are four principal routes to growing revenue and profit:

1 Cutting costs

2 Increasing occupancy

3 Increasing demand for F&B

4 Increasing prices

Cutting costs

If £20,000 can be taken out of the cost base the business becomes far more profitable even at 60 per cent occupancy. This could be achieved by:

1 Postponing any necessary R&R projects, providing the physical state of the hotel is up to standard. However, cutting back on the upkeep of the property might well store up even more expensive problems in subsequent years.

2 Saving a further £10,000 through better deals with suppliers but with such a small hotel, such savings verge on the unrealistic.

3 The owner could reduce his own drawings from the business.

Even if these savings can be achieved hotels have an unwelcome habit of incurring more rather than less cost when they have just been purchased. Because of this, a contingency fund of £10,000+ is advisable with any hotel purchase.

Increasing occupancy

At 70 per cent, the hotel should certainly attempt to increase occupancy. Setting a target of 75 per cent within 12 months would be a sensible first step, to be achieved by a bigger investment in sales and marketing which would, firstly, concentrate on promoting two and three night short break offers, especially in the off peak months. The use of past records and the development of a viable data base would be an important element in this promotion (see Chapter 17).

The ultimate aim would be 80 per cent occupancy. This is not impossible – there are hotels that reach 90 per cent occupancy – but in sustaining such a high level these hotels have to be in an outstanding location and be offering an exceptional and original standard of food, service and accommodation. In addition, they also have to be fashionable, which implies that they have attracted an extensive amount of media coverage.

Jolly's Resort Hotel does not fall into this category.

Increasing F&B sales

The growth of Jolly's business depends as much on developing its F&B operation as on any immediate increase in occupancy. At 70% occupancy, F&B already represents 50% of total turnover but in theory this could be increased as there is space in the restaurant to accommodate up to 30 chance diners as well as all the hotel guests.

Lunchtime is an area that could be exploited. If the number of lunches can be doubled £30,000 additional revenue would be raised, yielding some £12,000 EBITDA. Just as important, more customers at lunchtime would also provide the hotel with greater animation and activity during the day which many small hotels lack.

Operating a restaurant can yield significant returns providing it is properly costed and controlled, provided it has the right menu which is correctly priced, and provided the food is of the right standard and the restaurant has the right ambiance – but that's a lot of provisos.

What would be critically important in Jolly's case is that the hotel would have to lure every overnight guest into the restaurant for every night of their stay, which is what we have generously assumed in the example. This is unlikely to be achieved but even if ten more dinners could be sold for 60 per cent of the year, a further £61,000 in revenue or £18,000 in net profit would be generated.

However, there is little point in raising the standard of food and service in a restaurant that is totally out of keeping in terms of ambiance and style – or vice versa. Diners come for the total meal experience, not just for the food.

This could not be achieved without a skilled chef, a changing menu, special lunchtime offers, high quality service standards and an ambiance that is designed to attract the eating-out market. Considerable expenditure in the fabric and furnishings would be needed, in marketing the new facility and in upgrading the skill sets of the kitchen brigade, all of which require further investment.

Increasing prices

In theory, the higher the occupancy, the higher the price the hotel can charge.

Those operating at 85-90% occupancy are able to charge a premium price because their target market is willing to pay over the odds for the privilege of staying there. This is exceptional and in Jolly's case is unlikely ever to be achieved; at £240, the price is already challengingly high for what the hotel offers. If occupancy remains at 70% or below, it would be unrealistic to assume that there would be scope for increasing room prices significantly.

The danger of boosting occupancy by discounting lies in the fact that discounting does not necessarily boost occupancy sufficiently to compensate for the loss in income.

Jolly's Hotel could lower its B&B rate to £200 or even less but unless this boosts occupancy to compensate for the decline in income, such a move would have a wholly negative impact on profitability. Conversely, the higher the occupancy, the greater the scope for increasing tariffs. At 80 per cent, the hotel would be trading so strongly that it could consider raising its rate by £10 - £20 or even more. Managing the price at which rooms are sold, as well as keeping track of occupancy levels, are critically important management functions but they need to be carefully considered as part of the whole marketing plan.

Another alternative would be to charge extra for breakfast and sell rooms at a room-only rate.

This is, in effect, a 12.5 per cent tariff increase which would be noticed by regular guests but probably not by new customers. However, charging £270 for an overnight stay (which would be the price if two breakfasts were taken at £15 each) makes the hotel more expensive without any marked improvement in the standard of comfort and service. Implementing this policy immediately would be likely to damage occupancy and might lose the hotel a marketing advantage as most customers are more willing to pay an all-inclusive price than be faced with a string of additional costs as they leave. On the other hand, offering a room-only rate would suit those guests who don't want breakfast, although these would be in the minority and mainly in the corporate market.

The sale price, at £1.1m, is over seven times EBITDA at 70 per cent occupancy – a premium price for a hotel of this character that relies for its future increased profitability on skilled F&B management. To achieve higher profits, the hotel would have to provide a commercial restaurant rather than a hotel dining room which means that it would need to be given a separate identity.

> Anyone buying a hotel must analyse its strengths and weaknesses. The wise purchaser would see the dangers in Jolly's scenario. *Managing a restaurant demands different staff, different skills and different aptitudes to those needed for running a hotel.* A buyer with an extensive experience and interest in F&B would find Jolly's challenging enough; a buyer without F&B experience would be wise to give it a miss.

Other ways to value a property

There are some quick rule-of-thumb methods of assessing a hotel's value, one of which is expressed as a multiple of EBITDA – anything between five and nine times; the higher the multiple, the more valuable the hotel though this, again, is only an approximation and in London at least such a calculation is fairly meaningless. Such is the demand that hotels in the capital can be sold for significantly higher valuations. Valuations can also be highly subjective as Queen's Moat Houses proved in the early 1990s. Here, two reputable firms of valuers valued the QMH portfolio of hotels at widely differing levels – one was almost twice the other and undertaken only a year later. A third valuation agreed with neither of the previous two.

Professional hoteliers are often guided by the cost per bedroom to agree a valuation but this can range hugely depending on style and location. Some London hotels exchange hands for well over £700,000 per room while those in the provinces can be valued at under £50,000 – less if the property is poorly located and its business potential is doubtful. On average, most independent hotels fall in the £50,000-£85,000 per room category but such calculations are often thrown awry by the degree of food and beverage revenue, the quality of the rooms and whether they all have en suite facilities, the general level of upkeep and the need for renovation and refurbishment, the amount of grounds that a hotel owns and whether the owner's accommodation is included. In London, property values are much higher and the eagerness of hotel groups to own a property in the capital makes these calculations something of a nonsense anyway.

In the final analysis, the only satisfactory means of calculating an offer is go through the process that the potential purchaser of Jolly's Resort Hotel went through.

Five points to remember . . . .

This example illustrates not only the critical importance of occupancy but the main considerations in any purchase.

1   **Consider the present trading position of the hotel and analyse its strengths and weaknesses.**

2   **Analyse these accounts against industry norms – if there's a big difference in any items, why?**

3   **Consider how you are going to improve the business – in what areas can it be developed and which markets will be denied because of the hotel's physical limitations?**

4   **Play to your own strengths. A hotel that depends on developing its F&B business, for example, is going to demand more talent and more commercial commitment than a hotel that just relies on room sales.**

5   **Be prepared to refuse to buy. If the figures don't add up, if the trading pattern is unsuitable and if the prospects are limited, look elsewhere.**

. . . and finally

After visiting a property, you will come away with the feeling that either the hotel is definitely not the place for you or that it could be your ideal hotel.

Avoid the danger of rationalising the drawbacks and highlighting the advantages – a dangerous exercise in any important commercial decision.

Ten more pieces of advice!

1 Occupancy is important – but the room rate is even more important.

2 Any increase in occupancy feeds directly into the bottom line – but so does an increase in room rate. Balance the two for the greatest yield.

3 Recognise that discounting room rates is now a reality.

4 Don't forget to budget for a commission to agencies – allow 12.5 per cent of room rate as a minimum.

5 Calculate payroll costs accurately – they vary from department to department.

6 Engage additional staff only when absolutely necessary – they cost you money! Organise work patterns of existing staff more effectively.

7 Budget realistically: better to overestimate costs and underestimate revenue – that way you won't get a nasty surprise.

8 Never forget – food and beverage costs should not exceed 30 per cent of food and beverage sales.

9 Check that the vendor's costs and revenues match the industry norms in Tables 8.1-8.6. If not, why not?

10 Don't rationalise the drawbacks of any purchase – remember, you will only have to overcome them later.

8

9 Is the purchase feasible?

"There are many types of hotel – commercial, town centre, seaside, country house, boutique – your first step is to know what type of establishment you want to buy.

When I bought The Cottage in the Wood in 1987, I researched the trends and discovered that the overseas holiday market was a major threat to our traditional seaside resorts. I drew a map of anything south of a line from the Mersey to the Wash, excluding seaside and poor old Wales. We had already decided we wanted to run a country house hotel but one with a point of difference that we could market.

I signed up with the commercial estate agents and scanned the trade press for properties, only to discover that my requirements were broadly ignored by the agents. I only visited a handful of hotels; most did not match my criteria.

We were regarded as 'unknown' by lenders so I was pushed towards a finance broker. This proved to be excellent as he was helpful and responsive and effected an introduction for me. There are many brokers available and the large agents have their own finance division; normally a fee is payable to the broker and sometimes to the funder. They will also advise and guide you - they can often obtain funding when your own efforts have hit the buffers.

You need a good and responsive solicitor to undertake the conveyance and ensure your interests are fully protected and, don't forget, you become responsible for insurance at exchange of contract stage. I would always appoint a chartered surveyor to check out the property.

Read Chapter 21 carefully! In 27 years of hotel ownership we have continually upgraded and improved the property including a major re-development plan which saw the removal of eight inadequate bedrooms to be replaced with a new building that added 10 bedrooms taking us from 20 to 30.

And remember - there is a real danger that once the hotel is known to be for sale, the staff will become unsettled, weddings are cancelled, and the locals stop coming to drink and eat. Factor this in when buying any property."

John Pattin
Proprietor, Cottage in the Wood, Malvern, Worcs

The accounts have shown how the hotel has traded during the past three years. The vendor's answers to your questions have provided important information about the physical structure of the building and about the business. Now, we have to look to the future. How will the business develop in the first few years of your ownership? If you are to obtain funding for the purchase, the finance source will certainly need to understand your plans and how you are going to achieve them. In other words, you have to prepare a business plan to ensure that the purchase is viable.

If a hotel is making good profits with high occupancy, you need to satisfy yourself that these profits will continue to grow. The hospitality industry is one in which the personality of the owner plays a significant part in the success of any business. The smaller the establishment, the more likely it is that the owner attracts customers by the strength of his own personality. This is particularly true of restaurants. You should expect some decline in trade until regular customers have become accustomed to your new style of ownership. A proportion may never do so but, to compensate, you should be able to attract new customers of your own.

Even with a profitable hotel, opportunities for future expansion and development should not be overlooked. It is a cliché to say that a business that stands still goes backwards but it is true, nevertheless. A new conference room could open new markets; the addition of more bedrooms might be possible; if you have the space, a health spa might be an added attraction for hotel guests, particularly if it is a resort or country house hotel or one that attracts a younger clientele.

If the hotel is not fulfilling its potential – or maybe is making a loss – the need for such developments may be even more urgent but there may be a simpler explanation for poor performance: the management of the hotel is just not up to scratch.

In the following example based on a real purchase, the ownership and management of the hotel were sadly lacking: investment had been cut back, staff were de-motivated, the standard of food and service had declined and the business had become more of a drinking pub than a hotel. Some or all of these factors apply to many hotels on the market because owners and managers frequently do not have the ability to maximise the hotel's potential.

So, whatever the state of the accounts, you have to look to the future rather than the past. In doing so, the accounts will show the way; an analysis of them will show the weaker parts of the business. You have to show how you can put the business right, how much investment you need and how long it will take you.

This is the basis of the business plan. Its benefit to the potential purchaser is that it concentrates his mind wonderfully on the solution to the challenges of the business and makes him think of the opportunities that are presented. **Setting a goal gives focus and direction.** Like every plan and target, the objectives may not all be reached at the right time but the exercise of putting aims and objectives on paper, of carefully reasoning them through, is a highly beneficial and necessary discipline.

9

It is also essential if you need to raise finance to buy the hotel. The bank or finance house will want to know where you see the future of the business and you will need to have a reasoned and realistic business plan to support the application.

Your business plan will, if properly carried out, give you a picture of the business in the first two years of operation under your control. This, in turn, will confirm that the asking price is realistic and the business proposition is sound.

The White Harte

Business Plan: an example

The following plan is based on a 16-bedroom hotel in an English market town. The hotel, which we shall call The White Harte, was purchased by a professional hotelier whom we shall call Nigel Jones and it was prepared for two reasons:

1   To give precise reasoning to back up his initial enthusiasm for the hotel.

2   To help raise finance for the purchase.

The example has necessarily been shortened and some of the details of the hotel have been omitted or amended.

The plan began with a full description of the hotel and its facilities, the number of bedrooms (all with bathroom en suite), the services and other physical amenities. It then explained the geographic area of the town, noting its close proximity to other major centres by road and rail, its state of prosperity and its future business and industrial potential. It also examined the competition – what markets they were in and how much of a challenge they posed.

He found that the hotel was located in a prime position in the middle of the town – a good sign because it implies it is the centre of the local population for shopping and other amenities. A leisure centre had been recently built and there were sporting activities available including shooting and a nearby racecourse. Although farming was the major activity (perhaps a promising source of potential business for dinners and banquets) there were a number of well-known national companies with big factories on the outskirts. The town also attracted tourists in the summer because of its historic and scenic connections. Colleges and a university nearby and one or two boarding schools promised a raft of business.

Jones wrote in his report: *"Such a profusion of education establishments suggests a flourishing resident population and also indicates a flow of people into the area, visiting offspring at the various establishments. All must be potential users of the hotel's services..."*

Looking to the future, a visit to the local planning office enabled him to discover that a national company was planning to build a new office complex scheduled for completion by the end of the following year, which would employ 600 people, all of whom would be living in the area. There were several major new housing developments in the town.

Jones then looked at the hotel he was considering buying. The White Harte was the only significant hotel in town – a very unusual situation – which made his business forecast easier. There were a number of small guest houses and one or two pubs with rooms but the nearest branded hotel was nine miles away. The town had so far escaped the incursion of a budget hotel. There were the usual numbers of pubs and some small unlicensed restaurants but only a few of the pubs had a strong line in bar meals. There were two other restaurants that provided dinner and the town hall provided space for large functions.

This information was gleaned from visits to all the pubs and restaurants in the town where Jones talked to the landlords and locals about the area. From all these investigations into the locality he concluded that the town was:

"A market town with a prosperous farming community, expanding industrial developments and a centre for leisure and sporting facilities.

"A number of factors have acted together to produce an increasing demand for hotel and catering facilities. These include:

1. Increasing population

2. Movement of industry into the town

3. Proximity to other large towns and their easy accessibility

4. Tourist attractions

5. The provision of sports facilities in the town and local sporting events such as horse racing

6. Existence of colleges and boarding schools

"The lack of any other hotel and the small number of good licensed restaurants means that the hotel, under professional management, could exploit the market for a complete range of hotel and catering services."

The hotel was owned and was being run by a small brewery under a manager and it was clear from the brief summary of the turnover for the previous three years (Table 9.1) that, taking inflation into account, it had not achieved growth over the period and that its potential was totally unrealised.

Table 9.1: The White Harte: Turnover for year ending September 30

	Year 1	Year 2	Year 3
Liquor	262,222	272,464	280,624
Food	165,172	160,290	155,620
Rooms	80,708	82,628	82,212
Sundries	10,972	9,250	9,610
	519,074	524,632	528,066

According to the accounts, Gross Operating Profit (EBITDA) in Year 3 was £20,692, though no allowance was made for repairs and renewals which, if properly allocated, would have turned the profit into a net loss.

Bars

As this was brewery owned, it was not surprising that bar revenues exceeded all other revenues put together, despite the fact that the building had 16 letting bedrooms. The brewery's primary aim was to sell beer. Even so, between the first two years, bar turnover rose by 3.9 per cent and between the second and third years by 2.9 per cent. In other words, turnover hardly kept pace with inflation which, at the time of the purchase averaged 3.0 per cent.

Food

Between the first two years, food turnover decreased by 2.9 per cent and by a further 2.9 per cent between the second and the third year. Taking inflation into account, this apparently small fall in food sales in current terms is infinitely more serious in real terms. The decline in food sales indicated something was radically wrong with the food being provided and the way in which it was being promoted.

Rooms

Between the first two years, turnover increased by 2.4 per cent and decreased by 0.5 per cent between the second and the third year. Allowing for inflation, there was no growth in room sales in the three year period, yet this department was potentially the most lucrative.

Sundries

Most of this revenue was from the machines in the gaming room, but it also included revenue from tobacco and telephone sales.

Total turnover

In the first period, turnover increased by 1.1 per cent and in the second period by 0.6 per cent. Again, the increase in turnover had not kept pace with inflation.

The study examined all four areas in detail, with the following conclusion.

"The hotel is doing little more than treading water. It has lost six per cent of its food revenue over three years and room sales actually declined in Year 3."

The accounts – such as were provided initially – revealed a fundamental weakness in the hotel's trading position. For a sixteen-bedroom hotel, the unit was totally dependent on bar and bar food sales. The rooms, proportionately much more profitable, were producing only 15 per cent of revenue. Why was this? Of the 16 rooms, 14 were doubles and two were singles – all had en suite facilities but they needed upgrading. The average number of rooms sold per night was seven, giving an average room occupancy of 43 per cent but almost all the rooms were being sold as singles, so sleeper occupancy was lower. There was little weekend occupancy when a demand for double rooms would be expected. In spite of the low tariff (averaging £33 per person) the hotel was still not attracting customers.

In the restaurant the average spend per customer at lunch and dinner was reasonable for the establishment but the number of covers sold was very low and little chance business was attracted yet the potential for building up these food and beverage sales, given the location of the hotel in the middle of the town, was clear.

A closer examination of the hotel produced the following information:

Business travellers

Monday to Thursday only; poor occupancy due to dated room standards, poor hygiene, lack of promotion, indifferent food choice and poor standards of cooking. Very little occupancy at weekends which, given the hotel's location, was a lost opportunity,

Lunch and dinner business

Very low numbers all week; no chance trade in spite of being in the town centre – due to an unattractive restaurant which lacked atmosphere and any warm ambiance, as well as the poor quality of food provided.

Bar trade

Busy bar trade all week from locals and residents but for a hotel in a prime location in the middle of the town much of the potential was not being realised and takings could be improved; no "hostmanship" was being displayed.

Bar snacks

Only served Monday to Friday although Saturday was a market day when the bar was very busy. The take-up was poor because portions and presentation were indifferent and unattractive.

Gaming machines

They were available every weekday evening in a function room that had been converted into a pool hall with fruit machines and a pool table. The room had a bar but produced poor takings and tended to attract under-age drinkers. This deterred other locals from using the facility (even if they wanted to) and gave the hotel an unhealthy image. Worse, it made the room unavailable for letting for more lucrative functions.

In general, the standard of housekeeping and cleanliness was poor and the bars lacked supervision; Jones' experience led him to conclude that pilferage would be rife. Little leadership was given. There was no promotional literature and no advertising was undertaken; the website was poor and browsers were unable to buy directly off it. There was no regular maintenance programme. Redecoration was necessary in almost all main areas and all the bedrooms but none had been undertaken in the previous three years.

Jones' summary of business was:

"The hotel represents a totally unexploited business. It has been run as a public house with emphasis placed on earning revenue in the bars and associated outlets such as gaming machines. Little effort has been made in the past to exploit the demand for hotel accommodation despite the extensive facilities that the hotel possesses. Advance reservations for rooms and catering are extremely poor. Opportunities for pilferage abound through lack of supervision and security. The hotel has a very poor reputation with local populace."

Jones realised he would need to provide a sound business plan with targets and realistic forecasting if he was to be successful in obtaining the finance he needed.

Looking at the market opportunities, he divided them into a number of different areas and his feasibility study stated:

Weekday occupancy

"Build up existing slim trade by providing higher standards of comfort, food and cleanliness. All bedrooms and bathrooms to be refurbished to bring them up to standard and £10,000 per bedroom to be allocated to this project – this to be put into immediate effect on the purchase of the hotel; bedrooms to be taken off floor by floor (there are three floors) to avoid unnecessary disruption. Four bathrooms to be refitted at a budgeted cost of £5,000 each.

Weekday occupancy to be increased by promoting 24 hour conference packages in conjunction with the upgrade of the function room, and by building up corporate trade.

In order to build up occupancy, the website to be developed into a more aggressive sales tool, with the ability for guests to book online; local companies and organisations to be contacted both by mail and in person; use of social media and hotel guides and other promotional media to be optimised.

Once refurbishment is completed prices to be adjusted so that rates are placed on a per room basis, with proposed room rate at £100 (inc VAT) per room, breakfast (£15) extra; once demand strengthens and is sustained, prices to be increased to £105 in Year 2.

Total budget for refurbishment of rooms: £180,000

Budget for conversion of three staff bedrooms is £80,000 to be implemented late in Year 1 from earnings, including an allocation from the capital budget."

Weekend occupancy

"Weekend packages to be introduced with special deals including such offers as three nights for the price of two, special themed weekends – some run in conjunction with local attractions or local events; weekends to be promoted through the website, by advertising, social media and web-based agency sites."

Chance restaurant trade

"To be built up by converting the dining area into a brasserie-style restaurant, making it a more attractive venue with a better design and softer lighting; new tables to be used without tablecloths (to make the room more informal and to save on linen and laundry costs). Floor covering to be reconsidered – existing carpet to be thrown away but floor boards to be examined and, if appropriate, sanded, stained and polished in keeping with brasserie ambiance. Also critical is an improvement in food standards and the introduction of two/three course lunchtime menus and other offers to be promoted through local advertising, in-house and exterior promotions, 'A' boards outside, and by direct mail shots to local businesses. Before implementation, a new chef to be recruited to oversee the creation of new dishes and new menus.

Budget for the refurbishment of restaurant: £20,000. (Jones recognised this was on the low side and might need to be increased.)

New items of equipment required for the kitchen (new tabling and one new oven, as well as some other minor equipment) which was estimated at circa £30,000; further investment required in future years. Work to be postponed until the new chef has settled in and a joint decision is taken on what is required and how the flow of work in the kitchen can be better planned. This work to be deferred to Year 2 but planning is a key activity in Year 1. It is intended that the investment can be funded out of earnings in Year 2."

Increase bar snacks

"To be developed by improving food standards and presentation, providing greater choice and variety of snacks, with more effective merchandising particularly exploiting the hotel's prime trading position on market day – Saturday. One aim: to convert 25 per cent of those taking a lunch-time bar snack to eat in the restaurant."

Morning coffees and teas

"Both aim at the female audience and, if successful, will greatly extend the White Harte's attraction. To be developed by introducing appropriate menus with choice of coffees, pastries and biscuits and sandwiches, scones and cakes in the afternoon. Promotional signs outside the hotel, including 'A' boards and in-house promotion; some advertising to be introduced."

Functions

"Take out the uneconomic gaming machines and pool table, which gives the hotel a poor image; refurbish the room so that it is suitable for meetings and functions; new décor, carpet, furnishings; the new facility to be promoted by direct mail shots to local businesses, advertisements in the local press and through in-house promotions, as well as through the website and social media.

Budget for refurbishment: £20,000."

Friday and Saturday evenings

"No attempt has been made to develop business in the restaurant on Fridays or Saturdays, the principal evenings of the week; with an average of four covers on a Saturday night, the restaurant is completely uneconomic. The room can accommodate 90 diners and trade to be developed by promoting special menus, with special offers such as a 'free' glass of champagne or half a bottle of wine (cost to be included in the price), and higher food quality and better service. Local advertising to be undertaken but word of mouth advertising will be more effective; improved weekend room occupancy will also increase demand.

Private dinner dances to be promoted for the function room."

Special promotions

"To develop package promotions to the nearby race course, during race meetings, possibly in conjunction with a local coach firm."

Rotary and others

"Fortnightly lunches to be encouraged because they attract local people and local business-men into the hotel. Other organisations to be targeted include Lions, Round Table and the Masons. Although difficult to increase prices for this market, with better standards of food and service the meetings will act as an effective means of enabling the hotel to become known amongst an important section of the local business community; full advantage to be taken to meet Rotary members to sell on other hotel services."

One of Jones' first acts was to join Rotary while he encouraged his chef to join the Lions – encouraging key members of the management team to join local associations is an effective way of networking and getting the business known locally.

Other development opportunities

The plan also looked at the medium term, with two further development opportunities:

1 To turn three of four unused staff bedrooms into guest rooms all with bath and shower; the remaining room to be used for management sleepovers.
2 To convert a large, empty barn at the back of the hotel, which fronted on to a back street, into a wine bar.

In the longer term Jones was anxious to acquire adjoining premises in order to add more bedrooms to the hotel. This latter aim was in the distant future and dependent on availability and cost. This did not form an integral part of his business plan but both the medium-term projects were included because they were relevant and scheduled for early implementation; they also showed his commitment to the purchase.

These plans gave the bare outline of Jones's immediate objectives. What they show is that he had a clear idea of the challenges and of the solutions. The aim was to turn the establishment from a bar-orientated business into a hotel with a much broader food and accommodation base. He aimed to become more food-led, attracting a greater share of local business entertaining as well as building up the leisure eating-out market. Equally important, he aimed to make the hotel a centre for social activity in the area.

The budget for the immediate improvements was £220,000 which he needed to include in his loan application to his funding source as this was an integral part of the application. He also needed a further £80,000 to convert the three staff bedrooms; these funds were also required for Year 1 as he planned to start work on this project in the first year so that the bedrooms came on stream for Year 2.

The hotel was on the market for £650,000 – clearly a high price for a business that, in reality, was operating at a loss and which required considerable re-investment but the hotel's location, and its unrealised potential, were both highly attractive; the opportunity to convert three of the four staff bedrooms into letting rooms provided a valuable additional revenue stream.

Jones was able to invest £400,000 into the purchase, leaving a balance of £250,000 plus a further £220,000 in order to bring the premises up to the standard demanded; this excluded the £80,000 required for the bedroom conversions. In total he required an advance of circa 70 per cent, a very high loan to value ratio for a business that had potential but was currently unprofitable.

He realised that the amount of investment that was required to bring the hotel up to scratch would be a negative factor in any loan application; on the other hand, his experience of the hotel industry would be held in his favour. If his application could show that he knew exactly what he was planning to do, and why, and how profitable the business could be, he believed that it was possible that he could raise the necessary funds. The improvements he planned would be the decisive factor in the hotel's future profitability; without them, the purchase was not viable.

What were the targets?

How were these plans to be achieved? Jones divided them into the short-term (up to one year) and medium-term (the second year). He believed that any plans beyond two years would be meaningless at the present stage of the hotel's development.

He decided to set himself some specific marketing objectives for each of the two years with a brief description of how he would achieve them. This, in turn, was turned into a budget P&L account for 12 months and a cash flow forecast

The Year 1 targets were:

1 Increase room occupancy to 75 per cent.
2 Increase weekday lunches to 10 per day.
3 Increase Sunday lunches to 30 per day.
4 Increase Monday-Thursday dinners to 12 per night.
5 Increase Friday and Saturday dinners to 50 per night.
6 Increase lunch spend to £15 per head (Sunday £30 per head).

7   Maintain dinner spend at an average of £20 per head.

8   Increase beverage spend for weekday lunch to £3 per head.

9   Increase beverage spend at Sunday lunch to £5 per head.

10 Increase beverage spend at weekday dinners to £5 per head.

11 Sell £80 worth of snacks in the bar every day.

12 Develop the function room as a revenue stream.

13 Increase function numbers to 80 per month at average spend of £25, plus £5 per head for beverages.

14 Increase main bar takings to £900 per day.

15 Appoint new staff in key positions and retrain remaining personnel.

Targets are useful only if they are realistic and achievable. Jones considered these targets were tough in the first year of operation but he considered they were attainable provided the necessary investment in the property could go ahead and sufficient emphasis on sales was undertaken. To achieve these 14 objectives he would:

1   Raise standards of comfort and style of bedrooms/bathrooms through a refurbishment programme to be implemented immediately.

2   Raise standards of comfort and ambiance in the restaurant and bar through upgrading the areas, making both areas more attractive.

3   Introduce weekend special offers, some themed, to be promoted locally and nationally.

4   Introduce special weekday overnight offers on dates that were traditionally weak.

5   Introduce special lunch-time offers.

6   Create special menus for weekend dinners and Sunday lunch.

7   Employ a more highly skilled chef and kitchen brigade.

8   Improve bar sales through better bar staff training and hostmanship.

9   Introduce morning coffee/afternoon tea service in the bar area.

10 Recruit new staff in the front of house, restaurant and rooms departments and ensure they have the right skills.

11 Provide 'standards of performance' manuals so that all members of staff know what their job comprises and what standards are expected.

12 Set up a system of simple on-the-job training, keep training records and develop a training programme in social skills for waiting and front- of- house staff designed to maximise their effectiveness.

13 Find and exploit all sales opportunities including internet sales.

14 Introduce strict cost control systems especially in the F&B department.

15 Develop the website as a powerful sales tool.

Looking further ahead, the Year 2 plan consisted of 19 new targets:

1   Increase room occupancy to 78 per cent.

2   Increase Monday-Saturday lunches to 20 per day.

3   Increase Sunday lunches to 40 a day.

4   Increase Monday-Thursday dinners to 20 per day.

5   Increase Friday and Saturday dinners to 60 per night.

6   Maintain Monday-Saturday lunch spend at £15 per head.

7   Maintain Sunday lunch spend at £30 per head.

8   Maintain beverage spend for Monday-Saturday lunches at £3 per head.

9   Maintain beverage spend for Sunday lunch at £5 per head.

10 Maintain beverage spend for Monday-Thursday dinners at £5 per head.

11 Sell £120 worth of snacks at the bar every day.

12 Develop the function room as a conference/meeting room.

13 Increase function covers to 120 per month.

14 Increase bar takings to £950 per day.

15 Staff turnover not to exceed 10 per cent once new staff have been appointed.

16 Increase room rates by five per cent.

17 All staff to have a minimum of two 30 minute training sessions per week.

18 Convert three unused staff bedrooms to letting rooms.

19 Plan and introduce new kitchen layout.

He set out the following methods by which he would achieve these objectives:

1   Ensure the hotel makes full use of social media.

2   Continue to develop weekday and weekend occupancy through internet booking agencies.

3   Increase the catchment area from which local business is taken.

4   Consider joining a marketing consortium or set up marketing arrangements with some other hotels.

5   Use special promotional events to attract more business – for example, gastronomic weekends, racing weekends, wedding promotions.

6   Promote the hotel to all new businesses moving into the area.

7   Develop more function business by introducing 8/24h conference and meeting packages; a minimum of two wedding promotions per year.

8   To achieve recognition by such organisations as Good Food Guide, AA Guide, Trip Advisor (in particular).

Improving standards

Jones added a brief note explaining exactly how he would raise the standards of the hotel:

◆ **Food standards:** To be improved through more highly skilled staff, correct purchasing, correct storage, correct presentation, good hygiene.

◆ **Bar standards:** To be improved by better training, better hostmanship, correct pricing, correct price purchasing, tight stock control, correct storage, correct presentation, good hygiene, good security.

◆ **Accommodation standards:** To be improved through complete refurbishment programme, improvement in décor and decoration, correct cleaning, hire of linen stock, training of staff and a regular maintenance programme.

◆ **Service and staffing standards**: To be improved by hiring appropriate staff, increasing staff motivation, introducing good conditions of employment, ensuring good discipline through training.

These targets indicated how Jones was going to develop the business. After improving standards and quality in the first year, the second year would give him the chance to consolidate. Occupancy would be improved through more aggressive sales promotion and by using more on-line agency websites.

The function room would drive the small conference and meetings business. Through higher standards Jones would be in a position to increase prices for the rooms in Year 2 thus yielding more revenue per room. In Year 1, he recognised that the improvement of the website and the introduction of sales literature would incur higher sales and marketing costs than in subsequent years; similarly, recruitment and training costs would be higher in Year 1.

How to increase revenue?

As we saw in the Jolly's Resort Hotel example, once the maximum number of overnight guests or diners has been reached, there are only a limited number of ways that a hotel can increase revenue:

a) Raise prices

b) Increase in-house sales

c) Undertake structural alterations by adding rooms through extensions.

Jones was already planning to add additional rooms but prices can be increased only if there is a sufficiently strong demand. Increasing in-house sales is feasible only if the staff have been given appropriate training. In fact, most hotels will attempt to add a few percentage points of occupancy by discounting rather than increasing their prices in order to boost demand. In effect, this is what Jones was planning to do by introducing special three-nights-for-the-price-of- two and similar offers in order to gain those extra room sales. But once guests are in the premises, they can be encouraged to drink at the bar and spend in other ways, thus helping to make up for the income lost by discounting. Providing the deals are costed properly they will still be profitable.

Encouraging diners to have a cocktail beforehand, side orders with their meal, wine, dessert, liqueur or coffee can add as much as 15 per cent to F&B revenues. Up-selling these additional items, providing the staff are properly trained, can be hugely profitable but the opportunities need to be carefully handled to avoid diners having the impression that they are being pushed into spending more.

While Jones recognised that special deals are less profitable than full rate bookings, he took the view that higher quality rooms and a more attractive ambiance generally would enable him to price the rooms at a higher rate in the first place, thus gaining higher REVpar. He believed that the upgrade of his rooms and of the whole hotel would attract new markets; in other words, provided the hotel offered value for money, he could increase prices to levels that could not only be sustained but enhanced.

All the objectives relied on the fact that he had to recruit new key full-time members of staff. A head chef would be needed, plus two sous chefs if they were to cope with the expected increase in demand; a restaurant manager to be responsible for food service and a head receptionist to deal with bookings and to oversee the development of the website and social media would also need to be recruited. This would probably take several months though Jones already had a head chef in mind – someone who had worked for him before and who was willing to join him.

His own role would combine the oversight of the refurbishment programme with his wife, and for both to handle the recruitment of new staff and the training of the staff that remained. He would also devote one day a week to visiting local businesses and meeting potential local clients. His wife, who was also an experienced hotelier, would spend most of her time in the first year on the design aspects of the refurbishment programme and day-to-day control but would be available to help out front-of-house at times of peak demand.

With his plans outlined, both of them realised that the purchase of the hotel was a full-time commitment, particularly in the first year. Both recognised that they would be living and breathing the hotel for 24 hours every day – a daunting thought but one to which they were prepared to commit.

Finally, he set out his principal objective which he regarded as an essential goal: to provide value for money: this must be the primary objective of every hospitality enterprise. No matter what price is being charged, the customer must always believe he has received value for money; if he does not, he will never return and, worse, may well complain about his experience on TripAdvisor, Twitter or Facebook, thus compounding the problem facing the hotel.

But what about the sales forecast?

Jones recognised that these plans and objectives only took him so far. A sales and costs forecast was also required for the first two years of operation. This would show how much extra revenue would be produced by the successful implementation of his plans. But extra revenue also implies extra costs. It was necessary, therefore, to look at projected costs and revenues to verify how much profit the hotel would produce if all his plans came to fruition.

Costs are certain but revenues are only estimates. The example shows the steps that need to be taken to prepare a trading forecast as the core element of a business plan. Any funding source will want to know how you intend to develop the business and what the likely trading position will be in the first few years of operation. Above all, it will want to know whether you can repay the funds being advanced over the timescale of the loan period. The business plan must explain all.

Such a forecast in the form of a budget can only assume that the business meets the targets set out, some of which might not be achieved although others might be exceeded. In this particular hotel, raising occupancy levels to 75 per cent would be a tall order and would be difficult to achieve in the first year but Jones believed it was an important goal to aim for and he had confidence that it was achievable with his upgraded rooms. On the other hand, it was likely that if he succeeded in attracting forty covers for a Saturday night he would be able to increase to fifty people with word of mouth advertising and some local promotion. Success tends to breed success – but this is only true if value for money continues to be provided.

So Jones prepared a sales and costs analysis which itemised as accurately as possible how much money he would earn in the different sectors of the F&B department - see Tables 9.4 and 9.8 (see pages 115-118).

He prepared a separate estimate for payroll costs because they represent such an important part of any hotel's general cost structure – see Tables 9.3 and 9.7. In Year 1, the projected payroll costs amounted to 28.9 per cent of revenue – a somewhat low figure and one that might not be met. This increases to 29.6 per cent in Year 2, reflecting the hotel's three additional rooms and more active F&B revenue. Maintaining these percentages would be a challenge, however, and Jones recognised that he might have to allow some leeway; experience would guide him in the future.

Jones also prepared a budgeted profit and loss account with all known and assumed sales and costs, together with the major operating ratios (see Tables 9.4 and 9.9). The accounts show that he expected the hotel to achieve EBITDA of £214,491 in Year 1 (20 per cent) and £327,786 (23.3 per cent) in Year 2. Against these sums, Jones would need to subtract loan interest and capital repayments, directors' fees and an amount for depreciation, leaving a net profit of £73,848 (6.9 per cent) in Year 1 and a healthy £164,551 (11.3 per cent) in Year 2.

What was the outcome?

Experience subsequently showed that most of Jones's projections were correct. All the important percentages were more or less achieved in Years 1 and 2. Bedroom and restaurant revenue more than doubled and takings in the bar increased compared with the turnover under the previous owner. The wage percentage evened out at 27.8% in the first year but rose to 29.5% in Year 2 (very close to his budgeted cost) while energy, water and insurance costs were higher and there were variations in other costs including laundry, music and entertainment and rentals.

There were also variations in his budgeted expenditure. His bedroom refurbishment programme came in £20,000 under budget partly because he joined a buying consortium and was able to buy furniture and furnishings at discounted rates; his wife took control of the programme and they did not employ a design consultant. Although this was personally time-consuming, it saved on consultancy fees and, in order to save more time, they decided not to individualise every room but to make them as standard as possible, with furniture and furnishings of identical style.

A similar approach was taken to the upgrade of the four bathrooms that required a complete refit. Jones also decided to blitz the programme by shutting all the bedrooms for a four week period rather than implementing the programme room by room. The loss of income was sustainable as revenue from the rooms was so low that losing it for a month was balanced by the advantage of having all his rooms upgraded and brought on stream at the same time.

In fact, Jones considered closing the hotel entirely for a six week period in order to upgrade all the areas, including the restaurant, function room and bar, but this would have been a step too far. Losing the income from the bar for six weeks would have lost at least £30,000 at a time when every penny counted. Besides, he did not want to deny his regulars access to the bar for such a long period of time as this would only encourage them to find an alternative hostelry with the danger of losing them completely. In any case, the layout of the building enabled work to be confined to the various areas so the workings of the hotel would not be unduly disrupted. An added benefit was that if it was evident that work was being undertaken to upgrade the hotel's facilities, word would spread throughout the town – a considerable PR benefit.

The subsequent upgrade of the restaurant and function room, which was started after the bedroom refurbishment was completed, overran the budget by some £5,000 and took longer than planned because of the time taken deciding on the new designs and décor, changes in the lighting and then ordering and taking delivery of the new furniture – three months in all, which was far longer than planned. Once the carpet was removed, the floorboards were found to be in excellent condition; after sanding and polishing, they complemented the casual brasserie-style theme. The restaurant had to be suitable for both lunch and dinner so the bright and cheerful ambiance for breakfast and lunch was more subdued for dinner – mainly achieved by using some table linen at dinner, changing the lighting, and using candles extensively.

Six weeks after Jones took over the White Harte, the new head chef, Andy, arrived – a welcome appointment. Jones was keen to integrate Andy's ideas with his own in order to ensure that the restaurant refurbishment was in line with his aim of introducing a brasserie-style menu. One of Andy's first tasks, however, was to oversee the cleaning of the kitchen which had been left in a very poor condition. Contractors were brought in and only a very limited food service was available for the two days that it took to deep clean the equipment, floors and walls. Once completed, thoughts turned to compiling the new menus and the recipes to be used.

At the same time, Jones recognised that marketing and selling the new facilities was an even more pressing need. He decided to modernise the White Harte's image by hiring a graphic designer to produce a new logo and print design; using the new designs he engaged a website designer to upgrade the hotel's site and to enable it to take on-line bookings. These were budgeted costs for Year 1.

Jones recognised that, even though he and his wife were totally preoccupied with the refurbishment programme, he needed to spread himself around the community, visit potential clients to boost corporate weekday business, devise weekend packages, prepare the wages – and meet and greet guests, all at the same time.

For four months, neither he nor his wife took a day off – a situation made worse by the fact that the other key appointments, for a receptionist and restaurant manager, took much longer than he anticipated; he was determined to make the right choice and many candidates were deemed unsuitable.

During this period, it became clear that only one of the two barmen should be retained and Jones was mightily relieved when the other gave his notice giving the opportunity to recruit a new person who could display a much better attitude to customers. Similarly, the one room maid also departed and advertisements for two part-time replacements generated a positive response.

Five months later

Five months after his takeover of the White Harte, the receptionist and restaurant manager posts were both filled and Andy had decided to train up the young commis who remained while recruiting a sous chef two months later. He approached final year students in the local catering college for a replacement commis; although this did not yield an immediate result, a subsequent enquiry from a student was positive.

Jones then had time to turn his attention to his other major project: planning the conversion of the four staff bedrooms to three guest rooms and one room for management sleepovers. This became more complicated than he envisaged and took three months, much longer than planned, and required the services of an architect because of the need for structural alterations and new plumbing and electrical lines. It was only towards the end of Year 1 that the conversion began. The project, which was budgeted at £80,000, overran by £30,000 because of the additional structural work involved.

More importantly, Jones decided to upgrade these rooms to a higher specification than the hotel's 16 rooms which he had just refurbished, reckoning that it would be more profitable to market and sell them as high quality, boutique-style accommodation than as more run-of-the-mill hotel bedrooms. Fortunately, the size of the rooms allowed him to introduce walk-in showers as well as baths in the bathrooms and to use more luxurious furniture and furnishings, including ultra high quality mattresses which, he believed, would more than compensate for the somewhat unattractive outlook of the rooms which overlooked the dilapidated barn. He paid particular attention to soundproofing and lighting as well as wi-fi, internet access and other equipment such as television, CD players and music systems.

Although the cost of conversion significantly overran the budget, Jones believed that it was money well spent.

The rooms would have a minimum life of five years before any refurbishment would be considered necessary; he could also sell them at a premium price. He planned to assess demand in Year 2 before increasing the rate for the three rooms in Year 3 to £130 (inc VAT) per room – still good value. In Year 3, he also intended to increase the rate for the other rooms to £110. It was important that the capital investment made in the hotel generated additional income quickly but the danger of increasing prices too far too soon was recognised. The situation would need to be closely monitored and the rates that other hotels in the area were charging would have to be checked before deciding to go ahead with any increase.

During Year 1, Jones and Andy re-planned the kitchen but, before this, the menus had to be planned and the style of cooking agreed. Clearly, if pizzas were to be on the menu a pizza oven would be necessary; similarly, if fish and chips was to be a staple dish, suitable deep fat fryers were required; and if home made scones and cakes were to be offered for afternoon teas, a baking and pastry section with its own ovens was needed.

All the options were discussed but space was at a premium in the kitchen which limited the extent of the variety of dishes on offer. It was decided to offer a choice of brasserie-style dishes some of which changed daily and weekly but with some regular items such as steak, fish and chips, and steak and ale pie, sausage and mash, together with dishes that reflected Andy's interest in South Asian and Chinese cuisine.

Once the restaurant was refitted and Andy's new menu introduced, Jones invited the local press to visit and cautiously undertook an advertising campaign in the local papers. It became the top story on his website and he used Facebook and Twitter; a leaflet drop to businesses in the area was also completed.

It was towards the end of Year 1 that Jones began to consider the conversion of the barn at the back of the hotel into a wine bar. He was convinced that the proposal was viable as there was no wine bar in the town and the facility would offer a choice to pub-goers. He recognised this was a significant project that needed an architect to

9

plan and to oversee the building work. The estimated cost - £90,000 - was another major investment and his experience of other areas of the hotel led him to believe that an overrun would be likely; the difficulty lay in the need to cope with problems that could not be foreseen. In fact, although it was clear that the roof had to be replaced, it was discovered that the foundations of one wall were insufficient to carry the weight of the new roof, and this led to an additional £10,000 cost.

But, although he was keen to move ahead with the project he decided to put it on hold for another year. Cautiously, he was anxious to ensure that the improvements he had already made were successful and he wanted to ensure that all four departments – rooms, functions, food and beverage - were operating at optimum efficiency. He was aware that having brought the hotel up to standard, in Year 2 he had to concentrate on building up the business. His domestic circumstances had also changed as his wife had become pregnant and had less time to spend on helping to operate the hotel. He recognised that sooner or later he would have to appoint a manager who could take day-to-day control.

He decided that Year 2 would be a year of consolidation. Planning the barn conversion would, in any case, take time and planning permission was needed; he would also have to undertake a cost benefit exercise: what trade would the new wine bar attract, what trade would it take away from his existing bar operation, what food would he need to serve, what would be the best design, what would be the payback time?

How Jones calculated his purchase

Jones's successful ability to forecast sales and costs accurately was due largely to he and his wife's previous experience of hotel operations but their experience of the first year of ownership had taken them aback – even they had not realised quite how all-consuming in time and effort the purchase would be. For a newcomer to the industry, such an introduction to hotelkeeping would have been a baptism of fire.

His experience also gave him knowledge of hotel accounts which enabled him to more easily compile his budgeted P&L accounts. This would be a handicap for a newcomer but the examples that follow show how revenues and costs can be estimated which, in turn, will indicate whether any potential purchase is viable.

Tables 9.2-9.5 illustrate Jones' initial calculations for Year 1:

Year 1

Table 9.2: Room revenue in Year 1 at 75%

	Gross £	VAT £	Net £
16 rooms x 365 days x 75% occupancy = 4,380 x £100	438,000	73.000	**365,000**

Average net room rate is £365,000 ÷ 4,380 = £83.30

Table 9.3: Payroll costs in Year 1

	£
Rooms: 20% of room revenue (£365,000 x 20%) Assuming no night porter	**73.000**
Food: 35% of food revenue (£375,816 x 35%)	**131,535**
Beverage: 16% of beverage revenue (£329,050 x 16%)	**52,648**
Management/Admin: 5% of total revenue (£1,072,266 x 5%)	**53,613**
TOTAL	**310,796**

These calculations enabled him to prepare budgeted P&L accounts for Year 1, which appears as Table 9.5.

Table 9.4: Budgeted F&B revenue for Year 1

	Income £	VAT £	Net £
FOOD			
Breakfast 4,380 rooms x 1.8 sleeper occupancy x £15	118,260	19,710	98,550
Weekday lunches 10 x 6 days x 52 weeks x £15	46,800	7,800	39,000
Sunday lunch 30 x 52 days x £30	46,800	7,800	39,000
Weekday dinners 12 x 4 nights x 52 x £20	49,920	8,320	41,600
Friday/Saturday dinners 50 diners x 2 nights x 52 x £25	130,000	21,667	108,333
Bar Snacks £80 x 365	29,200	4,867	24,333
Rotary lunches 10 x 2 x 12 x £25	6,000	1,000	5,000
Function lunches 4 functions x 20 people x 12 months x £25	24,000	4,000	20,000
			375,816
BEVERAGES			
Main Bar: £900 per day	328,500	54,750	273,750
Weekday lunches 10 diners x 6 nights x 52 weeks x £3	9,360	1 560	7.800
Sunday lunches 30 diners x 52 weeks x £5	7,800	1,300	6,500
Weekday dinners 12 diners x 4 nights x 52 weeks x £5	12,480	2,080	10,400
Friday/Saturday dinners 50 diners x 2 nights x 52 weeks £6	31,200	5,200	26,000
Rotary lunches 10 diners x 2 lunches x 12 weeks x £3	720	120	600
Functions 4 functions x 20 people x 12 months x £5	4,800	800	4,000
			329,050
TOTAL			**704,866**

Table 9.5: Budgeted P&L accounts for Year 1

	£	£
REVENUE		
Rooms	365,000	
Food:	375,816	
Beverages	329,050	
Room hire	2,400	
	1,072,266	1,072,266
DIRECT COSTS		
Payroll (28.9% of total revenue)	310,796	
Food @ 30% of food revenue	112,744	
Beverages @ 30% of beverage revenue	98,715	
Commission @12.5% of total room revenue	45,625	
Total direct costs	**567,880**	**567,880**
Gross Profit		**504,386**
INDIRECT COSTS		
Rates and water rates	34,000	
Energy	40,062	
Insurance	8,000	
Telephone	6,000	
Music and entertainment	20,000	
Sales and marketing	35,000	
Training and recruitment	10,000	
Repairs and renewals @ 5%	53,613	
Admin and General @ 4%	42,890	
Misc; Rooms @5%	18,250	
Misc: Food @ 5%	18,790	
Misc: Beverages @ 1%	3,290	
		289,895
Gross Operating Profit (EBITDA) (20% of total revenue)		**214,491**
Capital repayment	23,500	
Loan interest @5%	23,500	
Directors' Salaries	40,000	
	87,000	**87,000**
NET PROFIT (6.9%)		**127,491**

Year 2

By the second year of his operation, Jones has converted three staff bedrooms to letting rooms – all doubles – which increases his room revenue considerably; he also believes he can increase occupancy to 78 per cent and in view of the strong demand, he plans to increase room rates by five per cent to £105. As a result, his forecast room revenue is 19 rooms x 365 x 78% = 5,409 rooms @ £105 per room = £567,976 (less £94,662 VAT) = £473,313; this represents £108,000 additional income over Year 1 and if the rate can be moved up to £110, the increase in revenue is £130,000; he decides on the lower figure.

In Year 2, taking into account the increased revenues from the rate rise and additional bedrooms and the reduction in sales and marketing and training expenditure, he estimates he would be able to finance the kitchen refurbishment out of earnings and begin planning the barn conversion perhaps allocating some of the R&R budget to the projects. Jones also recognised that the exterior of the hotel needed redecorating, which was estimated at £20,000, but this became a Year 3 project. With the new rooms, his sleeper ratio is 36 divided by 19 = 1.9

9

Table 9.6: Room revenue in Year 2 at 78%

	Gross £	VAT £	Net £
19 rooms x 365 days x 78% = 5,409 x £105	567,976	94,663	**473,313**

Net achieved room rate is £473,313 ÷ 5,409 = £87.50 – an increase of £4.20 per room compared to Year 1, showing how much the increase in room numbers and room rate benefits the hotel's revenues.

Table 9.7: Payroll costs in Year 2

	£
Rooms: 20% of room revenue (£473,313 x 20%) Assuming no night porter	**94,662**
Food: 35% of food revenue (£529,296 x 35%)	**185,253**
Beverage 16% of beverage revenue (£370,357 x 16%)	**59,256**
Management/Admin: 5% of total revenue (£1,376,566 x 5%)	**68,828**
TOTAL	**407,999**

Table 9.8: Budgeted F&B revenue for Year 2

F&B Revenue	Income £	VAT £	Net £
FOOD			
Breakfast 5,409 rooms x 1.9 sleeper occupancy x £15	154,156	25,692	128,463
Weekday lunches 20 x 6 days x 52 weeks x £15	93,600	15,600	78,000
Sunday lunch 40 x 52 days x £30	62,400	10,400	52,000
Weekday dinners 20 x 4 nights x 52 x £20	83,200	13,866	69,333
Friday/Saturday dinners 60 diners x 2 nights x 52 x £25	156,000	26,000	130,000
Bar Snacks £120 x 365	43,800	7,300	36,500
Rotary lunches 10 x 2 x 12 x £25	6,000	1,000	5,000
Function lunches 6 functions x 20 people x 12 months x £25	36,000	6,000	30,000
			529,296
BEVERAGES			
Main Bar £950 per day	346,750	57,792	288,958
Weekday lunches 20 diners x 6 days x 52 weeks x £3	18,720	3,120	15,600
Sunday lunches 40 diners x 52 weeks x £5	10,400	1,733	8,666
Weekday dinners 20 diners x 4 nights x 52 weeks x £5	20,800	3,466	17,333
Friday/Saturday dinners 60 diners x 2 nights x 52 weeks £6	37,440	6,240	31,200
Rotary lunches 10 diners x 2 lunches x 12 weeks x £3	720	120	600
Functions 8 x 20 people x 12 months x £5	9,600	1,600	8,000
			370.357
TOTAL			**899,653**

Using these calculations, Jones prepared a budgeted P&L account for Year 2

Table 9.9: Budgeted P&L accounts for Year 2

	£	£
REVENUE		
Rooms	473,313	
Food	529,296	
Beverages	370,357	
Room hire	3,600	
	1,376,566	**1,376,566**
DIRECT COSTS		
Payroll (29.6% of total revenue)	407,999	
Food: @30% of food revenue	158,788	
Beverages @ 30% of beverage revenue	111,107	
Commission @12.5% of room revenue	59,164	
Total direct costs	737,058	737,058
Gross Profit		**639,508**
INDIRECT COSTS		
Rates and water rates	34,000	
Energy	41,000	
Insurance	8,000	
Telephone	6,000	
Music and entertainment	20,000	
Sales and marketing	20,000	
Training and recruitment	5,000	
Repairs and renewals @ 5%	68,828	
Admin and General @ 4%	55,062	
Misc; Rooms @ 5%	23,665	
Misc: Food @ 5%	26,464	
Misc: Beverages @ 1%	3,703	
		311,722
Gross Operating Profit (EBITDA) (23.8% of total revenue)		**327,786**
Capital repayment	23,500	
Loan interest	23,500	
Directors' salaries	40,000	
	87,000	**87,000**
NET PROFIT (17.5%)		**240,786**

9

The need for such a detailed exercise arises in almost all hotel purchases and even for those businesses that are so successful that it may be assumed that improvements in room, food and liquor sales are impossible. Improvements are almost always possible. Even though trading may be poor, it should be added that in some cases the purchaser may be quite happy with the present performance of the business because it gives him an adequate return on his investment. He may not want to work harder and seek more business. If this is the case, so be it. It shows how difficult it is to generalise about the hospitality industry.

The only accounts that Jones received from the vendor before drawing up his projected profit and loss account were the sales figures in Table 9.1. The full figures were not available until later. It needs experience of the hotel industry to be able to draw up a set of accounts without historical figures and still make them meaningful but with knowledge of the common operating ratios, it can be done for small hotels. However, the vendor's accounts, over a three year period, should show the true cost of such items as heat, fuel and power and insurance and must always be examined carefully.

The projected profit was more than adequate to cover interest and capital repayment charges. Although his personal bank refused Jones' application, he made contact with a broker who arranged a loan at six per cent interest over a 20 year period - a relatively high rate at the time but one which he could service providing all his calculations came to fruition. If the hotel continued to make profit on this level he would be able to invest more in the business. Alternatively, he could attempt to repay the loan more quickly.

After the exercise

If the figures clearly show that the hotel is not a viable business at the asking price you have two alternatives:

1   Forget about it and leave it to someone who has more personal capital to invest.

2   Put in an offer that will give you a viable return on the capital employed. The size of the offer could be so far below the asking price that you may not feel it worthwhile putting it forward, but remember how 28-year-old Richard Branson purchased Necker Island, his 74-acre retreat in the Caribbean which he visited in the late 1970s and quickly fell in love with.

When Branson visited Necker, the uninhabited property owned by Lord Cobham was on the market for US$5m. Branson put in an offer US$100,000 – needless to say, the offer was refused but over the next few months, Branson gradually increased it. Eventually, at a time when Lord Cobham was in need of short term cash; Branson's offer of US$180,000 was finally accepted – a 96 percent discount off the asking price. Branson then spent US$10m developing the resort.

The moral of the story? Everything has its price.

Depending on how long the hotel has been on the market and how keen the vendor is to sell, any offer may stand a chance of acceptance.

Once your offer is accepted, you will be asked to give a deposit of some substance to prove your interest. This should be given to the agent via your solicitor. The agent will need to know who is acting for you because of the preparation of the contract of sale. He also might be able to put you in touch with a lawyer experienced in hotel sales and purchases if you wish. Once that has been settled, you have to begin what may appear to be the most daunting part of the project: raising money.

Five questions you must answer -

1   What immediate changes in the business do you have to make?

2   What changes in facilities can you make for the better? What will they cost?

3   Look to the future – what steps can you take to make the profits grow?

4   Where are the new markets – but make sure you optimise the hotel's existing markets first.

5   Have you budgeted carefully? The bank will be checking your figures!

and five key points to remember

1   Payroll, food, and beverage costs should not exceed 30 per cent of relevant revenues.

2   Don't forget – your success will ultimately depend on your staff. Recruit wisely.

3   Remember – the commitment in the first year or so will be total.

4   Be realistic – don't offer more than the property is worth.

5   Be patient! Remember Neckar Island and Richard Branson!

9

10 Raising the finance

"I assume that you have secured some funding - possibly a mix of your own cash from other business successes, maybe some family money and, of course, some bank funding which now comes in the form of covenanted loans, and probably a very small working overdraft on your current account.

But remember - banks are suppliers. They just happen to sell a product called money. They want their money back. They want it when you have said they will get it. And they will want to know the progress of your business intimately. Expect, as standard, to provide monthly management accounts, balance sheet, and cash flow forecasts for the next 12 months delivered in a timely manner.

Make sure you understand the covenants that are part of your loan agreement. They will probably relate to a ratio of profit to loan repayments and or interest, or possibly both in terms of interest cover and capital repayment. Don't underestimate how important it is to be able to maintain those ratios, so work out what happens if your hotel underperforms for six months, and make sure you are covered. Breaking those covenants means the bank can increase the low interest rates you hopefully argued strongly for when setting up your borrowing. Worse, it can ask for its money back.

Make sure you understand the difference between cash generation and profit. Cash is king and it's the only way you can pay off your debts.

Finally, if you are required to have interest rate protection as part of your loan, don't rely on your bank for advice. It has no obligation to advise you in any way so take proper independent advice. Make sure that any interest rate protection you are required to take does not (or cannot) add to your liabilities on your balance sheet at any time in the future, thus avoiding the trap into which so many private hotels have fallen during this last recession."

James Bowie
Proprietor, Belmont Hotel, Leicester

You have inspected the hotel; you like the property; you have prepared a business plan; your offer has been accepted (subject to funding). Now comes the difficult stage – raising the finance. It is the key activity on which the whole enterprise of buying your own hotel rests. It can also be the most difficult.

Although their attitude towards financing has become markedly more cautious, a clearing bank will generally be the first port of call for most would-be purchasers. This might not always be the case as some purchases can be self-financed.Of course, the business will need working capital to enable it to cover its day-to-day running costs and it might also need additional funds to renovate and refurbish the property, so even if there is sufficient capital to purchase the business outright it might well be that additional funds will be necessary to enable the business to refurbish. An overdraft facility might also be necessary.

Most purchasers, however, will generally turn to their bank for a loan or a commercial mortgage.

A loan is what it says it is – for a small business it is an advance of money for a certain project to be repaid with interest on or before a fixed date, usually on a short-term basis, advanced against some security but which can be recalled at any time; a commercial mortgage is similar to a domestic mortgage – the loan is set against the value of the property over a given timescale (usually no more than 25 years) and cannot be called in unless the mortgagee defaults.

Here, potential purchasers must be realistic. A bank's caution is not only based on its experience of the hotel industry in the last couple of decades (which has not been wholly favourable) but on the need to reduce the risk to which they are likely to be exposed when lending to someone who is not (yet) a professional hotelier.

10

The bank's approach has changed in other ways, too, and not necessarily to the advantage of the applicant. If your business plan is persuasive and your business experience relevant, good quality mortgages and loans continue to be made into the hotel industry but the process is now likely to take much longer than it did in the past when branch managers had the authority to lend quite considerable sums of money. Today, most loan applications of any size, and certainly any loan that relates to a hotel purchase, will rarely be within the authority of the local branch manager; it will automatically be referred to the bank's business unit.

What considerations for the bank?

Banks have established business centres in order to amalgamate all their business accounts. From the prospective purchaser's point of view, this means that obtaining a loan from a bank will not only take more time but it will demand more professional expertise.

More than ever, obtaining bank finance depends on the strength of your business plan, the feasibility of the project, the size of the loan you need and the sum you can invest yourself, the valuation (by the bank) of the business you want to buy and finally, but no means the least important, the bank's judgment of your business abilities. Few hotel loan applications will succeed if the applicant does not have a business track record, preferably (but not necessarily) in the hotel industry.

For the first-time purchaser who is seeking to acquire an existing property, the bank will have a number of considerations:

♦ How much do you want to borrow?

♦ What is the location of the property?

♦ What is the hotel's occupancy?

♦ What is its turnover/profit record?

♦ Is the hotel already branded or part of a consortium, such as Best Western?

♦ Is the hotel suitable to become a branded property?

♦ What is the state of the property and how much work needs to be undertaken to maintain its competitiveness?

♦ How familiar are you with current trends in the hospitality industry? What experience do you have of working in the industry?

♦ Can you prove your financial and business acumen?

Loan to Value/EBITDA

Few banks are willing to fund more than 50–60 per cent of the value of the business and the higher the loan – and the bigger the risk to the bank – the more heavily you will pay for it in interest charges. No bank will provide 100 per cent purchase finance as effectively it will then own the business outright; banks are not into equity ownership. Much depends on how the bank values the business: some will take the total valuation, others may be willing to lend a higher sum but on the value of the bricks and mortar only, which will be much lower.

The Loan-to-Value (LTV) ratio expresses the ratio of a loan to the value of the hotel purchased. For example, if you borrow £1m to buy a hotel worth £1.3m, the LTV ratio is £1m to £1.3m or 77 per cent – too high a ratio.

The risk of defaulting on the loan is always uppermost in any lending decision . . .

. . . so the loan to value ratio is an important calculation in raising finance for a hotel purchase. With any agreed loan, banks will probably insist on borrowers buying protection insurance which increases the cost of the loan.

Whatever route it takes, a bank will price the loan against the risk. It will clearly take notice of the LTV ratio but it will be even more concerned at the profitability of the business and on the gross operating profit – earnings before interest, taxes and amortization (EBITDA) – in other words, the net income of the business without the effect of financing and accounting decisions. This figure is a good measure of core profit trends and is often used as a shortcut to estimate the cash flow available to pay debt. For a bank this is a significant calculation.

Essentially, debt servicing for a hotel should be relatively simple as hotel businesses are highly cash generative; people pay on departure (sometimes even in advance);

hotels do not have a time lag between selling their product and payment for it. On outgoings, it is true they have a weekly cash demand for wages but suppliers will generally not be paid for 28 days – sometimes longer – and debt repayment is likely to be on a similar timescale; payments for utilities, rates and insurance are on an even longer term basis. EBITDA will show how easily the business can service its debt repayments through cash generation, which explains why the bank is so concerned about the calculation. EBITDA is also influential in agreeing a business's overdraft facility.

Increasingly, however, the raising of finance has become a service undertaken by independent mortgage brokers who specialise in the hospitality industry. Lenders are able to offer funding to prospective hoteliers as hotels are usually freehold assets which offer good security.

Brokers have access to funds which are in addition to those of the major banks . . .

. . . and are able to offer mortgages albeit at a higher rate of interest and for a longer period than is possible through a commercial bank. Typically, a 60-70 per cent loan to business value ratio will apply with a 15-25 year mortgage term. Some brokers are able to offer an LTV of up to 80 per cent – possibly 100 per cent – over a period as long as 30 years, though repaying a loan of this size is onerous and will almost certainly demand some additional security; the charge to the broker will be up to one per cent with a similar sum to the lender, so it is important that these additional costs are budgeted.

Overdraft

You will also need funds in order to operate the business on a day-to-day basis.

There is no point in buying the hotel and having no money – working capital – to operate it.

Do you have sufficient cash flow? Do you have sufficient revenues to pay the food suppliers in time? Can you pay the energy bills? Can you repay the mortgage every month? What about the business rates? Are the wages covered? Unless you have sufficient funds from your own resources, you will almost certainly need an overdraft facility to carry you through the lows of the trading year; thus, the extent of your overdraft requirement should be clearly identified in the business plan. It is vastly preferable to negotiate this at the time of your purchase, even if you are not taking out a bank mortgage for the purchase. Because of their cyclical nature, most resort and country hotels have much lower trading in the winter months and need bank support during these periods.

The main purpose of an overdraft is to overcome the peaks and troughs of current trading and it can be called in at very short notice; interest charges can also rise and fall according to the current economic situation.

Bank loan

The advantage of a bank loan is that it is convenient to arrange, does not lead to any profit-sharing on the part of the business and is subject to tax relief. However, the bank will impose stringent lending criteria and will demand some kind of security or personal guarantee; in addition, if you break the conditions of the loan, it is normally repayable on demand or the bank is likely to add extra service charges. There is thus an element of personal risk. If you are unable to repay the loan the bank will call in the personal guarantee; you must carefully consider how you manage this exposure before you agree to the loan.

Commercial mortgage

Much like a domestic mortgage, this is a loan over a fixed period at either a fixed or variable rate of interest secured against the property. It is the most established method of purchasing a hotel. However, you will have to invest as much as 40-50 per cent and non-payment of the mortgage will lead eventually to a forced sale of the hotel. The mortgage might also impose restrictions as part of the loan.

Finance from friends and relatives

This is quite common and has the advantage of not needing an approach to a bank; it also means that repayments can be flexible with lower interest charges. A formal agreement is always advisable outlining the length of the loan and interest payments as this kind of funding always risks personal relationships. The loan might be demanded back even before the end of the agreed period just when the business is least able to repay it.

Directors' loans

If you are setting up a company with fellow directors to buy the hotel, then they might agree to help purchase the business by means of a loan or through some equity investment. A formal agreement is essential and it is important that the hotel's finances do not become mixed up with personal finances. Legal advice is essential.

Loan notes

A loan note is a form of deferred payment which enables a purchaser to buy a business but to pay only a proportion of the asking price upfront. In addition to the cash payment, the vendor also receives loan notes which are a form of an IOU. These enable the vendor to receive payments (usually with interest) over a set period of time, ending on the date at which the entire loan is to be repaid. There are tax implications for both the vendor and the buyer to this form of finance and the vendor (and the bank) must clearly be willing to defer payment in this way.

Mezzanine finance

Under normal circumstances, in contrast to equity investors who make a return when a company does well and can then sell their shares at a profit, banks lend money and make a profit by charging interest on the loan, As the name implies, mezzanine finance is something of a hybrid, combining conventional debt with a component that provides the lender with an additional payment when the borrower achieves certain performance targets. Under a mezzanine arrangement, the lender charges interest but also profits from the company's growth so the lender has a medium to long-term interest in the success of the business. The reason why mezzanine finance is growing in popularity is because it provides businesses with an opportunity to raise money in order to fund purchases that are seen as a risk: buying a hotel would fall into this category. Banks can provide mezzanine finance although venture capital funds are a key provider in the market. Mezzanine finance isn't generally available to small businesses.

For some larger purchases, mezzanine finance provides access to bank funding that might not otherwise have been available and is often payable over a longer period of time than normal credit terms, but it can be costly and its success depends on the growth of the company. The exit payment could put significant strain on businesses that fail.

From the bank's point of view, mezzanine finance provides the lender with a higher than normal interest rate (because the risk is higher), plus an arrangement that will allow it to share in the success of the company.

Business angels

Similar to finance from a relation or directors, business angels are private individuals who are keen to invest in companies that have good growth prospects. Their advantage is that they require no collateral and do not expect interest payments on their loan; instead, they will expect a share of the business and of the profits, so you lose some independence. The biggest drawback is finding them!

Venture capital

Similar to business angels, venture capital is a form of private equity investment but the disadvantage, as with a business angel, is that you have to hand over partial ownership of the business with the obligation to repay the capital and pay dividends for as long as the loan exists, according to the agreement. On the other hand, a venture capital company can provide other skilled services and you can use their expertise to build the company up. Venture capital funding is really only suitable for a sizeable acquisition by a professional hotelier.

Debentures

This is a loan, usually from a private individual, but it does not have collateral and is not secured against the asset of the hotel; the debenture holder has no rights of ownership but has the certainty of a fixed rate of interest (typically higher than other types of loan). Interest payments have to be met even if the hotel does not make a profit. Professional advice is necessary.

Share issue

By issuing shares, you are exchanging a share of the business for an investment in it. This is a formal structure which will need legal advice to set up but it is a means of excluding the cost of a bank loan, although bank finance might still be needed for working capital; however, some investors might be helpful in bringing outside skills to the business. You dilute ownership and control of the business and, depending on the structure of the shareholdings, you are likely to be accountable to other shareholders who might have a tendency to interfere with the running of the business and will expect a share of the profits.

SEED Enterprise Investment Scheme (SEIS)

Under the Seed Enterprise Investment Scheme, income tax relief is available to individuals who subscribe for qualifying shares in a company which meets the SEIS requirements, and who have UK tax liability against which to set the relief. Investors need not be UK resident. So if you have an investor who is willing to support you, then he could take advantage of the scheme which is aimed mainly at supporting the expansion of small companies – they must have fewer than 25 employees and have no more that £200,000 in gross assets, into which category will fall many small hotels.

The investment is medium term – the shares must be held for a period of three years from date of issue for relief to be retained – but relief is available at 50 per cent of the cost of the shares, on a maximum annual investment of £100,000. The relief is given by way of a reduction of tax liability providing there is sufficient tax liability against which to set it.

As it is very tax efficient for investors, the SEIS is an attractive way for people buying a business or expanding who do not have the necessary equity but who can raise money from friends and family.

Enterprise Finance Guarantee

This is a government scheme, launched in 2009, which aims to help businesses lacking adequate security or proven track record for a standard commercial loan. The scheme, which is run by the Department for Business Innovation and Skills, guarantees 75 per cent of the loan from an established lender, while the borrower pays a two per cent per annum pro-rata premium to BIS. The scheme does not provide the loan itself but guarantees it, providing additional security for the lender. The borrower is responsible for repaying the total loan, not just the 25 per cent beyond the Government guarantee. The scheme is open to businesses whose turnover is less than £41m. Loans can vary in size from £1,000 to £1m, with repayment terms ranging from three months to 10 years.

Promissory note

When a potential purchaser is short of the required finance to purchase a hotel, it is sometimes possible to arrange a promissory note which is a legally binding agreement with the vendor to pay the balance of the price over a given number of years. It is a form of an IOU and, as such, is difficult to arrange. For example, a purchaser may be paying £600,000 for a property but is £30,000 short. The vendor may be willing to accept a promissory note to pay back the final tranche over five years at £6,000 per year at a fixed rate of interest.

Other funding

Newer ways of raising money have emerged including funding from other finance platforms and challenger banks such as Crowdcube and Metro Bank. Internet 'crowdfunding' sources are independent investors who are registered on an internet site and who are willing to back small businesses either through equity or loans. Although there are a number of examples of crowdfunding in the hospitality industry they are typically for established businesses which want to expand; in some cases the funding comes from existing customers who see growth potential in the business and want to invest in it. It's unlikely that you will be able to raise money to purchase your first hotel by this means unless you have a proven track record and a specific project that would be of interest to investors. There are other sources, such as Business Cash Advance and MarketInvoice, but these are principally aimed at existing businesses who want to expand or refurbish.

10

Summary

In seeking finance, the bank or a mortgage broker will be the first step. In either case, getting to the front door is the easiest bit: your hardest step is to convince the lender that you are a good risk for their investment.

When you approach any lending institution, do it professionally and be fully prepared. If possible, take your accountant with you. Whoever lends you money will be judging you not only on the viability of the business plan but on your own professionalism. A proper presentation is therefore essential.

Any funding institution you approach, and that includes the broker himself, will want to know the answers to questions we have already raised in earlier chapters. As a first step in considering an application, a lender will require a professional valuation by a specialist hotel valuer as the value of the assets will comprise the security for the loan.

The valuation by the bank will cost you money as the bank will expect you to pay the valuer's fee (about 1.25 per cent), which will be one of the many fees that you will be expected to pay during the loan application process; other costs include Stamp Duty, legal fees, surveyor's fee, and arrangement fees. It is essential that you budget for them as these can add up to significant sums of money.

In deciding whether to provide finance the lending source will need to be convinced of your general business ability and will be looking for realism and commitment from you. The onus will be on you to prove that your objectives are sensible and achievable.

How the lender views the purchase

A senior manager from a finance house explains how he views the importance of the interview.

Obviously, the degree of experience required will vary with the nature of the business but generally we like to see applicants who have had a varied experience of all types of hotel, big and small, and can show us a CV which shows a steady progress in terms of managerial experience. My advice, therefore, to applicants is to prepare the ground carefully. Write down full details of your career to date and bring along as many testimonials as you possibly can. Ideally, we would like to see that you have experience of the type of hotel you intend purchasing.

It is important that you feel relaxed at the interview. We are really trying to assess your personality, the ease with which you can communicate with us, your business acumen and enthusiasm. We want to hear of your ideas and for you to convince us that you have really looked at the hotel in depth and can improve the present standard and level of business. It wants to be convinced that if it lends you money, its investment will be safe.

Is the money you are putting into the business all your own or are you having to borrow money from another source? Lenders will be concerned about your other source of funds if you are borrowing money from elsewhere. Banks, in particular, do not much favour purchasers raising money from a wide variety of different sources and some will refuse to offer funding altogether if they are not the sole source of finance, apart from your own personal funds. Money raised from your own family and immediate relations, providing the money is tied properly into the business and cannot easily be withdrawn, would be viewed as your own funding. There may also be the situation where one of you is able to bring in another source of regular income. This is particularly so in the case of a small guest house which can be run by either the husband or wife while the other earns a salary elsewhere. The income earned from this second activity might well be taken into account when decisions are taken on whether you can realistically repay the loan on the property.

All banks have sophisticated computer programs which help them price the loan but the interest charged will be between three and five percentage points above base rate.

Some banks might be willing to agree a capital repayment holiday on your loan or mortgage, whereby you pay back only the interest in the first year or so. Of course, the capital has to be repaid at some stage so you will paying for this facility with a higher repayment rate later on but it is a useful device if you believe that you need a couple of years to establish the business in its early days and to generate new earnings.

What will your bank, or lender, want to be told?

1 **Be clear about the amount of funding you need and what you want to use it for.** In your loan application, it is wise to assume the shortest possible loan repayment period as this will reduce the cost of finance but it is important to be realistic. Your business plan should have calculated the loan period. Any increase in interest rate can have a devastating effect on a business, particularly in the early days of ownership when borrowings are high and new sources of revenue-generation have not yet been exploited. Of course, interest on your loan can be charged to the profit and loss account; in addition, with inflation, the value of payments in future years will be much reduced. But heavy borrowings are a burden that must be repaid. You are working for yourself, not the bank

2 **Be sure that you have all the information that you need on the trading record of the business and that your projections are accurate.** False optimism here is fatal. Growth plans must be realistic and should not be so optimistic that they are unobtainable under normal circumstances.

3 **Banks lend on propositions and to people, and both are equally important.** Lenders need to be convinced that you are the right person to back. Many an application has been turned down because the project was suitable but the applicant was not; but even if the applicant is highly suitable no lender will ever lend on what it considers an unsuitable proposition. If you can show that you and your partner have worked in the industry, even if it is only as a waiter in the kitchen or in the bar, then that will help; just as important would be some evidence that you have attended courses or seminars in the industry and read the trade press and have knowledge of industry trends.

4 **Before any interview, try to predict the type of questions that you will be asked about yourself and the business**. If there is more than one of you, you should all come to the interview; lenders will want to be satisfied that you and all your partners have a more than equal chance of succeeding.

5 **Don't assume that rising property/business values will give you an exit route and enable you to sell on the business quickly**. Not every hotel appreciates in value.

6 **Remember - the value of the hotel will be what it is worth to another individual with access to funds as limited as yours.** The vast majority of small hotels will not be of any interest to a major group. When it comes to selling your hotel (a factor which you have to consider even when you purchase) the value of the hotel will be what it is worth to another individual with access to funds as limited as yours.

10

7 **An important point to remember in any purchase is that whenever you take over a new business, you rarely have enough money**. There is always something unexpected, no matter how carefully you have budgeted. Unforeseen new pieces of equipment are notorious for running away with costs; you might find that there is more work to be undertaken than even the most damning surveyor's report indicated. Budgeting for both the expected and the unexpected, with the full agreement of the lender, is critically important. At the time of purchase, you will have significant sums to pay out (see next chapter) and even when all these costs have been met the wise business will still have something left over.

8 **Finally, keep in close touch with your lending source and if you see any financial problems, don't wait to be overtaken by them** - hence the importance of generating monthly management information. A lending source wants you to succeed, so the earlier you talk to it in times of trouble, the better.

Insurance and pensions

Any lending source will insist that you take out sufficient life assurance cover because the death of you or your partners could create considerable problems for the business.

Other insurance may be necessary and the cost of these premiums should be included in your business plan. It may also be appropriate to re-emphasise the need to plan ahead for your pension arrangements. Clearly, your pension contributions will be dictated by your level of profit and available funds but pension planning is important, if only because many people coming into the industry are in their late 30s and early 40s – even later. At that age, and if no previous pension arrangements have been made, contributions have to be significantly high to ensure a satisfactory standard of living on retirement.

With a freehold or long leasehold property, the building itself will provide a significant sum of money when it is time to sell up, providing the business has been in ownership for sufficient length of time and there are no outstanding loans on the property, but no hotelier can rely on a high capital gain except perhaps in London. However, retirement and selling the hotel lie in the future. The immediate task is to secure your source of finance. As soon as funding becomes available, the purchase of the business can move ahead in much the same way as a house purchase.

The vendor's solicitors will prepare the contract for sale, your own solicitor will institute the necessary searches, contracts will be signed and the deal will be completed within 28 days of the exchange of contracts. You will also have to have the wet and dry stock valued on the day you take over by a firm of stocktakers. All this is in the hands of the lawyers with the hotel agents holding a watching brief. The next chapter looks a little more closely at the lawyer's role in this transaction

Ten points you need to consider

1 A business plan for the first three years is essential for any finance application.

2 Most finance houses will not consider loans of more than 60 per cent.

3 A finance house will look for an applicant's experience of work in the hospitality industry – or appropriate business experience in another sector – as a key factor in considering a loan application.

4 Loans are priced against the risk – the greater the risk, the higher the cost.

5 Banks lend on propositions to people: lenders need to be convinced that you are the right person to back.

6 Ensure you know all the answers to the questions you are likely to be asked when you seek your loan.

7 Make sure you have sufficient working capital in your loan application – and funds for any necessary planned refurbishments.

8 Don't assume that increases in property values will give you a profitable exit route.

9 If at first you don't succeed . . . . .

10 Keep in regular touch with your lending source – you may need more support at a later date!

10

11 Finding a good lawyer and some legal points

Buying a hotel is a complicated legal transaction. Make sure you have a good lawyer to help you on your way. There are plenty of legal hurdles to overcome and you need wise advice.

In buying a hotel, what exactly are you purchasing?

1 Are you buying a property (freehold or leasehold) which is either vacant or has been used for some other purpose, with the intention of converting it into a hotel?

2 The purchase of the assets and goodwill of an existing hotel as a going concern?

3 The shares of a company which owns and runs an existing hotel?

Of the three, the second alternative is by far the most usual for the first-time buyer. The purchase of a large house or other building for conversion into a hotel was common in the 1980s but it is less common now (but see Chapter 15). Nor is it usual for the first-time buyer to purchase a company that owns and operates a hotel.

This emphasises the importance of using a lawyer who is knowledgeable about business transfers and who can conduct due diligence. Good legal advice, on the biggest financial transaction of your life is not a luxury, it is a necessity.

The importance of due diligence can hardly be overstated as it can reveal problems that have not yet been uncovered. The best advice is to involve both an experienced consultant and accountant to cover the due diligence aspect of the transaction, especially with regard to the accounts, as these can easily be manipulated to show fluctuating levels of profit depending on how the vendor treats various charges. There is even more risk in a company acquisition where it is paramount that the lawyers/purchaser incorporate the necessary warranties and indemnities in the sale and purchase agreement so as not to expose the purchaser to contingent liabilities post acquisition, for example, outstanding tax or pending litigation.

In one purchase, it was discovered that the present owners had not actually registered the purchase when they bought it so, theoretically, the previous owners still had title to the property. This meant that there was a remote but still a real possibility that the relatives of the previous owner could make a title claim against the hotel. An application had to be made for a possessory title to the Land Registry office.

In another example, although planning permission had been granted for an extension by converting barn, stables and outbuildings, permission was only for holiday-let accommodation not for hotel rooms. The rooms could not be let during January through to March, which clearly had implications on future revenue. An application for a deed of variation had to be made to the local planning authority.

A good commercial lawyer who has preferably handled several hotel purchases, is what is needed. During the negotiations you must check his fees – in both the examples above, extra legal costs were incurred in resolving the issues.

Due diligence will also reveal what contracts exist between the hotel and various suppliers such as energy, television rental companies, office equipment, linen hire and laundry companies, membership of a consortium. These contracts indicate what the hotel is committed to when you take it over, what the terms of the contracts are and how easy it would be to release them if you did not feel they were appropriate.

Obtain copies of the contracts and read these before accepting them. If you feel that they are not suitable you can ask the vendor to terminate a particular contract prior to the acquisition so they don't become your commitment. This also applies to employees at the hotel, when it may be necessary for the vendor to make certain employees redundant prior to completion.

It is also important that the purchaser obtains all rights to websites, CMS systems, passwords to booking engines and TripAdvisor, together with an assurance that the accounts for online travel agents (OTAs) are paid up to date on the day of completion; OTAs will be quick to cut off the flow of future bookings. Likewise, the rights to company trademarks, logos, print and images need to be transferred to the purchaser. It is also wise to have an inventory of furniture and fittings attached to the sale and purchase agreement at exchange of contracts.

In brief, here's a list of the costs that you are likely to incur in purchasing the property:

♦ Survey fees for any surveys you have undertaken

♦ Valuation fees by your lender

♦ Stamp Duty

♦ Land registry fee

♦ Costs incurred by your lawyer in local authority searches and other searches

♦ Arrangement fees, if any, charged by your lender

♦ Legal costs

♦ Accountant's costs

♦ VAT, if payable (but this would be reclaimable if VAT registered)

The first point on which any lawyer will want to satisfy himself is the source and reliability of your funding. From then, the procedure varies depending on which alternative you adopt.

Purchasing to convert

If you do decide to go down this route – see Chapter 15 – perhaps with your own financing, the only asset being traded is the land and buildings. Your lawyer will want to make the purchase conditional upon:

1   The granting of planning permission for change of use to a hotel.

2   If leasehold, the landlord's consent to change of use to a hotel.

It is unlikely that you will be able to get plans approved before exchange of contracts so an element of doubt will always remain in a transaction of this type, even though outline permission for change of use might be granted. This is particularly so if the house, or parts of it, are listed. You can visit the local planning department with your architect to discuss any specific ideas you have prior to drawing up detailed plans. In this way, you will get an idea of what might or might not be allowed which, in turn, will affect the scale and nature of your plans and might lead you to withdraw your offer entirely even if planning permission is being granted.

Buying an existing hotel

If you are buying an existing hotel, you are buying its assets and goodwill, as well as the physical means by which the hotel operates –

the building, its fixtures and fittings, furnishings, linen and crockery, together with the benefit of certain contracts which the previous owner may have entered into. The sale and purchase agreement, which is drawn up by the purchaser's lawyers, will include all the various warranties/indemnities/guarantees; it is also the document to which the disclosures made by the vendor may be attached, for instance a list of the employees, start dates, salaries, fixtures and fittings. On the day of purchase, you will also purchase the stock at valuation. The procedure will include a disclosure letter from the vendor which will detail numerous matters, such as the following:

1   That the hotel has a Premises Licence enabling it to sell alcohol. However, before you are able to sell alcohol under your ownership you will have to obtain a Personal Licence or nominate someone, who is called the Designated Premises Supervisor (DPS), who is a Personal Licence holder. A Premises Licence is indefinite and can be transferred to you as the new owner but a Personal Licence is required to be renewed every ten years and can only be obtained through a formal qualification by attending a one-day course to get the Award for Personal Licence Holders (APLH). When you receive your APLH certificate, you must then apply for a standard Disclosure and Barring Service (DBS) reference. When you apply for your Personal Licence, local authorities will only accept DBS checks less than 28 days old so if you want to continue providing alcohol on purchase and you don't employ a DPS you will need to have obtained a Personal Licence beforehand.

2   The letter will contain a number of warranties which you may want to put into the sale and purchase agreement although it's often difficult to get vendors to agree to them, especially in a company sale. Other items included will be contracts entered

into by the vendor (for example any outstanding liabilities of the business), the terms and conditions of employment of the staff (their contract of employment), the legal ownership of the assets, the accuracy of the accounts and whether the business is involved in any litigation.

3   You will need to establish who is responsible for collecting outstanding sales ledger balances and you must remember to apply for PDQ terminals and paying-in books for the hotel bank account, well in advance of completion.

4   Between exchange and completion ensure that you have set up accounts with the hotel's suppliers so there is a smooth transition.

5   On completion, apart from the liquor and food stocktake, it is quite often the norm to include a stocktake of consumables and laundry which form part of the purchase cost.

6   The agreement will say what will happen to the name of the hotel if it needs to change, as company-owned hotels typically have branded names which have to change if the hotel is sold.

7   Similarly, it will explain what will happen to the hotel's logo, especially if it is a registered service mark.

8   It will identify who is responsible for the hotel's book debts. You will need to know if any debts carry forward into your ownership.

9   It will contain an obligation by the vendor to run the business between exchange of contracts and completion in the same way as previously, so that no goodwill is lost. This is a good reason for making the period between exchange and completion as short as possible. With the best will in the world, a vendor who has decided to sell up has made the decision and will want to get on with the rest of his life so his interest in the business will naturally wane the nearer the sale gets to completion.

10 It will provide for the purchaser to register for VAT before completion so that the sale of the business assets presents no VAT problem. The hotel's existing bank must also be kept in the picture.

11 It will state how the stock is to be valued and by whom on takeover (Chapter 9).

12 It will explain how existing customers and suppliers are to be told of your takeover. In fact, it's unlikely that many customers – unless they are very regular – will need to be told directly and one option is not to make any announcement at all. Key suppliers, like wine and drinks, meat and groceries will certainly be interested in you as the new owner and will want to know your credit worthiness.

13 If staff have not already been told, the disclosure letter will explain how they are to be told of your purchase, who tells them and when.

14 A detailed inventory of the items included in the sale will be provided. Once submitted, this must be carefully checked to ensure that all the items which you believed were included in the sale are actually included.

15 If the hotel is being purchased leasehold, it will be necessary to get the landlord's approval for the sale of the lease. This is likely to involve you providing references as well as an initial payment of rent together with a deposit.

16 A covenant by the vendor not to open or become involved with another hotel business within a certain radius of the hotel, and within a certain period of time, might be necessary. This is important. Much of the success of a hotel is often dependent on the personality of the owner; if he leaves to open a business nearby, much of the trade of the hotel could move with him.

17 The letter might also provide for an induction period during which the vendor will show you the ropes. Ideally, you should want to take control immediately; having the previous owner on the premises for any length of time could become an unhelpful diversion.

On completion, you are now the owner of the business with only the stocktaking to be undertaken before you can take full control (see the next chapter).

Finally . .

Anyone who has bought a house knows how long the legal process can take; buying a hotel will take even longer so allow sufficient time for the process. Your lawyer should keep you informed of progress and be able to prepare a pre-contract report so that various aspects of the purchase can be reviewed on an on-going basis.

Ten key questions to answer

1   Do you have confidence in your lawyer? If not, get another one!

2   Make sure you know what you are buying – property or company?

3   Will you be a company or sole trader? Decide before you purchase.

4   Are there any planning issues?

5   Have you undertaken due diligence?

6   Have you budgeted accurately for legal, licence and other professional fees? They will be high.

7   Do you have all the appropriate licences before you trade?

8   Have you checked the inventory?

9   Have you agreed to take over as soon as you can? Delay doesn't help staff morale or the business.

10 Have you told suppliers and customers you've taken over?

12 Taking over

The time between the day on which you exchange contracts and completion day will appear all too short because there is a great deal to be done.

The precise length of time will depend on the arrangements you make with the vendor. Normally it is not more than 28 days but it can be less; it is even possible to exchange and complete on the same day. If a longer time elapses, it may be prudent to re-visit the hotel before the exchange.

As soon as the contracts are exchanged the business is technically yours and you cannot withdraw from the deal without severe legal complications; it is slightly different in Scotland so make sure you are aware of this. Ask the vendor for a list of pre-paid deposits such as future weddings or parties. This money, which sometimes can be a substantial amount, must be handed over to you, as the purchaser.

The first objective is to take steps to insure the property from the day of exchange of contracts.

If you are borrowing money from a financial organisation, it will have probably made this a condition of the loan but you must also insure against both the structure and the contents of the building. Insurance against occupier's liability is also essential. You should also consider a profit protection policy which will provide you with a regular income based on past profits of the business if the building and its earning capacity is destroyed. You must bear in mind that the cost and scope of insurance can be affected by any personal guarantees that you may have given to the bank and whether you are operating as a sole trader or as a limited company.

It is usual to insure for three years' loss of profits based on the gross figure.

It is likely that the vendor will already have the property insured but you must ensure that the insurance is adequate for your needs if it is transferred to you.

The need for personal permanent health insurance cover and for cover on key staff should also be investigated. Buildings and contents insurance premiums are tax allowable and sensible insurance cover should be regarded as a prudent investment; so should suitable pension arrangements.

Licensing

If the property you are buying does not already have a Premises Licence, you will have to apply for one – and if you do not have a personal licence, you will need to take immediate steps to obtain one.

Inventory

The vendor will have already drawn up an inventory of fixtures and fittings of the business before contracts are exchanged. This will include items on hire or lease, and all the items in the building that are included in the sale, such as kitchen equipment, bedroom furniture, linen, carpets and curtains. To be certain, you should also ask for a list of items that are *not* included in the sale. Before this is agreed, ensure that all the items you understand to be included in the sale are listed in the inventory.

If the property is leasehold, there will be two inventories. One will list the fixtures that you are leasing from the owner of the freehold, such as fixed seating, and the other will include the fittings that you are buying from the leaseholder. On the day of the takeover, you will have to engage your own valuer to check the inventories as well as the wet and dry stocks.

Be sure that all the items listed in the inventory are still in the establishment and that no important item has been switched. It is not unusual for a purchaser to find that items of a poorer quality have been substituted in the time between the initial inspection and before the inventory is taken, so keep a sharp eye out and pay particular notice to the quality of the bedlinen, cutlery and china.

On takeover day, the wet and dry stock will be valued at wholesale prices.

In some cases (an exchange of tenancies, for example) both the vendor and the purchaser will employ their own stocktaker who will have to agree on the value of the stock. In many hotel purchases, the vendor and purchaser jointly appoint a stocktaker to act for both parties which saves one set of fees.

Most hotels are offered for sale complete with fixtures and fittings but in some contracts fittings are not included and have to be purchased at valuation. In this case, both your valuer and the vendor's have to agree their value before completion date. Valuing furniture and fittings is a skilled job but sometimes not even experts can agree. Your valuer will look after your interests and will bargain for you if that is necessary.

You will also receive a schedule of existing contracts and a schedule of current staff employed. This will give you a picture of the staff position and will indicate how much redundancy they will be entitled to if you do not want to keep them on (see Chapter 20).

On the morning of the takeover, the valuer and stocktakers will move into the hotel. They will measure and value all saleable liquor on the premises including beer, wine and liquor stocks in the cellar, in the optics and on the shelves. Food stocks will also be valued but the stocktaker will pay particular attention to stock which is out of date or not fit for consumption. Usually, the premises are assumed to be yours at 10 a.m. Depending on the size of the hotel the stocktaking will probably have finished by lunchtime, but in a larger hotel the stocktake can continue into the afternoon. When the value of the stock is agreed, a settlement will have to be made there and then on the premises. While the completion of the purchase is likely to take place in your lawyer's office (only rarely on the premises), the purchase of the stock will be completed in the hotel immediately after the stocktaking with cheques or money transfers used for payment.

Make sure that the electricity, gas, water and telephone meters are read on the morning of the takeover. The vendor is responsible for the payment of these.

The settlement will take account of this, the stocktakers' fees and other costs, some of which are rated for VAT purposes (reclaimable later). You will also have to pay your own valuer's fee (a percentage of the stock value or a day rate, whichever you have agreed). Either at the time of the settlement or previously at the time of the completion of the contract, money that has been accepted by the vendor as deposits for forward bookings will be credited to you.

On handover keys are very often a problem for purchasers. Frequently, many are untagged and they are often kept together in a box or on a large ring, some of them long since redundant. From a security point of view, you need to know which are the current keys, where they are, and that they are properly tagged. This applies particularly to master keys; you need to ensure that they are all accounted for.

Finally, obtain sufficient money from the bank for floats for all the tills – £300 in small change should be enough, depending on the size of the hotel.

Once the appraisement of the stock in trade is signed and you have paid for it, the hotel and all its stock is legally yours. The stocktakers will give you a copy of the appraisement. The vendor should be made aware that the property is now yours and he should be discouraged from stepping behind the bar. He will depart leaving you as the new owner of the property.

12

Six action points

1   Make sure the hotel's insurance is valid and up-to-date.

2   Do you have immediate funds to pay for wet and dry stock?

3   Ensure you have enough cash for floats for all the tills.

4   Check all current contracts with suppliers and guests.

5   Make sure you have adequate personal cover for death or illness.

6   Do you have adequate personal insurance and pension arrangements?

13 Budgeting

"I wish I had been privy to the wisdom of this chapter before we purchased our hotel. It only had 65 rooms, two restaurants, one bar and a spa. That seemed simple enough, until the first month's profit and loss account arrived. We had lost £100,000 and I didn't know why. We had departmental budgets of course, lined up alongside the month's actuals. We even had a third column that told me the precise difference between the two but I still didn't know why it had happened. Every head of department gave excellent reasons why they'd missed their targets, then left the room. I was left studying a historical document; the money was long gone. I realised then that running a hotel (or in my case trying to) was the most complex business I had ever been involved in, and that's more than a few.

During that first month I watched lots of employees milling around; they all seemed busy enough and the hotel was nearly full. The month-end would surely reveal some happy figures? It hadn't occurred to me that I should have ensured that each department's wages and consumable costs were running in line with its prescribed percentages of revenue. Receiving a daily snapshot of revenues versus costs seemed overkill too, but if I had, I would have seen how the month was evolving, and done something about it before the history was written.

I concluded we had taken on an untameable beast. We hadn't of course, we just didn't know how to tame it. This chapter tells you how."

Richard Whitehouse
Managing Director, Rudrum Holdings, (formerly managing director, The Cornwall Hotel, St Austell)

Having completed the purchase, your immediate task is to operate the business. You will be so busy in the first few days that you will not have much time to think but there is a need to plan for the future as well as to operate in the present.

Experience with your stocktaker will have served to emphasise the size of your financial investment in wet stock and the need to make sure that the investment is properly protected. Even in a small hotel, the value of the stock can be as much as £20,000; for a larger hotel, with a cellar full of wines, the stock value would be much more.

Where bar staff are employed, you should arrange for a monthly stocktake of the liquor stock. Shortages will be rapidly revealed in this way and the action will have the added benefit of showing employees that you intend to keep a close eye on pilferage and wastage.

If the hotel is so small that only you and your wife or family run the bar, the need for regular stocktaking is not so pressing but, even so, a quarterly stocktake is desirable just to check the accounts. Many hoteliers do their own stocktaking. In a small hotel this may not be an onerous task but by employing a professional company you ensure that the job is accurately carried out, leaving you time to do more essential jobs.

A more immediate task is to ensure that you understand the intricacies of VAT and PAYE.

Depending on the size of the business, you will either prepare the hotel accounts yourself or employ a bookkeeper in-house; alternatively, you can hire an external accountant. The cost of hiring a bookkeeper may appear to be an unnecessary luxury but the advantage of having one is likely to far outweigh the costs; he will ensure that the accounts are properly compiled and enable you to concentrate on other activities which will inevitably grab your immediate attention. Without a dependable bookkeeper, you have no control over your revenues and outgoings.

A good idea is to set up a separate VAT account. Each time you pay revenue into your bank, transfer 15 per cent to the VAT account (you will have some VAT claims to set against the total VAT payments). This ensures that when the quarterly VAT payment is due there are no cash flow surprises.

13

Your bookkeeper's most important job is to prepare regular accounts and to keep you informed of the business's progress.

In a large hotel, daily trading accounts are compiled but in a small business a weekly or even monthly profit and loss account is likely to be sufficient. Regular accounts are important to any hotel or catering business because there is no point in knowing in July that you made a loss in the previous February. You need the information by early March (i.e. ten working days) so that you can take remedial action.

In the simplest system, the accounts will show revenue and outgoings, the balance being the earnings before interest, taxes and depreciation (EBITDA) – see Chapters 7 and 8. Annual payments such as rates and insurance and quarterly charges, such as electricity, gas and telephone, need to be allocated to the accounts on a monthly basis so that a proportion of the total annual expenditure on these items is set against every month's income.

Budgets

Your business plan will have provided you with a budget for the year but the annual figures need to be refined to a month-by-month basis.

There is no point in having budgets that are completely unattainable; they should be realistic and provide an incentive for you to reach your business objectives. At the same time, they provide a measurement of your financial success.

Before you take over you should work out the hotel's projected income and expenditure for the first year on a monthly basis. Some months may be poor – January is typically the worst hotel month for most hotels – so you cannot take an annual figure and simply divide by twelve. You should look at each month and realistically estimate your income and expenditure for that period. You will find that you are budgeting for a loss in some months. At the height of the season, however, you will hope to make a profit and you need to budget for that as well by estimating your occupancy levels, your room revenue and other income.

12 Economic Levers

The 12 Economic Levers (see next page) provide the key statistical information that will enable you to operate your hotel profitably. They provide the financial framework in which to operate your business but there are other activities that should be undertaken. These will provide you with other information on how the business is performing on a daily and weekly basis; more important, they enable you to take remedial action if key percentages, such as food costs, beverage costs, room occupancy, are not being achieved.

Because you want to monitor your financial position regularly, your monthly profit and loss account should relate actual performance to budgeted performance. The simplest way of doing this is to have three sets of figures side by side in the monthly accounts – the actual figures achieved, the budgeted figures and the variance. In this way, the figures are easily compared and you will be able to see instantly whether business has improved or declined compared to the budget. Your first few monthly budgets may well be somewhat inaccurate but with experience they will become much more precise.

Accurate budgets, regular costings and performance reviews, together with up-to-date monthly accounts are essential activities throughout the life of any hotel. Unless you know how the business is performing on a monthly, weekly and daily basis it will not be possible for you to introduce any immediate remedial measures to rectify any overspend on food costs, declining margins, higher wage costs or falling occupancy.

A budget also helps you plan your R&R (Repairs and Renewals – see Chapter 21) schemes and ensures that you undertake only what can be afforded. If you take over a hotel that needs major improvements, the temptation will be to spend considerable sums of money on the property immediately. If you prepare an R&R budget, it will act as a realistic brake on your enthusiasm because you will probably not be generating enough cash flow in the first few months of ownership to be able to afford to spend much money on renovation. Of course, if considerable renovation and refurbishment is required and you have included this in your loan application, then you will want to get the work underway quickly. If this is the case, and it means that rooms are out of commission, then budget accordingly as it will affect your projected revenues and cash flow.

12 Economic Levers

In any hospitality business, there are 12 economic levers which can be implemented to measure the success of the enterprise.

ANNUALLY

Budget: This enables the unit to calculate the potential gross operating profit and, at the same time, sets financial goals and targets.

QUARTERLY

Food costings – These are carried out by the head chef for each dish to ensure gross profit margins are being achieved; they must include all ingredients, condiments etc.

Beverage costings: A similar exercise on minerals/wines/spirits/beers.

MONTHLY

Profit & Loss Accounts: These produce monthly financial results against budget.

Beverage stock take: This ensures margins are achieved and identifies discrepancies.

Food stock take: This checks purchase prices and ensures stock levels (5-7 days) are maintained.

WEEKLY

Sleeper ratio: Knowing the number of overnight guests helps control restaurant and room maid wage costs.

Sales forecast sheets: The forecast number of overnight bookings will indicate whether immediate sales action needs to be undertaken.

Wage forecast sheets: Wage cost percentages can be checked against future business.

DAILY

Daily analysis sheets: Allows management to compare, on a daily cumulative basis, how sales are performing against budget, leading to remedial action if discrepancies appear.

Average room rate: Taking the rate charged and deducting breakfast, dinner and VAT (if applicable) enables management to improve the net room rate

Flash food cost: Enables management to know on a daily basis the cumulative month-to-date food cost, enabling remedial action to be taken if necessary.

13

Expressing occupancy

For new owners, it is important to understand how occupancy is calculated and expressed.

There are three economic levers that are most relevant to the first-time buyer:

◆ Room occupancy

◆ Sleeper occupancy

◆ Average room rate (ARR)

We have already looked at these in Chapter 2 but the following calculations emphasise their importance.

Room occupancy

Most hotels use room occupancy as the total number of times a room is let expressed as a percentage of the total number of rooms available. This is a reasonable calculation but in a hotel with a large number of double and triple beds such a percentage disguises the fact that a double room is frequently let for single occupancy. More accurate, therefore, is the number of sleepers (guests) which shows how many people are actually staying in the hotel. However, it should be noted that many hotels now sell on a per room basis, whether with single or double occupancy; alternatively, they sell on a per person per room basis.

Taking a 16 bedroom hotel, room occupancy is calculated as follows:

Rooms available	16
Rooms sold	8

Room occupancy is 8 / 16 × 100 = 50%

Sleeper occupancy

Rooms available		16
Rooms sold		
Double	6	
Single	2	8
Sleeper ratio:		
Doubles	(6 x 2) =	12
Singles	(2 x 1) =	2
		14

Sleeper occupancy (the number of sleepers) is 14 / 8 = 1.8 (rounded up).

Average room rate

We have already emphasised the importance of correctly calculating revenues with regard to breakfast and VAT charges:

	£
Room charge (B&B)	100.00
Less: Breakfast charge	12.00
TOTAL	88.00
Less: VAT (£88÷1.2)	14.67
TOTAL	**73.33**

The relevance of these three economic levers becomes apparent when the total room revenue is calculated:

16 rooms @ 50% occupancy × ARR (£73.33) = £586.64.

These calculations will be sufficient for most first-time buyers. The principal reason why they are so important is that they enable you to calculate the cost of housekeeping staff and breakfast staff wages, which is critical to your revenue assumptions and wage cost control.

In our examples of industry norm wage costs (Tables 8.2, 8.5 and 8.8 - pages 84, 86 and 88), wage costs are 20 per cent for rooms (25 per cent with a night porter), 35 per cent for food, 16 per cent for beverage and five per cent for the manager and bookkeeping/administration costs.

In fact, these can be separated out even more precisely by assuming that of room wage costs reception staff account for 12 per cent and housekeeping staff account for eight per cent. These percentages will vary from hotel to hotel but are industry norms.

In our example of ARR, we would need to deduct eight per cent of room revenue – £46.88 – to calculate the housekeeping wage cost of servicing the rooms.

Similarly, in calculating the breakfast wage costs, and using the industry norm of 35 per cent wage costs, it is assumed that food service represents 12 per cent and the kitchen represents 23 per cent of food costs. Using these averages, the wage cost in our example is as follows:

15 sleepers @ £12 (breakfast charge) ÷ 1.2 (VAT) = £150.

Foodservice wage cost @ 12 per cent of £150 =   £18.

These calculations will help you set your tariff which is one of the most important decisions that you make. In addition, they will also allow you to forecast your weekly wages correctly – vital with the ever-increasing upward pressure on payroll, which remains any hotel's largest cost centre.

13

An understanding of all the costs and revenues involved in operating a hotel will ensure that a hotel's losses can be curtailed – and its profit potential can be achieved.

As we have already seen (Chapter 8), hotels have high fixed costs. If the hotel is full, these costs will still be incurred but you will also incur other costs – called indirect or variable costs – which vary in direct proportion to the amount of business that the hotel is enjoying.

The fixed costs include such items as rates, utility charges, insurance, manager's salary, some staff costs, loan interest and repayments, maintenance contracts and other items which do not vary in relation to the number of guests or the level of business achieved.

What of variable costs? With more guests in the hotel, more bed-linen will be used and so laundry charges will increase in direct proportion to the number of guests accommodated. The same applies to food costs for breakfast; heat, light and power and wages; more staff will be required to service the guest needs. These costs will add up to a considerable sum of money over a year but to highlight their impact on profit, it is always helpful to break them down on a cost per guest basis. This, however, is a difficult exercise to undertake and would best be undertaken after you have some experience of managing your hotel.

Of course, hotel guests will buy other services once in the hotel, such as drinks at the bar and additional meals, which will increase revenue, particularly if rooms have been discounted. If the hotel does not have a restaurant or a bar, then the opportunity for additional sales is extremely limited – something potential purchasers must consider before buying a guest house or small hotel with limited facilities. Clearly, no hotelier can afford to neglect any sales opportunity that pushes his revenue as high as possible. Even a couple of pounds extra spent servicing guests will drag down profit, just as every pound extra that you encourage them to spend will boost profits.

This is particularly true if you are buying a resort hotel where the relationship between fixed and variable costs will be the crucial factor in deciding whether to close during the winter months.

Will it cost more to stay open in the winter with a skeleton staff to serve a few guests (almost certainly at a reduced rate) or should you decide to bear the entire burden of the fixed costs without any income, close the hotel for the winter and lay off all the staff?

Immediate challenges

Wages

Calculating staff wages will be an early task you have to face particularly as they will claim up to 30 per cent of your revenues. The HMRC's introduction of Real Time Information (RTI) means that you have to post PAYE returns on a weekly basis. This means that employers (or their accountant, bookkeeper or payroll bureau) will:

◆ Send details to HMRC every time they pay an employee at the time they pay them.

◆ Use payroll software to send this information electronically as part of their routine payroll process.

This is a significantly more onerous obligation than the previous regime of an annual return and means you have to be organised to deal with it from your first week. There are a number of companies which offer specialist wage systems, the cost of which should be balanced against their greater speed and efficiency.

"Profitability is the lifeblood of all successful business. Hotels are no exceptions to this. Without profit, you will not be able to invest in the essential ongoing maintenance and upgrading of your hotel to keep pace with your guests' ever rising expectations. It's easy to fall in love with the idea of being a hotelier and even to think that it is worth putting up with a few months of poor performance because it will get better with the season/weather/economy. The reality is that those few months can become permanent and that there is never enough spare cash left to invest. The result can be a discounting spiral that can become impossible to reverse.

This chapter sets out not only the analysis essential before purchasing a property but also the need to constantly ensure that operations are profitable. It is very easy to set prices and do the analysis at the beginning of the year but your costs will vary (almost invariably upward!) and seemingly, without notice, your margins will be eroded. If you couple that with some subtle discounting as well as the siren voices of the Online Travel Agents and your profit has gone.

You can use discounting as a sales tool. Indeed, to try and ignore the market reality in the internet age of immediate price transparency, is as doomed as King Canute. However, you must intimately understand your costs, particularly the marginal cost of every aspect of having guests in your hotel and to know how to price. To do otherwise is to become a busy fool!"

Adam Fox-Edwards
Proprietor, Arundell Arms Hotel, Lifton, Devon

13

Energy

Energy usage in a hotel can be high and even if you are on an economic tariff at the start of the year that is not necessarily always the case at the end of the year. Most suppliers enable businesses to change their tariff within a three month window but if you miss this (which, in a busy hotel, is easily done), then you might be rolled over onto a higher tariff which could cost hundreds, if not thousands of extra pounds. By shopping around, the potential for saving money is considerable. This can be a task outsourced to one of the many price comparison companies or websites such as Make it Cheaper. Using this site, one small pub company saved over £3,000 in a year. Most sites will also regularly monitor your usage to ensure you keep on top of the problem and they can reduce telephone, insurance and Chip and Pin costs as well.

At a time when businesses are under extreme cost pressures, the ability to switch suppliers is one way by which budgets can be kept under strict control and using these sites should be a permanent feature of your budgetary control.

As the new owner - ten pieces of advice

1 The budget is your financial framework – use it as your financial discipline.

2 A monthly P&L account within ten working days is essential – otherwise you are driving blind.

3 Make sure your staff know the weekly/monthly target figures.

4 Make sure you understand how VAT works – and keep VAT revenues in a separate account.

5 Can you organise the payroll – or do you need to bring in help?

6 Don't forget – PAYE returns to HMRC must be weekly. Make sure you have the funds.

7 Arrange for a regular monthly stock take – stock and cash can wander!

8 Make sure you have sufficient funds set aside to pay the quarterly utility bills.

9 Check your energy suppliers by shopping around.

10 Be aware of all the costs in room sales – commissions can be onerous.

14 Sole trader or limited company - and some legal points

One factor that you will have already considered is whether to form a company to run the business or whether to operate is as a sole trader or as a partnership. But there are other legal considerations.

The simplest way of running a business is as a sole trader, but there are legal and tax implications. The proprietor (the sole trader) becomes personally responsible for all the debts incurred and his own personal possessions can be sold to realise sufficient money to pay these debts if the business goes belly-up; the private home of a sole trader can be sold to raise money to pay his debts.

The same applies to a partnership which is created when two or more people act as sole traders together. The same principle of unlimited liability applies and the partners will be jointly and severally responsible for the debts incurred according to the partnership agreement regarding the sharing of profits and losses. A sleeping partner (someone who invests money into the business but who usually takes no part in its operation) will also lose his investment if the business goes under.

Both these forms of trading provide little protection to a businessman and most hoteliers take the view that it is commercially prudent to form their own limited liability company or to buy a company that is already registered 'off the shelf'.

Your lawyer can advise you which course of action to take. As the name implies, a limited liability company limits the liability of the shareholders of the company to the amount each has invested in the business. However, if a bank loan is involved, the shareholders would usually have given their personal guarantees as part of the financial conditions and these would be called on in the case of insolvency. A company is a legal entity of its own irrespective of the number of shareholders. Whereas a sole trader employs people personally, a company, not its directors, enters into a contract to employ staff.

Forming a company may also have tax advantages. Basically, the sole trader will be taxed on his net profit as income. If this exceeds a certain amount he may be better off to trade as a limited company and pay corporation tax. There could be an optimum mix between company tax and directors' fees and your financial planning and tax adviser or accountant will advise.

Your lawyer will help you in the steps that need to be taken to form a company. The fees involved are not prohibitive but your lawyer's and accountant's charges will be a cost element and should be budgeted.

Red tape

The longer you own and manage your own hotel, the more aware you will be of the rules and regulations that govern the way you manage the property – in other words, red tape. These regulations exist in almost every area of the operation of the hotel but especially in employment and in food safety/kitchen hygiene which are outlined in following chapters. Here are some of the key rules and regulations that you will have to deal with as soon as you take over the property.

1   You must keep a **register of guests**. This can be in the form of a book or separate sheet or electronically, and must be retained for 12 months after completion. The information required for all guests over 16 years of age is their full name and their nationality and date of arrival. For those who are not British, Irish or Commonwealth guests a passport or other documentation which shows their identity and nationality must be provided; in addition, you should obtain details of their next destination, including the address, if known. (In fact, the 1972 Immigration (Hotel Records) Order on which these regulations are based is now considered obsolete and is being considered for repeal as part of the coalition government's Red Tape Challenge, but it remains a legal requirement while it remains on the books and the records can be inspected by the police or anyone authorised by the Home Office.)

    Incidentally, it is not an offence for British people to sign under a false name. Although these requirements might appear somewhat onerous it is in the hotel's interests to know who is staying on the premises if only to be able to create a visitor profile. Who are your guests? Where do they come from? What age are they? How did they find you? Are they willing to be kept in touch with future promotions? It is not unusual, therefore, for hotels to have tick box forms asking guests to provide this information which enables the hotel to build up a picture of visitor profiles which will, in turn, influence its marketing and promotional programmes.

2   If you receive **deposit payments from customers**, they should be accounted for (for VAT purposes) as being received then, not when the guest subsequently stays and pays the balance due.

3   A hotel must display in reception **a notice under the Hotel Proprietors' Act 1956 which sets limits on liability for guests' stolen or damaged belongings**. Without the notice, a hotel's liability may be unlimited. You must also display the correct notice: one for Greater London, one for the rest of the UK.

4   This brings us to the **Data Protection Act 1998**. Before you purchase your hotel, it would be wise to read up on this Act. A very useful guide is published by VisitEngland – *The Pink Book 2014: Legislation for Tourist Accommodation*. This booklet is an invaluable source of reference for all legal aspects of managing a hotel and should be one of the first additions to your business library. In brief, the Act is designed to protect the privacy of individuals by preventing the misuse or unauthorised use of personal information that is held by others. The Act applies to hotel data bases, whether they are computer or manual filing systems, index cards, files or visitor books.

5   It is no longer a legal requirement that the room tariff is displayed at reception but the Consumer Protection from Unfair Practices Regulations 2008 (CPR), means that **hotels are under an obligation to be open and honest in their pricing** and not to omit information which might affect someone's purchasing decision. In order to comply with CPR, hotels should exhibit their prices (chiefly single room, double room) and prices should include VAT (if you are VAT registered), any compulsory service charge and state whether meals are included in the price. The Act applies to all statements of price, whether advertisements, on line, in brochures, or orally by phone.

6   **Licensing law** is complex and far reaching and will have a direct impact on your business. It also varies between England and Wales and Scotland, so it is important that you understand the regulations that apply to your hotel, both with regard to the people you can serve and the staff you employ. In brief, a licence holder must not sell liquor to anyone under the age of 18 or allow the sale on his premises and must ask for proof of age if he is in doubt. Under-age drinking poses problems for licensees for they are held responsible if it takes place on their premises. For a brief resume of the rules and regulations, VisitEngland's *Pink Book* (see 4 above) is an excellent guide.

7   Your premises will no doubt already be registered with the local authority through its environmental health office under the Food Hygiene (England) Regulations 2006 and similar regulations in Scotland, Wales and NI, but you should put in place and implement your own **food safety management system** in order the satisfy the local environmental health officer. The system is based on Hazard Analysis and Critical Control Point (HACCP) assessments under which you must assess all potential food hazards and how you deal with them. The Food Standards Agency publishes a guide – *Food Hygiene: A Guide for Businesses* - which can be downloaded from the Agency's website (www.food. gov.uk) and which should be required reading for any newcomer to the industry.

14

Local environmental officers carry out routine inspections and the frequency of visits will depend on the risk posed by the business and its past record, so if the vendor has had a chequered history with regard to food hygiene you can expect the local authority to take a keen interest in you; in any case, as the new owner the local environmental officer will want to meet you and check your understanding of the requirements in order to ensure that standards are being maintained.

The environmental health officer's powers are quite draconian – he can issue a hygiene emergency prohibition notice, which effectively closes down the kitchen if there an immediate risk to the public – so it is in your (and your chef's) interest to understand what is required.

As a result of your inspector's visit, you will either have the existing food hygiene rating confirmed or a new one will be issued. The National Food Hygiene Rating Scheme, commonly called Scores on the Doors, will rate your premises between 0 and 5 (a similar scheme in Scotland has only three categories). Although you are not obliged to display the score (except in Wales), those premises with high scores often do, using it as positive marketing tool. A guide to food inspections – *Food Law Inspections and your Business* – is available for downloading on the FSA website. One aspect of the Food Safety Act 1990 also relates to allergies - EU regulations have been introduced which force premises to provide information on allergens in the food being served.

8   You must ensure the **safety of your customers**. Under the Occupiers Liability Act 1984 you are responsible for the physical safety of everyone who comes on the premises, not just guests but postmen, suppliers and others who are lawfully on the premises. This liability can be covered by insurance. Not all the rooms need be covered as there are parts of the hotel which guests are not entitled to enter.

Public liability insurance is not mandatory but it would be a foolish businessman who ignores it; if successful, a serious claim against the hotel could be disastrous. You must also cover yourself for your liability for any harm suffered by employees at work under the Employer's Liability (Compulsory Insurance) Act 1969. There are a number of insurance companies who can offer special insurance packages for hoteliers which include public liability insurance, employers' liability insurance and property and contents insurance.

9   You must describe your goods and services accurately. The **Trade Descriptions Act 1968** makes it a criminal offence to apply a false trade description to goods or services and covers descriptions given both verbally and in writing. It covers any factual statement about the physical qualities of the product, e.g. size of bedroom. The Trade Descriptions Act is enforced by Trading Standards officers. The Consumer Protection Act 1987 governs both the pricing of products and product safety. The way in which prices are presented to customers is controlled by a very detailed code of practice. This covers most forms of promotional marketing. There are rules which deal for example with how sale prices can be claimed, introductory offers, recommended prices and free offers.

As a result, be careful of the description of your hotel in your brochure. The Advertising Standards Authority recently won a case against a restaurant that advertised a welcome New Year's Eve cocktail reception as 'serving guests exclusive cocktails from our world-class mixologists' whereas only one cocktail was offered; eight other statements were judged to be misleading. Pricing should include VAT and should not confuse potential guests, nor should additional charges be added at the time of purchase unless previously notified.

10 The **law about accepting bookings** is complex and VistEngland's *Pink Book* is an invaluable introduction. Broadly, a contract to reserve a room can be oral or written and must include a definite offer of accommodation by the hotel and an unconditional acceptance by the customer within a reasonable time. This causes little problem for bookings undertaken weeks in advance. More difficult are telephone bookings where there is no time for written confirmation. In fact, most telephone bookings are now credit card reservations; if the guest does not appear the credit card is automatically debited with the room charge providing the room cannot be let to a late arrival. For a single night's accommodation lost by a no-show, the ill-will created pursuing a claim is probably not worth the financial recompence, though larger hotels may well have a policy of automatically charging the credit card.

A valid contract can only be cancelled by agreement of both parties, so a guest can claim compensation if he arrives to find that the room he has booked is not available. In this situation, which can happen in city centre hotels during busy periods (over-booking is commonplace) the hotel is obliged to make every effort to find alternative accommodation of the same standard and to pay the taxi costs for the guest to get there. For a resort hotel, where a family of four has booked a fortnight's accommodation at full board, a cancelled booking at short notice can lead to a much greater financial loss. Even in this situation, the hotel must make every effort to relet the room. If this is not successful, the hotel is entitled to claim compensation for the loss of accommodation income, less an allowance for food not consumed.

Some bookings require a deposit and one of the most common cancellation procedures is to have a fee that varies according to the amount of notice given – the nearer to the time of arrival, the less deposit is returnable. In the booking process, you must make clear what your cancellation policy is and under what circumstances some or all of the deposit is returnable.

11 **Finally, remember you are not alone – even if it may feel like it**. Consider joining the local hotel association if there is one and the national trade association (The British Hospitality Association, Queens House, 55/56 Lincoln's Inn Field, London WC2A 3BH – www.bha.org.uk). The BHA can give legal advice to its members. The Institute of Hospitality is the professional body for the hospitality industry and membership is available by qualification. Many local colleges also run short courses in various aspects of hotel and catering management – full details from People 1st, the industry's Sector Skills Council (www.people1st.co.uk)·

14

Ten keys pieces of advice

1   As a sole trader, you are personally responsible; as a company, your liabilities are limited.

2   Keep a register of guests . . . .

3   . . . and display the Hotel Proprietors' Act 1956 notice.

4   Use the guest register to form the basis of your data bank . . .

5   . . . but beware of the Data Protection Act!

6   Include VAT in all your prices (if you are VAT registered.)

7   Food Safety – never ignore it!

8   Describe your hotel accurately – beware of the Trade Description Act.

9   Remember – you're entering into a contract when you accept a booking.

10 Get hold of a copy of *The Pink Book* – read it and keep it by you.

15 Starting from scratch - some thoughts on conversion

Many people consider entering the industry by converting an existing building
– a large country house, for example – into a hotel. There are a number of
understandable attractions in this but the pitfalls may not be so obvious.

Country house hotels

In the 1970s, many country houses were converted into country house hotels; similarly many town houses were turned into town house hotels, frequently called boutique properties. These conversions, which were typically extremely expensive and resulted in some very high-priced accommodation, continue to this day as newcomers look upon conversion as one way into the industry. The advantages are fourfold.

1 It may be easier to find a private house of style and character.

2 A large house may be less expensive to purchase than an established, successful hotel because you are buying a building, not a business.

3 In opening a hotel you don't have to live up to – or dispel – a previous owner's reputation. You start with a clean slate. You can plan your hotel in your own way, restricted only by the structure of the property, your financial resources and your marketing objectives.

4 A country house hotel offers a tantalising glimpse of gracious living.

These are considerable attractions and there are many examples of private houses being converted to hotel use; in London, too, many terraced houses have been converted into hotels.

However, there are pitfalls:

1   Planning permission is likely to be difficult to obtain and if the building is listed there will be restrictions on what you can do.

2   Depending on the state and suitability of the building the cost of conversion can frequently be higher than budgeted. Indeed, it can be more expensive to convert a building into a hotel than buying an established hotel.

3   The availability of finance will be greatly restricted.

4   The cost of upkeep of country house hotel grounds is an additional burden on the business though they might, eventually, be one of the hotel's strongest selling points.

It would be cautionary to note that all the established hotel groups have expanded through new-build properties and very few are now converting other premises to hotel use though there are examples of office buildings being converted into hotels; these are on a much larger scale than a first-time buyer would be able to consider. **It might also be noted that the larger hotel groups do not regard the country house hotel market as a prime sector.**

The availability of suitable properties is more limited today than it was in the 1970s at the height of the explosion in the number of country house hotels. Many large private houses have since been bought up by high net worth individuals for residential use. Those that are available are likely to be in more remote areas which will make the marketing of the property difficult.

The cost of conversion also means that the hotel will be forced into the five star or deluxe category and the market for rooms at £300+ a night is necessarily limited. However, those same high net worth individuals have money to spend and they will spend it on quality products. Country house hotels are a popular lifestyle destination for them, as they are for those less wealthy individuals celebrating special occasions, such as birthdays and anniversaries. Attracting – and sustaining – this market demands the highest standards and the competition is strong.

In any conversion, the number of rooms that can be created will dictate its economics; in this market, rooms must be spacious in line with increasing customer expectations, Double or family rooms are essential. You will also need adequate space for public areas and kitchens.

It is almost *de rigeur* for a country house hotel to have a restaurant that aims to provide noteworthy food. Few people will be attracted to stay at such a hotel without the promise of fine dining. Of course, such a restaurant should also attract local diners and this will boost the restaurant's profitability – something that the business will need if it is to be successful. If the restaurant helps the hotel to be included in the various food guides, including Michelin, then that is all to the good.

We should add here that catering and hotelkeeping are entirely separate businesses. Not many hoteliers are great restaurateurs but in the country house hotel, where food is a key attraction, there is a need for the owner to be both. Recruiting and retaining key staff in the country thus becomes is a major challenge. In London, some hotels have let out their restaurant to a celebrity chef who takes the burden of managing the restaurant off the owner's shoulders – a trend which is now not unknown in the country house hotel market.

Another facility that many country house hotels offer is a health spa, some having been installed for many millions of pounds. The benefit of such an amenity will depend on how many local paying members it can attract and how much of an attraction it is to guests.

Whatever the location of the property, it is certain that conversion will be expensive – £100,000 per bedroom upwards – while equipping and fitting out a commercial kitchen would not to be less than £250,000. There should be a generous contingency budget to take care of unforeseen problems. As a result, tariffs will inevitably be high so an understanding of the connection between price and value is the key to success in this market.

Broadly speaking, the higher the price, the greater must be the value offered but the higher the tariff, the smaller is the market (though there is some evidence that this market sector is, indeed, expanding.) Competing in a more demanding and more sophisticated market means that lapses in the level of comfort, quality of food and standard of service are not easily tolerated or forgiven. So while value is paramount it is not just dictated by price. There are many very expensive hotels that achieve high occupancy levels because they provide great value; there are many inexpensive hotels that suffer from low occupancy because they do not represent good value.

Town house conversions

Conversions of town houses offer slightly different challenges. There are no extensive grounds; they are also easier to market because people visit a town or city for purposes other than to visit your hotel, whereas a country house hotel tends to be a destination in its own right. Business for a town hotel will also fall into a different booking pattern being busier in the weekday than at weekends; the country hotel's challenge is that weekday occupancy is typically lower than weekend occupancy, which is frequently high.

A town house conversion also has less flexibility in its pricing as it is easily compared to competitive establishments in the town; a country house hotel, as a stand-alone property, can be more flexible in its pricing.

There is also the possibility of converting a town property into a guest house rather than into a hotel. This is a viable option for many although one drawback is that the term guest house has a slightly pejorative connotation – hence the growing use of the term B&B. With nearly 400 five star guest houses listed by the AA, all with bathrooms en suite and offering a high standard of comfort and furnishings, this sector of the market is expanding.

15

The tariff of five star guest houses typically compares with those of the higher-rated hotels in the area but the owner's unique advantage is that he can offer a home-from-home to his guests rather than a branded hotel product. It is warmth and hospitality that encourage people to return and, more importantly, encourages them to tell their friends and neighbours about their stay.

B&Bs are also staff-light. Most offer only bed and breakfast so outside staff and high level kitchen skills are not required. Prices can also be kept down if the establishment can avoid VAT by keeping below the £82,000 VAT threshold. Running a small town or city guest house can thus be profitable but because of their short season, those in resorts have more questionable economics. Occupancy in guest houses and smaller hotels (see page 23) is also generally much lower than in larger properties.

In operating any hotel or guest house, it's as well to remember that guests want greater comfort, more attractive decor, more comfortable furniture and fittings and tastier food than they would find in their own home.

And, almost above all else, the establishment should be clean. Survey after survey points out that cleanliness is the greatest imperative of every hotel. An owner forgets that at his peril.

Starting from scratch – ten questions you need to answer

1 Have you researched the competition?

2 Is the location right?

3 Is planning permission likely to be granted?

4 How many rooms can you provide?

5 Who will use them?

6 At what cost?

7 Do you need a high quality restaurant?

8 What other facilities do you need to provide?

9 Can you recruit the right staff?

10 Do you have access to sufficient funds? Builders' budgets are always exceeded!

16 Building up the business

> *"I always ask new recruits what is more perishable a tomato or a room? The answer, of course, is a room. , I can make soup with an overripe tomato. I can't sell last night's unoccupied room today!"*
>
> *Gavin Ellis*
> *Proprietor, Knockomie Hotel. Forres, Scotland*

What are your aims and objectives?

Don't confuse marketing and sales. Marketing identifies specific groups of people (potential clients) and identifies and satisfies their specific needs. It's a process that involves thinking, analysing, questioning. The actions you take to exploit the markets that you have identified will represent your sales activities. So you need to know your markets before you can successfully sell to them.

Every hotelier needs to establish both long-term objectives and short-term aims.

The short-term aims are mainly concerned with ensuring that the hotel immediately trades profitably, that sales opportunities are maximised and costs are contained. These aims will have formed a key section of your business plan so that your finance source knows where you are going, how you are going to get there, and how long it will take.

Your long-term objectives, which will be enshrined in your marketing plan, will identify exactly who your target markets are now and whether they are likely to change in the future. Will you be seeking new markets? How will you reach them?

Because a hotel is a small, individually-owned unit it does not mean that long-term objectives are unnecessary, but there are hotels that survive profitably from year-to-year without any plans for development or expansion.

There are many hoteliers who believe that further development is either impossible or unnecessary – the former because there are physical limitations on the business which prevent expansion or growth, the latter because the owner is making sufficient money for his needs and does not want the additional work involved in expanding the business. Generally, these are conscious decisions. Most purchasers, however, will have definite ideas about the future of their acquisition and will have a clear idea of the development of the hotel, showing what kind of customers the hotel can best attract, what their needs are and how the hotel is going to satisfy those needs over a specific period of time. Sales promotion techniques – the tools in the marketing toolbox – will be used to implement this plan.

Before you can promote your hotel, therefore, you need to be sure you are promoting it to the right market. So, consider:

1   Has the potential of the business been realised as the business stands now?

2   Once the present potential has been realised, how can the business expand in the future?

Every new hotelier wants to stamp his own personality on his hotel and to achieve this he may be tempted to make a violent change in the hotel's direction which could upset the established clientele. Unless new and more profitable customers replace those who are driven away by the change, the hotel will lose business. Leave a prosperous and successful hotel well alone until you have sound reasons for making changes.

However, the majority of hotels pose more difficult problems. A hotel may be reasonably profitable but may have shown little growth in the volume of business during the last three years; the rooms may be busy but the restaurant and bars empty, or vice versa. Alternatively, a hotel may be in an area where the holiday trade is declining and where there is no other potential source of revenue. Yet again, a hotel may be busy in the week but empty at weekends. All these situations pose classic hotel marketing challenges and there is no single – or simple – answer to any of them.

The initial exercise is to define exactly what the challenge really is. This may not be easy. A hotel may be suffering from declining occupancy, but is it because the area itself is declining in popularity or is the hotel losing out to other hotels in the area? If the latter, why are the other hotels more successful? Have new hotels emerged which are taking business away?

Many people who take over a hotel believe that, by an enormous personal effort, they can substantially improve business. Often, this is the case but sometimes there are more fundamental challenges to overcome.

Hotels can be sold at the bottom of a cycle because the vendor knows he is selling and is unwilling to spend large sums of money on a property that he will shortly not own. It's tempting to assume that you, as the new owner, can boost business merely by raising standards of service but this is not always the case; it is wise to dig a little deeper. What is the competition offering? This might reveal the other factors that account for your declining profits.

Stamping your own personality on the business makes your hotel unique – an advantage no competitor hotel can match. But you need to be able to meet all your guests' other needs as well: primarily, value-for-money accommodation, an attractive ambiance and good food.

> *"So often I have seen owners of small hotels forget they are their hotel's most important sales and marketing resource. They are the holders of the business's vision and direction and therefore its marketing message.*
>
> *Because the owner is the most vested in his hotel business, he is the most aware of its costs and therefore is best placed to create sales policy. And as he is the one who usually pays the bills, he tends to be the best negotiator when it comes to taking a booking. Unless you are a chef proprietor, you wouldn't dare to think of cooking for your guests; very rarely are owners the housekeeper, restaurant manager or barman. We normally employ people with their unique expertise to handle the major hotel areas.*
>
> *But when it comes to sales, when it comes to getting people excited about your product, helping them to see how great their stay will be with you and, most assuredly, what great value your hotel is - then, without any doubt, you are your hotel's best sales person."*
>
> *Jeffrey Epstein*
> *Chairman, Hotel Business Improvement Management*

It is impossible to overestimate the value of competitor research, not only before you purchase, but on a continual basis. Do your competitors have better facilities – larger rooms – better equipped bathrooms – more attractive toiletries – livelier restaurant – busier bars – more spacious public areas – better equipped conference and meeting rooms – a swimming pool and gym – more extensive parking – free wi-fi . . . ? The list could go on.

Many of these may be factors in encouraging people to prefer the competition but none of them will have been anything to do with what you might have thought was the problem of your falling occupancy: declining levels of service.

Marketing recognises that most hotels offer more than just a room – they offer a guest experience . . .

. . . . in which there are a great many different sales opportunities – from the sale of a room to a booking for dinner, from breakfast to afternoon tea, from morning coffee to lunch, from a drink in the bar to a bottle of wine in the evening, from a commission on a local tour to a car hire booking. The guest experience covers a multitude of sales opportunities and they will all be identified in the marketing plan. How well you sell these experiences will influence your revenues.

Franchising is the main engine for growth by major hotel groups. Franchised properties have thus muscled into the independent hotelier's traditional source of business as a result of which more franchised hotels are grabbing a bigger share of

16

the same-sized cake. Free wi fi in the bedrooms, for example, might not be feasible for an established hotel to offer but even some budget hotels are offering this facility and it is now widely expected by guests. It is far easier and less expensive for new–build hotels to meet expanding customer demands than it is for a hotel built many years ago.

Nevertheless, just as en suite bedrooms became an essential provision for any half decent hotel by the mid to late 20th century, so will advancing technology and changing customer expectations impose similar urgent challenges for the independent hotelier in this century. If he is to maintain his share of the market there is really no alternative to investing in his property.

Domestic leisure market

In general terms, holiday makers are more concerned about price and value for money than the businessman on an expense account. The introduction of new, budget hotels, all having bedrooms with private bathrooms, has raised customer expectations in every section of the market. A child in a parent's room at little or no extra cost will be welcomed by many guests but keen pricing may not be entirely the deciding factor in choosing the hotel in the first place. A hotel with children's play and games facilities, a swimming pool and regular entertainment might be more of an attraction which will enable it to charge a higher price than one without these amenities. It will certainly attract a wider clientele.

As it is clearly easier to generate business for a hotel in a popular area than in an unpopular area, it follows that hotels in successful resorts tend to be more expensive to purchase and are in greater demand than those in other areas. Wherever you buy the property, you must also consider whether you can develop the business. Can the season be extended at either end of the year - the 'shoulder' months of April, May, September and October? Are there other hotels spending time and effort extending the season? How active is the local tourist office? Is there scope for developing conferences and meetings and what improvements or additions would have to be made to cope adequately with this sector of the market?

Marketing and promoting a resort hotel can be a difficult undertaking because the hotel is dependent on only one type of customer and more and more leisure travellers are increasingly taking longer holidays abroad.

Resort hotels have thus become a victim of shifts in customer tastes and preferences as well as changing holiday-taking patterns. The thousands of people on the prom may look encouraging but they may also turn out to be day-trippers or staying in self-catering accommodation; they are of little use to your hotel.

Experience of staying in well-equipped overseas resorts also means that that the leisure traveller has become more demanding and less forgiving of perceived lower standards (and lack of sun) in UK resorts. A destination that does not provide the kind of facilities that people want will inevitably lose popularity which will, in turn, create difficulties for its hotels. However much promotion its hoteliers undertake it will be difficult for them to attract new customers – so much so that in many resorts, hotels have been converted into self-catering flats because the traditional market has so fundamentally changed.

A major growth area: short-break market

Success in attracting a share of this market primarily depends on the location of the hotel and the effort put into the promotion of short breaks.

People on a short break generally first decide to visit the area and then choose the hotel; the destination is typically the key factor in the purchase decision. Weekend business can thus be built up in a hotel in London because people want to visit the capital which has much to offer in terms of entertainment, restaurants and general animation; it is much harder to generate weekend traffic into an urban environment that has few such attractions. Even so, this doesn't inhibit group hotels, largely business-based in towns and cities, from trying to grab a share of the short-break market by heavily promoting discounted breaks in on-the-page newspaper advertising and through their web sites. Some extra attraction is frequently used to boost demand, such as a special interest weekend, but basically price is the main determinant.

Unfortunately, these packages can create high promotional costs and they take time to become popular and profitable. Primarily, the discount needs to be seen to be both genuine and attractive; it can take the form of offering an extra night free, a reduction on normal rates, a deal in the restaurant (one diner free, for example) or some other enticement, perhaps an upgrade to a better room, which convinces the guest that he is getting a better deal.

However, with additional income generated through the restaurant and bars (don't forget, you are selling that customer experience) weekend or weekday packages are vastly preferable to empty rooms and are an essential part of any hotel's total business mix. In fact, rooms don't always have to be discounted; a hotel's popularity may enable it to charge near full rate for weekends as well as weekdays leading to high week-long, year-round occupancy. Such hotels are exceptions and are usually well-located establishments with a high reputation for good food but, even for these properties, some enticement might be required to attract guests in the quieter periods.

16

Coach tour market

Coach tours also constitute an important part of the British holiday market but it is extremely price-conscious and profit comes from high turnover at cheap rates with very efficient catering, so food costs have to be strictly enforced. It is also a high risk area.

Coach companies will book up blocks of rooms early in the season in contracts that have late cancellation clauses – in some cases only two weeks before the arrival of the coach party. That 50-person coach tour which you expected may turn out to consist of only 20 people and you might not be able to fill the 30 vacancies with chance customers.

Providing the coach company is able to sell its seats, coach bookings can represent a regular source of income and some coach companies (Shearings for example) even own their own hotels. However, while this market has its advantages – the hotel benefits from the coach company's sales and marketing effort – negotiations with the coach company will mean that you have to let rooms at a considerable discount. Again, this is where your calculation of breakeven point is important. Of course, some guests will order drinks at the bar and wine with their meal, which will represent additional income, but this will vary from party to party and for some elderly parties may not be particularly significant.

The Fully Inclusive Tour (FIT) market, in which independent travellers purchase inclusive travel packages, is also important and growing; it is generally lucrative, fuelled as it is by consumers valuing the security and cost effectiveness that package holidays provide. At the same time, the market is also evolving in order to offer greater choice and sophistication to holidaymakers as well as more tailor-made itineraries. If you can negotiate your inclusion in domestic and overseas FIT tours you can build up a significant business but, as with coach tours, very small properties with a limited number of rooms (unless you are operating at the top end of the market) will make penetration of the market difficult. The lead time in building up an international tour market is also generally much longer than the domestic market. American incoming tours, for example, will allocate rooms in April or May for the following year.

Business market

Business travellers need services that other guests may not require…

… free wi fi, a writing area, either in the bedroom or elsewhere where they can prepare reports, good bathroom facilities, satellite television and radio in the bedroom and in-house movies in large city centre properties, good quality food in the restaurant and fast service at breakfast. Other facilities may attract but may not be crucial such as a health and leisure club and an indoor swimming pool.

In this market, whether a room is £80 or £180 a night may not matter too much as the customer is not paying out of his own pocket and VAT will normally be recoverable. The difference between £180 and £280 would be much more significant but still may not be critical for some business executives using bigger hotels. In other words, hotels in the business market have a greater degree of flexibility in pricing than a leisure hotel, though the hotel's location remains the key consideration. The corporate market provides the solid base on which to build up weekend or conference business but beware: your local competitors are seeking to attract the corporate traveller, too.

Conference market

Many hotels in the business market also attract residential meetings, seminars and conferences. The needs of the businessman and the conference delegate are broadly similar and not only major hotels with large conference rooms successfully exploit this market. In fact, the number of very large conferences is small and the market for small meetings is large.

The location of a hotel seeking to exploit the conference market is not as important as that of a hotel aiming at the business market. Businessmen go to a town for a specific reason - to do business there. This is not the case with a meeting or conference. Indeed, companies hold them in hotels often to get away from their own business environment and to be in one that is conducive to learning, thinking or decision-making. Of course, local industry needs to hold them, too. Price, however, is a more important factor than may appear on the surface. There are a large number of hotels specialising in residential conferences so competition is stiff. If it does not matter where the conference is held, price is frequently the determining factor in a company's choice of venue.

Whether a hotel is able to exploit the conference market depends on its facilities and the nature of its business. A twenty-bedroom hotel full of businessmen from Monday to Thursday night will not need to develop residential conferences even if a meeting room is available. There is no point in replacing ten per cent discounted commercial business with even more heavily discounted conference business. But if a meeting room is available there would certainly be scope for attracting non-residential meetings particularly from local companies; in the long term, building extra rooms to cope with residential conference accommodation requirements might be a viable option. Non-residential daily delegate rates including VAT averaged £43 in 2013 (£46 inc VAT in 2008) which is indicative of the competitive nature of the market (£136 inc VAT for overnight rates including dinner and breakfast - £138 in 2008).

Leisure facilities tend to be viewed by some conference organisers as important even though they may not be used by delegates themselves. The ability to offer golf at a nearby golf course can also be an attraction and would open up the holiday market, too. An additional benefit in attracting residential conference and meetings delegates is that they will normally consume more at the bar than the typical business traveller and this spend will go some way to offsetting any discount that you have had to agree on the room rate.

16

Overseas visitor market

The question facing every independent hotelier is how he can attract a bigger share of the overseas visitor market. The expense of selling directly to overseas countries is high and unless a hotel is part of a marketing consortium (see page 182) or unless local hoteliers co-operate in promoting their area overseas, few independent hoteliers can reach this market directly. It is possible to advertise in specific overseas newspapers and magazines but this needs careful attention and follow-up. Of course, your own website will be helpful though this depends on potential guests discovering the site in the first place. Experience may be your best guide here and national tourist boards will be able to advise you.

Location again is the key factor for overseas visitors. Overseas tourists are interested in Britain's historical and cultural past but they do not necessarily stay overnight in all these towns. Over 80 per cent of tourists stay in London and visit Oxford and Stratford in day trips by coach. It is only when they travel further afield that they need to have overnight accommodation. But, as London hotel prices are increasing at a faster rate than those of hotels in the provinces, more tourists, particularly those on return visits to Britain, will be encouraged to travel to other parts of Britain.

However, the introduction of sea and air links from the Continent to major provincial centres has been highly beneficial and air services into regional airports and ferries into such ports as Portsmouth, Plymouth, Harwich and Newcastle, for example, bring visitors directly into the provinces thus by-passing London. Many hoteliers in these areas have capitalised on these services by promoting directly to the countries concerned and it is significant that most of these towns have seen an increase in the number of new hotels.

Whether your hotel can take a bigger slice of the overseas visitor market is something that you must investigate. Major hotel groups will already have close contacts with overseas tour operators and travel companies and they are attracting a major share of the overseas visitor market but what is left is a profitable segment. The individual overseas visitor, who travels by car or train and who needs good quality hotel accommodation, is a valued – and valuable – customer

Dining-out market

Recognising that a guest's stay is not just for the night's accommodation but for a complete experience, building up the restaurant as a source of profitable income is an important consideration – covered more completely in Chapter 19. But here, you must be realistic. A small resort hotel, unless it is in the centre of the town, will find this difficult because of space and skill requirements; local people just do not view most small resort hotels as a dining out destination. Even more important is the growing competition from independent restaurants which aim directly at the dining-out market.

Most small hotels will face similar difficulties, but there are hotels in town and country locations which generate trade in their restaurant and in their function rooms. If your hotel is not already exploiting this market but has the facilities to do so you should certainly investigate whether building up a restaurant trade is feasible.

What other restaurants exist in the area? What type of food do they serve? How much do they charge? How late do they stay open? Is there a noticeable gap in the market that you can fill? Would your hotel with the right menu be able to fill the gap as an interesting, value-for-money restaurant? Have you got the right ambiance to encourage dining-out? What type of food could you serve most effectively? Would a 'good food' reputation help you to fill more bedrooms?

In some cases, the answer to these questions might encourage you to place your restaurant as an important part of your marketing strategy. Not only would it produce revenue and profit of its own, provided it is properly costed, controlled and marketed but it would get the hotel talked about locally. This is important because most hotels outside London depend on local trade for the broad base of the business. Don't, however, overestimate the amount of business from chance trade as this will take time to build up – and competition from branded restaurants gets stronger by the day.

A hotel offering cheap and simple accommodation is unlikely to be successful in offering high quality, expensive food – the markets clash. So while a hotel can successfully mix its market in terms of types of customer – business, conference, tourist and holiday maker, for example – it can only rarely mix it in terms of price and standard.

Function and wedding market

One further and related potential source of business needs to be investigated: banquets and other functions, such as weddings. These can be highly profitable and can develop enormous customer goodwill (or ill-will if carried out badly). They can also result in extra bedroom business. Their success is dependent on the facilities provided, the quality of the food and service and the planning that goes into the organisation of the event.

It's frequently the case that one hotel has become established as the main function venue in the area but this should not necessarily be a deterrent. One more hotel may be welcomed because it gives customers a choice. Even if the existing hotel is successful and popular, another venue on the scene will provide a choice that will be attractive to many. After that, you stand or fall on your own efforts.

One hotel in a town may be successful in banqueting because it provides cheap but cheerful food; a high quality but much more costly menu may not attract people away because they don't want a better meal experience. A much higher quality menu, on the other hand, could be welcomed by some customers and would open up a new market of people who want a better – or different – standard of food and service. If you do have a banqueting room, how can you boost business in the face of local competition? Do you need to improve the standard of food and service? Do you need to enhance the ambiance so that the room becomes a more attractive environment? Are your prices right?

Again, this emphasises the need for understanding the local market as well as recognising the need for researching what is available and how you can provide a viable alternative.

16

"Don't be a busy fool! Study all the sales channels that funnel business into your hotel:

* *Direct food and beverage*
* *Direct bookings, telephone and online*
* *Corporate - local and national*
* *Online Travel Agents (OTAs)*
* *Ground Handlers often representing other travel agents in overseas markets (F.I.T) and Incentive groups.*
* *Global Distribution Systems*
* *Discount Data Houses, for example Groupon.*

Review all the present use of such channels and decide whether to open more up tactically or close some down because they are diluting your yield. Only time will tell. But never be scared to experiment in different market segments and in seasonal peaks and troughs. Just because you needed to make a tactical discount last year do you really need to do it this year?"

Gavin Ellis
Proprietor, Knockomie Hotel, Forres, Scotland

Five pieces of advice...

1   Don't confuse marketing with selling.

2   Stamp your own personality on the business.

3   Never forget – guests are buying an experience, not just a room or a meal.

4   Short breaks are important – but regular full tariff guests can be even more critical for many hotels.

5   Regular investment in marketing and selling is the key to long-term success.

... and five questions you must answer

1   What market/markets are you aiming at?

2   Who will be responsible for exploiting them?

3   Has the hotel exploited its existing markets to the full?

4   How are you protecting your existing market? Remember, more and more hotels are grabbing a share of the same size cake.

5   What added value offer can you introduce to maximise occupancy?

17 Boosting your sales

"If your newly acquired hotel is a cold, rectangular box-shaped building where every room is the same, you have little if any staff, your restaurant serves food to a formula from a never-changing menu and you want to minimise your interaction with guests - then do not read on.

On the other hand, if your hotel is situated in a stunning location with beautiful grounds, in a building of character, with each bedroom different to the point of being quirky, and you aspire to create wonderful tasting and visually appetising cuisine realising that your guests are human and in search of a connection, kindness even – certainly hospitality – and are seeking a unique experience that creates a life-long impression with a memory they will share with others (which is potential business) - then every aspect of your sales and marketing must strive for personalisation.

When your guests are long gone, what will they remember?

The room or the small kindnesses; when you saw that, after their hike, a cup of hot tea was waiting for them by the fire? The fantastic starter at dinner or your restaurant manager giving a short master class in your region's cheeses?

But it is not only when your guests arrive at the threshold of your hotel that personalisation comes into play. It starts well before that, when they first get an inkling that they want to come to your hotel. That first contact may be inanimate - a web search on Google that throws up an image of your hotel. Or they may have been tweaked by a comment from a past guest on a review website.

Your task is to get your potential guest to interact with you directly, and as quickly as possible. You might think they do not want to. You might think that everyone wants to be anonymous, hence they book on-line. But it is not necessarily so and runs counter to why you bought this kind hotel in the first instance.

With each real interaction comes the opportunity to add real value and increased sales."

Jeffrey Epstein
Chairman, Hotel Business Improvement Management

Sales promotion is not just a question of getting customers to use your hotel. If you know where your markets are your sales promotion efforts will be effective; if you do not, much of your sales effort will be wasted.

The most noticeable revolution that has occurred in the hotel industry in the last decade is the advent of the internet. This has brought about the development of company websites, the introduction of social media and the use of entirely new and immediate methods of communication between hotels and their guests. In turn, this has changed the way hotels sell to the guests, how they generate contact with them before their stay and maintain that contact afterwards, and how they encourage them back for a return visit.

The increasing ownership of smartphones, tablets and other mobile devices also enables people on the move to book hotel rooms directly on-line, to plan itineraries and to change bookings if necessary. These applications did not exist even ten years ago but their use is now so common that a high percentage of hotel bookings is now made over the internet – a figure which will certainly grow. The hotel industry is truly part of the global communications revolution and major hotel groups in particular are taking full advantage of it.

The impact of this technology on the hotel industry is hugely significant.

It has enabled hotels, at little or no extra cost, to widen their sales thrust on a global basis, with a greater chance of penetration; it allows special offers to be created and marketed within hours rather than days – and without the use of expensive print material; it enables booking decisions to be instantaneously completed with no 'people' cost; and it allows hotels automatically to create a database of customers that can be readily accessed and used.

These are, indeed, significant advantages but there is one word of caution: while it provides the independent hotel with new channels of communication, it provides these channels to *every* hotel – so the competition which the independent faces has grown that much stronger; ignoring these developments, which includes such applications as Facebook, Twitter, is not now an option for the independent. If the major groups exploit the internet and social media to the extent that they do, then it is vital that the independent owner/operator does likewise.

The advantage is that many of these applications are free.

Your website, for example, once established, is basically cost-free and will be a prime tool in selling your rooms with pictures and stories that you hope will irresistibly drive the browser to book your hotel on-line. Of course, a website needs time and effort to keep up-to-date (something frequently ignored by too many hotels) but incurs little additional cost; using most social media accounts is also free. Many of the costs of print and staffing, which have traditionally been involved in marketing and selling, have thus been reduced or even eliminated.

The emergence of commissionable on-line hotel booking agents such as Booking.com, Laterooms.com and Expedia have opened up the market enormously, giving hotels many new and more powerful ways of reaching their public.

Using them can represent an important element in your sales strategy but you need to balance the greater exposure that you receive by allocating rooms to an agency with the discounted return you receive when the room is sold. In effect, the discount is the price you pay for the agency's efforts in selling your rooms. If the room sales are significant, then the commission will represent a considerable sum of money. The question to ask is whether you would have sold those rooms without using the agent. If the answer is negative then the commission is a worthwhile price to pay, always providing the rate is above your breakeven point. The impact of these costs is shown in the examples in Chapter 6.

The fundamental point to recognise here is that sales promotion is an essential part of any hotelier's job.

There is too much competition in the hotel market, all of it clamouring for the guest's attention, for any hotel now to sit back and wait for the customer to come through the front door, unbidden. Every other hotel in your neighbourhood is looking to steal your business. The power of the brands is such that people looking for a late room will be attracted to a branded property before they think of your less well known hotel; alternatively, they will turn to an on-line booking site for information and easy booking – hence their importance.

But how about in-house selling?

Selling is not just a question of getting people into the hotel in the first place . . .

. . . . vital though that is. It is also about generating the maximum possible revenue from every customer who uses the hotel's facilities, but done in such a way that the customer is totally satisfied when he or she leaves.

Every member of your staff is thus an essential part of your sales promotion effort. An able receptionist is your front line sales person as she sees all the guests and all the communication you have with them. She can also maximise occupancy by her skill in letting the available rooms to the best advantage, perhaps by withholding a sale for a single night when she knows there is a demand for three night stays. She can also encourage F&B sales by encouraging a booking for lunch or dinner. The waiter, by his skill in selling side orders or a dessert or a bottle of wine or a liqueur, can increase F&B revenue significantly. The room maid, through her contact with the guests, can encourage guests to return. The barman can develop regular trade by his personality.

The hotel is nothing but a series of interdependent sales areas that all need to work together if the unit as a whole is to exploit its true potential. This is what we mean by selling the whole experience.

17

Where to start?

Any promotional effort needs to start at home – with your existing customers and with the locals.

Most commercial hotels depend on the people who live in the town to help generate demand, so local residents must be encouraged to use the hotel's facilities. Maintaining your standards, at whatever level you decide, must be your prime business objective.

The hotel's website and social media are the principal places to explain your new ownership as well as your plans for the future and these will remain the most important means of communication with your market. Nevertheless, this should not deter you from using methods that have traditionally been a fundamental part of hotel marketing. For example, a personally signed letter to all the important companies in the area and to nearby shops and offices is one way of getting in touch with present and potential customers. This implies you have a list of these outlets; if you haven't you will need to undertake some research using local sources. An e-mail is less personal but is much cheaper to generate and easier to organise particularly if you need to communicate the same message to a wide audience.

However you deliver it, your message should provide some positive information on the improvements or extra facilities that you have introduced or intend to introduce, with perhaps some information about your background. Always address your message to someone specific, the managing director or chairman, for example, and find out his name; always personally address and sign the message – anything unnamed and unsigned will go straight into the waste bin.

This highlights a fundamental point of any sales promotion campaign: you must make contact with the person who makes the buying decision and this may not be the most obvious person.

If you don't get to the decision-maker you can waste an enormous amount of time and effort. The chairman's secretary, for example, may make all hotel bookings for a company but in a large company, individual secretaries may make reservations for their own boss. In one factory of a company, for example, it was discovered that seventy-two secretaries each made hotel bookings.

> To avoid this duplication of effort, accommodation buyers and most large companies, now use hotel booking agents, such as Thomas Cook or Expotel (a list is available from the Hotel Booking Agents Association) so that all bookings for the company are channelled through the one agency.

An advertisement in the local paper or radio station is another way of letting the public know of your new ownership but an advertisement that simply says 'Under new ownership' means little. Try to get the story across in a more positive manner by, for example, publicising the new menu in the restaurant, or a new deal you are offering.

It is difficult to quantify the success of advertising precisely but what is certain is that it is all too easy to spend a great deal of money on this method of promotion. If, for example, an insertion in a local paper for your restaurant costs £300, then it will have to generate at least £900 worth of business to pay for itself, taking the food and labour costs into account; put another way, if the average spend is £30 per head net, the advertisement will have to attract 20 new customers just to break even. Will the advertisement attract this number? And over what time period? Some people seeing the advertisement may not decide to visit immediately but may come several weeks later. The same analysis must be made of your room promotion advertising. It is important to keep a record of customers together with their average food and beverage spend per head (net of VAT). In that way, you can trace the success of your efforts.

Delayed reactions make tracking the effectiveness of advertising very tricky. One-off promotions for particular events can be highly effective providing they focus on the event itself, and their success or failure will be immediately apparent, but to promote the hotel or its restaurant more generally demands a more consistent approach with more regular promotion over a given time-frame. This is naturally more expensive and will need to be carefully planned and monitored to ensure that the advertisements continue to be cost-effective.

Effective advertising, like public relations, works on drip-feed – it involves a regular activity over a period of time.

However, many smaller hotels fill up with one-off campaigns on their website, sales through agency websites, social media activity, and even through classified advertisements in national newspapers such as the Saturday edition of the *Daily Mail*.

To try to assess how effective your promotion is, ask your guests how they heard of your hotel. Was it by visiting your website, by social media, by advertising, by word-of-mouth, by an article in a newspaper, by reference to a guide?

Replies received will be a valuable source of information in helping you to plan your future sales activities but beware of cancelling all advertising if your replies indicate that advertisements did not influence any of your guests' decisions to stay. The question can be interpreted very subjectively and people's memories can be misleading. They may well have been influenced by one or more of your sales activities but they could have completely forgotten which one – particularly relevant for major hotel brands which advertise regularly; or they might (or might not) admit to being influenced by a variety of different sources, with no indication of which source was the most important. As a result, even answers to this one vital question can be confusing and potentially misleading.

E mails, letters, advertising, your website, Twitter, TripAdvisor and other social media are all effective sales tools but everything depends on their style and content

17

and the way the recipient reacts. TripAdvisor is particularly valuable and customers should be encouraged to use it and describe how much they enjoyed their stay (but see page 44).

Perhaps the most effective sales method for corporate business is the face-to-face sales call because here you have an immediate response and can gauge exactly how your message is getting across.

A telephone interview can be equally successful if properly conducted and it has the advantage of taking less time. For major pieces of business, hotel companies make extensive use of personal visits and telephone calls but many independent hoteliers believe that they do not need to use such methods. This is unwise. The public is not going to beat a path to any hotelier's door; he has to attract customers and personal sales calls can form a key part in any sales promotion campaign. They may be time-consuming but they can also be very effective and long-lasting.

The principal advantage of such calls is that you can actually discuss the customer's real needs. You may, for example, know that a local company needs regular over-night accommodation for its important visitors without realising that every week it holds a seminar for twenty people (some of whom need accommodation) and that the chairman gives regular monthly dinner parties for important clients. If you can win some of this business which is going elsewhere, the value of the sales call will be much greater than you initially appreciated. You will also be able to find out what the company thinks of your hotel from past experience and you will be able to correct misunderstandings and misconceptions or effect improvements.

Once the initial contact is made, it's important to follow it up at a reasonable inter-val. Someone who says he will contact you in a month's time may just be trying to put you off: don't let him. If you think there is business there, invite him and partner to join you for lunch or dinner one day so that you can show them the hotel and the standards you are trying to achieve. Entertaining in this fashion can be a sound investment but don't waste their and your time by trying to sell them something that they will never use. Get to know their needs.

Local vicars, clergymen and the local Registry Offices can also be important if you want to develop wedding party business as they have information about future weddings; people may also have to stay overnight for funerals, so make contact with local undertakers. One hotel near a crematorium hosts two or three wakes every day – very good businesss. Keep an eye on the engagement columns of the local paper and write a personal letter to each couple, offering your hotel's services for the wedding reception if you have the right facilities for this market. If the hotel is big enough host a Wedding Fair promotion with other interested suppliers.

A systematic database is a basic requirement for any effective sales effort. In this way you can check the success of your sales promotion and keep on producing more business. Keep the data base under their specific markets – for example, conference and meetings, business, leisure so that access is easier.

Getting to know people . . .

. . . . in the local industry and community, and being seen as a key player in local affairs, must be the primary objectives for any hotelier.

Only in this way will you be able to maximise your position as the social hub around which the local community revolves. This requires almost no financial investment but it does demand your time as you mix with local society and get to know the most influential people.

Do I need a printed brochure?

The answer is possibly not but you are still expected to have one.

With the growing power of the internet and need for instant communication with your market, your brochure must be accessible on the website and this will be its primary purpose and use; the number you send out in the post or give away in the hotel will be comparatively small. So a printed brochure must be regarded as a useful sales tool although their disadvantage is that many people don't believe what they say because most of them say exactly the same thing.

In fact, most people considering staying at a hotel will now look up the hotel's website, hence the need for the brochure to be downloadable, and then access comments on TripAdvisor and other websites (which they *will* believe) before making a purchasing decision. Of course, not all the population (yet) has access to the internet but those who have are those who are more likely to travel.

Any brochure that you produce should be in the same 'house style' as your website, as should notepaper, bill heads and other literature. Their style and content are critical but care must be taken over cost; they are expensive to design and print as they need professional input.

It is instructive to examine the websites and brochures of competitive hotels (and of major groups) to analyse what they are saying and how they say it; a great many leave a lot to be desired in terms of copy and design. This also applies to company websites, and particularly those of US-based hotel companies, which are far more concerned with their use as an on-line booking tool rather than as a source of useful guest information. On-line booking is now an essential part of most hotel websites and for most independent hotels the website represents their brochure in electronic form, so it should be exciting, enticing, informative and easy to use.

Too often, the brochure will sell the positive virtues of a hotel without alluding to the beneficial effect they have on the customer. The most successful brochures sell a dream; too many British hotels are selling bedrooms. The difference is significant.

If you are aiming at the holiday or weekend break market you are not so much selling beds as a holiday dream in an attractive and alluring environment. You are selling an experience.

17

Your brochure should therefore emphasise the benefit of staying in your hotel rather than the magnificence of the hotel's facilities. **Photographs of empty bedrooms and dining rooms are more of a put-off than an enticement – a hotel does not exist without people and you need to show that your hotel is popular and welcoming.**

People give life to pictures: a barman mixing a drink in the bar says more than a picture of a bar counter; a close-up of an attractive dish with the chef tells the reader more than a picture of an empty dining room. The customer needs to be able to identify with the hotel and this can only be achieved if you successfully highlight the benefits that the hotel offers.

Hire a good graphic designer who can also design your web pages to create a consistent image. The higher profile and the positive image that good design creates is well worth the cost. If you can make your hotel stand out as an establishment of character and individuality, which are the most desirable attributes of any hotel, then you will have taken a big step ahead of the competition. Design is only effective if it encourages the viewer to take further action.

Once your house style is established, it needs to be carried through particularly when promoting short breaks in national or local media.

Make sure the design of your advertisement is carried out by your graphic designer and is not left to the printer.

Tell the world about your activities!

Many hotels produce an annual or bi-annual newsletter which is sent as a reminder to all past guests and is used as an enticement to attract future guests. They are normally put on the website but they can also be printed and direct mailed which is more expensive but might be more effective. The 'might be' is important because even if past guests are interested in developments at your hotel, and even if they enjoyed their visit, that does not mean that they want to make a return visit.

There's no doubt that newsletters on a website are helpful as they bring up-to-date information on the hotel to a wide audience in a formal and concise manner; if attractively presented, they certainly add to the site's value. The information they contain will largely consist of the press releases you have sent to journalists as well as other developments in the hotel which might attract potential guests but which might have not been sent to the media. They can also highlight your activities as the owner.

But remember: newsletters quickly become out-of-date, as does the whole of the website, and they demand constant – almost daily – updating.

Don't forget that . . . .

. . . apart from your website, your telephonist and receptionist are front line sales people, yet many telephonists have a manner more calculated to deter people than to attract. Bad customer contact in front of house can lose a hotel a great deal of money by putting people off. Letters and e-mails to potential guests should be friendly and helpful – never 'Dear Sir' or 'Dear Madam' or, worse still 'Dear Sir/Madam', but 'Dear Mr Smith'. Sign them all personally with your full name, 'John Brown'.

These little points amount to one thing: a hotelier has to create a welcoming and friendly atmosphere if he is to succeed. Somehow, through all your various methods of communication, you have to build up an impression that makes your hotel totally irresistible.

Once gained, this impression needs to be cherished and developed because it is your most powerful sales tool.

Who can help?

In addition to your own personal sales efforts there are organisations that can help you. The local tourist authority or Local Enterprise Partnership may be able to advise you and it is worthwhile to be seen as supportive of their efforts. Your hotel then appears in the local tourist board guide and you will have the opportunity to undertake further sales activities through regional promotional programmes. You should remember, however, that you only get out of these organisations what you put in. All the national tourist boards publish an annual register of hotel accommodation and operate the voluntary hotel registration and grading scheme. Unless you take part in this, the local tourist authority will not list you in its register of accommodation.

In many resort areas, the local authority produces a printed hotel guide and a website version, typically in conjunction with the local hotel association. These guides might be their only publicity medium though many of them are frequently criticised for being unimaginatively produced and having a poor standard of hotel advertising.

You should also think about joining a marketing consortium (see page 182). For hotels in the right location and of the right size, a consortium can represent a major means of generating business through centrally organised domestic and overseas marketing and sales activities as well as through listing on their website. Some also offer very advantageous purchasing schemes while much can be learned from networking with fellow hoteliers who collectively have a wealth of experience and are often prepared to share it in the club-like atmosphere of a consortium.

17

And what about those editorial mentions?

There are many books about public relations (as there are about marketing). Essentially, PR is about communicating your story through articles and mentions in the national, local and trade press, which includes local radio. This means preparing press releases and making contact with local and trade journalists so that you get to know them. However, press releases are rarely sent out by post now – they are distributed more through the internet and social media – and it is hugely difficult to get any but the local papers to take notice, so don't underestimate the challenge here.

For a first-time buyer, the story to get out is the fact that you've bought the hotel. So a press release to the local paper and to the trade press saying this – explaining who you are, why you've bought it, what you intend to do with the business should go out with your photo very soon after you move in. You should also tell the various hotel guides and local tourist bodies.

You can either do this yourself or employ a PR agency – the latter will charge but will take the administrative burden off your shoulders as it will have the names and contact details of your target PR audience. It will also draft the release for you in a way that journalists will be able to use, cutting out unnecessary verbiage. Journalists want facts and concise opinions, not extravagant claims and over-the-top descriptions.

After your initial press release, subsequent releases can cover the improvements you are gradually making and any new innovations. Newsworthy items are always welcome: new key members of staff, any awards gained by staff, any award gained by the hotel, new menus, new bedrooms, any sponsorship are all legitimate items. Inviting local (and trade) press to stay at the hotel once your improvements have been made is also important and here you may also be successful if you approach travel editors of national newspapers. An editorial piece in a national newspaper is a prize worth having.

PR, of course, extends beyond your relations with the press.

Earlier, we've covered the importance of TripAdvisor and other sites where your hotel might be mentioned, in some cases negatively. It's vitally important to monitor these as they can generate very adverse PR if not handled properly. Replying to bad reviews on these sites is important as the review will only give one side of the story – you must give your side to balance the picture and thus ameliorate the damage. So important are comments made on the social media that at least one major leisure group has launched a **bespoke 24/7 social media monitoring facility,** which uses a specially trained team to monitor 'chatter' about the group's brands and to better record customer sentiment.

If you get to know key members of the local and trade press they will also be very useful in citing your hotel (and your opinions, perhaps) in articles they are writing. But there are some golden rules which anyone dealing with the press needs to recognise. The following panel, written by Caroline Murdoch, one of the industry's leading PR practitioners, gives ten golden rules for anyone dealing with the press. Of course, there is a similar set of rules for journalists dealing with the industry – but that can viewed on Caroline's website - http://redworksmedia.wordpress.com

Ten things journalists hate about PRs!

We PRs often get it in the neck from journalists. With no right of reply, the PR is an easy target. However, if we do our job properly and stick to a few simple rules, we should be able to avoid criticism and gain the respect of our journalist colleagues.

Here are ten mistakes you need to avoid making in order to create the right impression and build a good relationship with your media contacts.

1. Pointless press releases. Only send a press release if you have something newsworthy to say. Stick to the golden rules of 'Who, What, Why, Where, When and How' and avoid lots of fluff and puff. Answer all these questions, preferably within the first paragraph or two because press releases tend to get cut from the bottom – so don't leave the most important detail to the end.

2. Badly written press releases. Language is a journalist's stock in trade so make sure you get your spelling, grammar and punctuation right. If this isn't your strong point ask someone else to proof it for you. Ideally, at least two pairs of eyes should have looked at a press release before it is issued.

3. Badly targeted press releases. Don't blanket mail your press release. Only send it to journalists if you know that it's about something in which they are likely to be interested.

4. Inaccurate information. Make sure that anything you send to, or tell a journalist is accurate. Once it's gone to print, has been broadcast, or gone viral via social media it can't be retracted. If you get it wrong the journalist gets it wrong – and they won't thank you for that.

5. Evading the question. If you're asked a question and you don't know the answer, be honest about it. Don't pretend and make up an answer you think they'd like to hear.

6. Not calling back. If you say you'll call them back, make sure you do.

7. Missing deadlines. One of the most important questions to ask when a journalist calls with a query, is 'what is your deadline?' If you can't meet it tell them you can't. Otherwise, make sure you contact them in time.

8. Following up a press release with a phone call. Once you've issued a press release there's no need to chase it up with a phone call to every journalist on the list. They won't thank you for it. If they are interested and need further information, they'll contact you.

17

9. Pestering. Journalists work to deadlines so, before you call, check that you aren't calling on the day they go to press. When you get through, check first that it's a good time to speak and then get to the point. Don't rattle on endlessly.

10. Inefficiency. Efficiency should be a guiding principle in all your dealings with the media. Show that you can be trusted to do and say what you promise and that the information you provide is interesting and trustworthy. Journalists can be very quick to criticise us PRs, so don't give them the opportunity.

And finally . . .

1 Never view your marketing and sales promotion effort as a one-off activity. Marketing and selling need constant attention. Understanding what your market is and how it is changing is a prime essential. You must also promote your hotel at every available opportunity. The results of this activity may not be immediate but they will be cumulative.

2 Avoid selling 'a mile wide and an inch deep'. Make sure that your sales effort penetrates each area sufficiently so that the potential is fully exploited before you move on to develop new sources of business. Money can be wasted by spreading your sales resources too thinly over too wide an area. To prevent this, plan the year's marketing effort well in advance and prepare a budget for it. This will act as a valuable discipline for all your marketing and sales activities.

Getting the strength of a marketing consortium around you

With all the marketing consortia, members retain their individual identity as well as their operational and financial independence but, through their membership fees, they pool their marketing, sales and purchasing resources. Marketing and sales programmes are devised to benefit all member hotels at a fraction of the cost that it would take an individual hotel to tackle the same market effectively. All operate an inspection scheme for new members to assess their suitability and to ensure that they fulfil the consortium's criteria. Fees can be high but they should be regarded as a marketing cost and, in many cases, they obviate the need for a hotel to employ a sales manager – though no hotel should depend entirely on membership of a consortium to fill its rooms. **Hotels themselves have to make their own sales efforts in order to survive profitably.** Few first-time buyers will be able to join an established consortium unless the hotel is already a member though a hotel would be considered after a successful period of trading, providing it met the membership criteria.

Best Western Hotels

www.bestwestern.co.uk

Best Western is the largest UK hotel consortium with 270 or so members and is part of the US-based Best Western International, now one of the largest global hotel groups with over 4,000 hotels worldwide. Most of the UK hotels are three-star establishments, with some four-star properties now being promoted as specialist sub-brands. All hotels in membership are privately owned and keep their own identity though displaying Best Western name and logo prominently is obligatory. The group offers a full marketing and sales promotion service under the Hotels with Personality tagline with a wide variety of special breaks to suit the needs of all members. The cost of membership varies but this also includes membership of Beacon, Best Western's group purchasing arm, which enables members to pay discounted prices for goods and equipment purchased – the savings sometimes offsetting the membership fee itself.

Classic British Hotels

www.classicbritishhotels.com

Classic British Hotels is a collection of over 80 three and four star properties, each one graded first class, superior first class, deluxe or luxury. All hotels in membership are privately or small group owned and have more than 20 rooms. The consortium provides a variety of special offers with national and global corporate and leisure programmes as well as an on-line booking facility; advice on marketing is also available

The Independents Hotel Association

www.theindependents.co.uk

Founded in 1992, with 150 members, the association has two separate hotel tiers – Select Hotels (mainly two-star establishments) and Executive Hotels (mainly of three-star and above properties).

Small Luxury Hotels of the World

www.slh.com

Originally called Prestige Hotels, the group of 32 UK hotels merged with an American marketing consortium and now calls itself Small Luxury Hotels of the World, which accurately describes its character, with a global membership of over 500. Membership is limited to those hotels of the highest quality and suitable size (generally no more than 100 rooms) and inspection is rigorous. It is unlikely that a first- time purchaser would be considered for membership unless he had considerable experience of the industry and is acquiring a suitable first-class property.

17

Pride of Britain

www.prideofbritainhotels.com

A similar group to Small Luxury Hotels of the World but entirely based within the UK with over 40 member hotels mainly in the luxury category. As with SLH, membership is rigorous and it is unlikely that a first-time buyer without experience of the hotel industry would be accepted into membership immediately.

Relais and Chateaux Hotels

www.relaischateaux.com/uk

This is a French-based consortium of outstanding hotels throughout the world, with over 30 hotels (and some restaurants) in membership in the UK.

Leading Hotels of the World

www.lhw.com

Established in 1928 by several influential European hoteliers, it started with 38 initial luxury properties; it now has 430 worldwide – 13 in the UK.

Preferred Hotels and Resorts

www.preferredhotelgroup.com

A collection of luxury world-wide properties with 13 in the UK.

Great Hotels of the World

www.ghotw.com

Another collection of luxury properties – nine in the UK

In addition to these consortia, there are a number of publications which also offer on-line booking facilities as well as promoting special offers and deals for member hotels. These include Best Loved Hotels and Conde Nast Johansens Hotels and they principally include four and five star properties of some character and interest.

"Remember, if you are considering whether to join a hotel consortium or even re-flagging it with a recognisable brand, be aware that they are all different and have different strengths and weaknesses. They also bring with them disciplines and investment commitments. Nevertheless, the benefits of an existing sales network and reservations channels might be beneficial. Do your homework and be comfortable with the brand you select; it is a relationship that will be successful only if you work at it."

Gavin Ellis
Proprietor, Knockomie Hotel, Forres

Sale promotion - ten pieces of advice

1   Technology has revolutionised selling – use it, never ignore it.

2   Your website is a prime sales tool – make full use of it.

3   Keep your website up-to-date and use it to tell readers about events and developments in your hotel.

4   Make sure you can accept bookings from the internet.

5   Using hotel booking agencies makes sense – but it costs!

6   Don't forget all the other ways of selling – they are still important . . .

7   . . . and a printed brochure might still be needed for your hotel.

8   Selling is not just getting people through the door – it's maximising their sales potential . . . .

9   . . . so all your staff become key sales people.

10   Consider joining a consortium.

17

18 Harnessing social media to your business

by Caroline Murdoch and Jeffrey Epstein

> *"The person who posts, tweets, uploads comments or images for your hotel is as much a statement of the hotel as the hotel itself. You as owner and every member of your staff contribute to your hotel's brand. It is as much about how you say something as it is about what you say*
>
> *When using social media to broaden the awareness of your hotel, try to say as little as possible; instead it is far more relevant to get others to make your case for you. Your guests, your friends, your suppliers, travel writers or bloggers are far more compelling at communicating your unique selling proposition than you are.*
>
> *Remember, we are all social animals 24/7. Social media should be something you engage in every day in the same way you would engage with people in real life. It is simply another means of expression. It should be fun and easy. If is not pleasant for you it will show. If you view it as chore; your social media efforts will be doomed."*
>
> **Jeffrey Epstein**
> **Chairman, Hotel Business Improvement Management**

The development of social media means that hoteliers now have no alternative but to take advantage of social network sites such as Facebook, Twitter, Google+, LinkedIn and Pinterest as well as recognising the importance of review sites such as TripAdvisor.

If you have a complaint about a company's product the most usual response is to write to the company itself describing the nature of the complaint. Chances are that you will eventually get back a standard letter from the Customer Services team, which is rarely helpful. If, however, you post the same complaint on Facebook or Twitter, you are likely to get an almost instantaneous response that is many times more helpful. While private complaints can often fester in a company's archives for weeks before they are dealt with, companies hate complaints aired in public and take immediate measures to try to close them down – by responding quickly and accurately. The age of social media is upon us. Hoteliers must recognise this change in customer relationships.

More significantly for hoteliers, the use of social media platforms has now become an integral part of people's travel experiences.

Major groups have already recognised the growing relevance of social media and this is not a development that independent hoteliers can ignore.

People have become accustomed to researching holiday destinations thus significantly extending hotel choice, making on-line bookings, adding photographs for friends to see while travelling and posting reviews while they are still enjoying their holiday. What they say about their experiences influences the choices made by the people with whom they communicate – their friends and family. Although business travellers are more likely to use a hotel recommended (and booked) by their company, social media still plays an increasingly important role during their trip – for example, when interacting with other conference delegates via a dedicated Twitter hashtag or finding out a special happy hour cocktail in the hotel's bar.

Social media also has a significant impact on a hotel's website. Search Engine Optimisation (SEO) – the art of ensuring that the content of your website, blog, or social media sites appears as high as possible in search engine rankings for any given search term – significantly influences the effectiveness of a hotel's website. At the very heart of all SEO is relevance, which is shown through the quality and the immediacy of content. Every social media posting about your hotel is an opportunity to expand on your hotel's content. Search engines take account of social media interactions (such as retweets on Twitter, shares on blogs, likes on Facebook and plus 1s on Google+) to work out where an organisation will rank in the search results. This is particularly relevant when the number of people accessing these social media networks via mobile devices is increasing rapidly.

Which platform to choose?

For the unknowing it can be a daunting task deciding which of the many platforms to choose.

Because social media, like the internet, is a 24/7 phenomenon, it can also be overwhelming to try to keep on top of the constant flow of updates and changes and to come up with a regular stream of fresh 'content'. Going on a short training course would certainly bring you up-to-speed but if you do not make the time or have the aptitude to manage the day-to-day activity yourself, delegating it to a member of the team who understands how social media works would involve – and perhaps motivate – others in the team to provide ideas. Alternatively, outsourcing to a local specialist agency or independent consultant is a possibility but social media should

18

be an integral part of your marketing communications strategy and, as the owner, you need to take an active interest in it and be aware of the information that is published on your site. The key for any successful social media strategy is that it reflects your hotel's unique culture and ethos.

So which sites should you be on?

Spend some time researching each of the social media networks to get a feel for which ones are appropriate for your hotel. Facebook and Twitter remain the largest sites and, for reasons discussed below, it is essential to create a Google+ Business Page. Some of the other sites you should consider are Pinterest, LinkedIn, Instagram and YouTube. Look at what your competitors are doing and how they engage with their followers. Each platform has its own style, voice and content activity and needs to be addressed individually. How you post a comment or image is not the same across all the platforms. Look outside the hotel sector to see how other companies are using social media to achieve their business aims and read blogs and articles on the subject by hotel industry specialists.

What are your objectives?

How do you want to use social media? Social media is an extension of your hotel's marketing and public relations strategy. Does your hotel have an image problem that you want to improve? Do you want it to increase corporate or leisure travel bookings, attract weddings and conferences, promote a new restaurant, or recruit staff? Your marketing and communications objectives will determine which sites you choose and the content you post.

Who are your audiences?

Who do you want to engage with and who will want to engage with you?

Most hotels have a range of audiences – leisure and business travellers, conference delegates, brides and wedding planners, local diners, tourism organisations, journalists, bloggers and reviewers. Building an effective social media network takes time and is done through small daily interactions. There are few instant successes.

What about content?

It is important to keep each social media profile up-to-date, to regularly add fresh content and to interact with your followers.

This is one of the most important lessons to be learnt – and it relates to the hotel's website, too: **out-of-date websites are worse than useless**. If you don't keep your sites interesting, with new content added almost on a daily basis, they will appear dated which will have a negative impact on your hotel's image. By not regularly refreshing the site, you will also lose your hard-earned SEO leverage. Content can include news stories, blog posts, video, photographs and infographics, surveys, reports and presentations. Sharing content from related suppliers is just as important as your own.

How do I know it's working?

As with any element of your marketing strategy, you should monitor and evaluate how your hotel is performing on each social network both quantitatively and qualitatively. Most of the social media platforms provide a section on analytics, so you can monitor the day-to-day activity. You can also use one of the on-line (and often free) analytical resources such as Google Analytics.

Getting started

Make a plan

If you know what you want to achieve and who you want to target, you can develop a social media marketing plan that sets out strategies for each network.

One of your main objectives should be to use social media ultimately to contribute to the process of generating sales, so it is important to create strategies for converting followers into customers. Your strategy should also include a mechanism for responding to comments.

Responding to comments ensures that your site is being actively managed – which reflects well on your hotel, too.

Setting up a profile or page

The content of your hotel profile or company page is important for a number of reasons. It allows you to present your hotel in the best possible light and to provide readers with all the information they need. It also performs an essential SEO role enabling your hotel to be found by the search engines.

When you register on a social media site, you will need to create a user name. Make sure this name is as consistent as possible across all your networks. Then complete your company profile or company page as fully as possible. The more relevant the information, the greater the chances of being found by someone searching for the terms you have included. Basic information to include is your hotel's name, telephone number, links to your website, blog and other social media sites and your location. In addition, add information about your hotel's facilities and services and anything else you think will be of interest to your followers. Don't make the mistake of simply replicating the same profile description across all your social media networks. Tailor each one according to the different types of audience. For example, your Facebook profile might be more relaxed and conversational, while your LinkedIn Company Page will be more business-orientated. You can also add images and logos with your telephone number always on the first page.

18

Creating content

Good quality, unique and factually correct content, in the form of written information, photographs, presentations, videos and audio podcasts drives success on social media.

Tell your story: why are you passionate about your hotel? What is its USP? What do you particularly want to promote? Are there any great guest thank-you letters you can publicise? This sort of content has the most impact and will resonate with your audience. It will generate traffic to your website, encourage people to share information with others and improve your search engine ranking. The wider the engagement through shares, recommendations, likes, Google+ 1s and reviews, the wider your reach will be and the greater your authority will be with search engines such as Google.

However, don't fall into the trap of treating social media as free advertising nor focus exclusively on selling. Use it to build relationships by engaging with, listening to and responding to followers. If you provide unique content that is entertaining and informative you will earn a good reputation and achieve a loyal following of people who have a genuine interest in your hotel.

Using social media as part of your customer service strategy you can post information about services, facilities, events and attractions in your local area and you can update followers with news about the hotel, and run competitions and promotions. To avoid running out of ideas for fresh content it is helpful to draw up an editorial calendar. Visual storytelling has the most impact, so using lots of good quality photographs and images is very effective. You might want to position yourself as an industry expert by sharing interesting media articles and coming up with your own 'Top Ten Tips' on a given subject. Every so often you can invite a member of the hotel team to take over your Twitter account for the day, or invite a valued client or supplier to write a guest blog.

Whatever the content you post, always think before you hit send.

You can delete a post but if it's already been shared and gone viral, it will be too late to retract it. Before posting anything, go through a mental checklist: proof read for typos and bad grammar; check that it is factually correct; consider whether or not it might offend anyone (if the answer is yes, don't send it); and acknowledge original sources.

Building a following

Your hotel can have a presence on every social media network but if no one is following you, you are wasting your time. Therefore, once you have established your hotel on your chosen sites, tell everyone. Display social media icons on your website and blog on brochures, business cards and other printed material and add 'share' buttons to website and blog pages. Include icons with your email signature, emailshots and advertisements; and email your client database informing them about your new profiles. As you start to post interesting content, follow and interact with others and your following should begin to grow. If it doesn't, or the people who do follow you are not your target audience, the reasons might be that:

♦ Your content is not interesting or relevant to the audience.

♦ You are not interacting with your followers by sharing their content or responding to them.

♦ You are not following or linking people back.

♦ You are following and linking the wrong people or organisations.

♦ You have no credibility because you follow too many people in relation to the number of your followers.

♦ Your profile lacks a photograph or a description.

♦ Are you engaging with your audience at the times that they are online and receptive to your messages?

You might think that you don't have many followers but remember, a small number of the right people are better than a large number of the wrong people. It's all about quality.

Monitoring and managing

There is no one easy way to measure the return on investment or success of your social media activity.

Each platform has to be measured and evaluated individually and on its own merits. There are specific analytic tools for measuring traffic and conversations. For example, Facebook provides a built-in analytics area and using Google Analytics you can measure responses and conversions generated by links to your website from promotions on Facebook, Twitter or other networks. However, you cannot just measure the success of your social media activity in terms of bookings or links to your website.

In this respect, social media is much like PR. It is about relationships, building trust with your audiences and creating a positive image.

Managing and tracking activity across a number of different social media accounts is time-consuming but you can simplify things by using one of a number of management systems such as TweetDeck, or HootSuite. These allow you to manage single or multiple accounts from a single dashboard, including distributing messages, monitoring your brand, measuring the success of a marketing campaign and running reports.

18

Etiquette

As in other aspects of your business, when building a brand and a reputation through social media, it is important to respect certain etiquettes. You will soon learn what is and is not considered acceptable across the different networks but in general, it comes down to showing respect and being polite. For example, people do not like being ignored so if someone contacts you with a direct message, or tags you in a tweet or Facebook message, be sure to respond to them within a reasonable time. Generally it is also accepted that you should avoid overt selling techniques. If you have questions about any aspect of a particular social media network, you can find answers in the help section of each one.

Basic rule: use the same rules of courtesy or politeness that you would use if you were attending a social function on behalf of your hotel.

What is blogging and why should I be doing it?

Blogs are like a diary or journal that you can update as often as you like with posts on any subject and can be as long or as short as you like. As with a website, you can include text, photographs, video and audio clips, graphics, maps, links to other blog posts, websites and social media networks and slide presentations. Generally they are free to set up and easy to use. You can choose from a number of blog websites but some of the best known are Wordpress, Blogger and Tumblr. You can set up a stand-alone blog or, with the help of your web developer, integrate it into your hotel website.

Blogging enables you to communicate directly with your guests, clients and suppliers. When you post a new article, people can comment on what you've written, generating a conversation. They can subscribe to your blog by signing it up for it directly or via RSS (Really Simple Syndication). They then receive an alert whenever you write a new blog post.

Hospitality provides a wealth of potential things to blog about ...

... general news and updates, competitions and promotions, amusing anecdotes and photographs, news about your staff and guests, things going on in the local area, master class videos featuring the chef, flower arranger or wedding photographer. Just make sure that what you post is relevant, well written and up-to-date. Your blogs are another source of content that you can disseminate across your various social media profiles.

One of the benefits is that unlike your website, which you might have to pay your web developer to update for you, blogs are easy to manage and to update yourself or by a competent member of the team. Another benefit is that, as with your website and social media sites, a blog will be indexed and ranked by the search engines.

Major social media platforms

On-going innovations in the social media world mean that there are new developments on an annual – even monthly – basis and the principal purpose of this chapter is to highlight its importance to the hotel industry and, more particularly, to the hotel you want to buy. You cannot ignore it.

Facebook

www.facebook.com (Monthly views, 900m)

The largest in terms of signed up followers and most used of all platforms. Its large following is based on building a network of friends and family where they share info about every aspect of their daily lives.

Hotels can create their own presence, and share content from offers to pictures. Additionally they can purchase 'sponsored' listings ensuring their content appears in their follower 'friends' timeline.

How can it be useful to the hotelier?

➤ Almost like having an additional website with the ability to engage and update in real-time.
➤ Allows you to maintain a steady flow of new content.
➤ Builds and creates an audience of loyal followers and allow them to help you expand your hotel's brand.
➤ Builds audience by purchasing the ability to appear on demographic user timelines similar to your existing customer base.
➤ Should be the backbone of your social media activity.

Twitter

https://twitter.com (Monthly views, 310m)

Originally a text-only platform limited to messages of only 140 characters. Twitter now includes links to images and video. Because its messages are small, it is perfect for real time messaging to audience.

How can it be useful to the hotelier?

➤ Keeps your followers up-to-date with offers, events and a real time commentary of what is happening in your hotel.
➤ Can be irreverent in tone. The content when used well is like a virtual drinks party.
➤ Excellent for building and extending local and regional customers bases.
➤ When used consistently can be force for stimulating demand when you need it.

Pinterest

www.pinterest.com (Monthly views, 225m)

This social media platform was primarily an image-based platform where users share their own images as well as commenting and including any image on the internet under subjects of interest. Subjects are based on creating 'Boards' and dropping related images onto the boards. Very good for building networks of users for specific product segments such as weddings, food or Christmas.

How can it be useful to the hotelier?

➤ Provides an attractive interface to present beautiful imagery of your hotel.
➤ Engages others with similar interests.

18

> ➤ Has a far more female than male following. Think of it like reading and clipping magazine articles you want to save and refer back to.
> ➤ Great for the wedding market.

Linkedin

linkedin.com (Monthly views, 255m)

A professional business network with over 200m users, over 64 per cent of whom are outside the US. As well as a personal profile, you can create a separate company page, providing you with an opportunity to showcase your hotel to existing and potential clients from the business community. On it you can add updates, photographs and list the hotel's services and facilities. From your personal profile you can join networking groups, or create your own, in which people share ideas and ask questions. You can take paid advertising and use it as a recruitment tool.

How can it be useful to the hotelier?

> ➤ Can be really helpful in understanding and growing your corporate market.
> ➤ Want to know about a corporate guest; check out their LinkedIn profile.
> ➤ Also helpful for building up a network of like-minded hospitality industry contacts.

Google+

https://plus.google.com/ (Monthly views 120m)

Google has been playing catch-up on social media over the last few years. It has attempted to copy the various activities of Facebook. Primarily used by travel and hotel bloggers to extend their audiences. Hotels can have their own presentations and spread content about their services using texts (posts), images and video.

How can it be useful to the hotelier?

> ➤ Use in the same way you would Facebook but it has less impact.

Tumblr

www.tumblr.com (Monthly views 110m)

This more of a micro-blogging site where users can create and post short form 'blogs' (stories) to their page. These blogposts are multimedia friendly using text, images and video. Appealing because of its ease of use. Also allows for simple commenting on others blogs as well.

How can it be useful to the hotelier?

> ➤ If you enjoy writing and telling stories or have the budget to employ a writer to create stories about your hotel, Tumblr can be very engaging.

Instagram

www.instagram.com (Monthly views 100m)

Created as a image platform originally in response Twitter which was primarily textual in content. Are very similar today where the user posts an image as short content rich description which is sortable using keywords (hashtags).

How can it be useful to the hotelier?

> ➤ Lively and fun to use. But be aware this is a secondary platform to Twitter and Facebook.
> ➤ What you want to do is to use Instagram to post to both Twitter and Facebook simultaneously

Flickr

www.flickr.com (Monthly views 65m)

Similar to Instagram as they are both image-hosting platforms. The community of users engages and comments on posted images. Owned by Yahoo, the site is used to research images for bloggers and is a good place to catalogue images about your hotel

How can it be useful to the hotelier?

➤ If you have great images of your hotel, Flickr is a great repository. Writers and bloggers will use it to find out about you. Similarly you can use it to introduce yourself to writers and bloggers who may visit your hotel.

Vine

https://vine.co (42m users)

A video-based primarily smartphone platform which allows you, by using its App, to create and upload short (5-6 seconds) video. It was acquired by Twitter in 2012.

How can it be useful to the hotelier?

➤ Unless you have a young and highly engaged market for your hotel, we would stay away from Vine. The self-produced videos can be fun to share but are of low quality.

Snapchat

www.snapchat.com (750+m images and video shared per day)

Created to be spontaneous, this platform works with a smartphone app. It allows users to share short video and images as well as short text. Once an image or video is created it can be sent to a controlled list of users. The messages, once viewed, disappear.

How can it be useful to the hotelier?

➤ Similar to Vine and for the same reason not necessarily helpful to creating awareness or growing your audience.

> *"We live in an age when at the push of a button a customer can communicate with thousands of people on Trip Advisor, Facebook, Twitter. They are in a position to potentially destroy what you may have spent years building up. You gain your customers one at a time but you can lose them in thousands. The relationship you have with your customer should be unique to you, it cannot be copied."*
>
> *Harry Murray MBE*
> *Chairman, Lucknam Park Hotel & Spa, Wiltshire*

18

Ignore social media at your peril!

1 It's here to stay – so use it!

2 Get some training in it – and harness the skills of your staff. If you haven't got the time, delegate.

3 Remember – customers complain on the internet, rarely face-to-face . . .

4 . . . . and they use social media sites to air their grievances publicly.

5 Social media is now the key way to keep in touch with your clients . . .

6 . . . . and for them to keep in touch with you.

7 Make a plan! What do you want to achieve? How best can you achieve it?

8 Monitor your success.

9 Blogging enables you to communicate directly with your guests.

10 Never ignore a criticism on TripAdvisor – always reply, and apologise if necessary.

19 What to do about the restaurant?

"Recognise that the customer will have different tastes to yours. You need to try to give every customer what he or she wants. Just because you or your chef don't want to serve chips in your restaurant doesn't mean that the customer will see it from your point of view. You need to train your staff to think the same way and empower them to make decisions based on this, without having to refer to you."

Tim Hassell
Proprietor, Ilsington Country House Hotel , Devon

'Food, glorious food,' sang Oliver in Lionel Bart's musical but the hotelier needs to take a less joyous and more calculated attitude towards his food and beverage operation.

A well-run restaurant can be highly profitable; a badly-operated unit can make a terrible loss. A good restaurant can be an excellent advertisement for your hotel and will get the establishment talked about throughout the area and perhaps further afield; a poor restaurant can give your hotel such a bad reputation that people will be deterred from staying with you altogether.

In no other department of the hotel does so much control have to be exercised nor are there so many traps for the unwary. Food is a high cost perishable commodity and the competent staff needed to prepare and serve it are difficult to recruit, expensive to employ and (all too frequently) a headache to manage.

Which market?

First you need to decide what kind of food and beverage operation you are going to run and whether a market exists for it in the area.

An analysis of the competition may lead you to conclude that there is a strong case for not providing a meal service at all, except for breakfast. Taking this route turns your hotel into more of a rooming operation but that may be no bad thing: you maximise your room revenue and eliminate any likely losses on your F&B operation. You can still provide a bar and some snacks without having to hire skilled staff. In effect, you provide exactly what your guests want: a room. However, if you believe you need to offer lunch and dinner, there are a number of different markets.

Gourmet cooking, à la carte

A restaurant in this, the most difficult of all markets, depends for its success entirely on its ability to produce high quality food with an appropriate standard of service on a continuous basis. Having an off-day in this market is not an option. Your own personality is likely to be an important factor in the restaurant's success.

Most country house hotels fall into this category and there are plenty of examples of success, some of them revolving around the cooking skills of the proprietor himself but, increasingly, on the skills of named chefs. Prices in these restaurants are high with the target audience being resident guests, although outside custom is extremely important; a successful restaurant gets the name of the hotel talked about locally which, in turn, encourages other business as well as boosting room sales.

If there are no such restaurants in your area there may be an opportunity to create one in your hotel but the fact that one does not exist does not necessarily mean it is a wide-open market—others might have started in the past and failed. The market just may not exist. However, eating-out has become such a lifestyle choice that it is unlikely that the area would not support at least one high quality restaurant that offers the right food at the right price; and even if one exists, that should not necessarily deter you. This shows that locals have acquired the eating-out habit and if they patronise other restaurants they can also be attracted to yours.

Once opened, you would expect to attract the majority of your resident guests to take dinner in-house; the economics of running the restaurant should be based on that assumption.

However, the menu will need to change regularly (or be very extensive) if you are to attract them every night of their stay. Just as important, you must attract local diners and encourage them back after their first visit. The level of repeat business dictates the success of most restaurants and the level of demand from outsiders will be a major factor in their profitability.

One challenge, however, is that while demand for dinner may be more or less in line with room occupancy, lunch-time trade will be almost entirely dependent on generating demand from the nearby locality. Few resident guests will take lunch and dinner on the same day. Only in the most exceptionally high standard (and high priced) hotels, which have a destination restaurant of distinction, will a hotel's trade at lunchtime be as profitable as dinner. Even with these establishments, special offers of a discounted two- or three-course lunch are now commonplace; in fact, increasingly, restaurants (both stand-alone and in hotels) now offer special, reduced priced, limited choice table d'hote lunches to encourage trade; these are marketed extensively through on-line restaurant booking agencies.

The economic consequences of limited lunch demand quickly become apparent. The cost of employing a skilled kitchen brigade and expert waiting staff has to be covered by one main source of income – dinner – although revenue from breakfast (and perhaps from afternoon tea) can be important. Because of this, many hotels, if all the costs are included, lose money on their F&B department. Nevertheless, customers (and hotel grading schemes) expect hotels to have a restaurant. Of course, the best answer to this is to build up local lunch-time trade so that it becomes worthwhile but the success of this will depend on location (it is much easier in a busy town centre), pricing (you will have to compete with nearby restaurants that offer special lunchtime menus), and the quality and variety of your offer (which depends on your marketing and kitchen skills.)

Cheaper, but still high quality

Hotels can rarely divorce their food and beverage operation from their rooms.

They must complement each other. As most hotels are not in the luxury category it follows that most hotel restaurants aim at the middle market. There are practical advantages here. The skills required are not as demanding or as costly as those needed by a critically rated restaurant; at the same time, the food costs are lower and easier to control.

Because of the growth of the restaurant industry in recent years, the competition facing mid-market hotels from independent restaurants, pubs and casual eating outlets is intense.

Figures from HotStats show that average food revenue as a percentage of total turnover for English hotels has fallen **from 24.7 per cent in 2003 to 22.2 per cent in 2012**. Food revenue (and beverage revenue, too – also down) is becoming gradually less important in hotel revenue streams while room revenue is becoming more important. The increasing number of competing independent restaurants and pubs is attracting the business away from the traditional hotel dining room; nor, with higher operating costs, can hotels match the aggressive menu pricing of many popular restaurant chains.

One other factor should be mentioned here: the need for surprise.

Too often hotel menus serve the same dishes in the same style without showing much innovation or imagination; they tend to be rigorously traditional, offering menus that might be popular but which offer no element of surprise. The same menu, with only a limited change of dishes now and then, is not the way to build up the eating-out market. It's important to introduce an element of surprise into menus so that new diners are attracted and are offered a new excitement when dining out.

19

Simple table d'hôte menu

For many small hotels it is better to consider concentrating on providing great food for the resident guests if they are on half board terms and to ignore lunch service altogether.

For this type of operation the menu is likely to be simple and brief – a choice of three or four starters and the same number of mains and desserts; or, in some cases, no choice at all. The quality will still need to be high but commensurate with the price being charged; it is all too easy to spend more on food than the price being charged warrants. Use of convenience and frozen food will probably be made because the kitchen will have only basic cooking skills.

> **Remember - trends in the restaurant sector are fast-moving and continually evolving; no sector of the hospitality industry is more dynamic.**

Restaurateurs react to changing customer tastes and trends far more quickly than hoteliers simply because food is their primary concern; food to hoteliers is generally of much less importance but demands far more management time; few hoteliers have the level of expertise in food that most restaurateurs possess.

Restaurateurs continually try to entice customers with new flavours and styles of service, sometimes with more focused and themed restaurants which have more specialised menus, at other times, reintroducing well established themes with a new twist. Even well-established and popular restaurant groups, while staying close to their original offer, change their menu on a regular basis and few restaurants survive five years without significant refreshment of both the ambiance and the offer.

Not every dish will be popular and those dishes that 'stick' take up space for dishes that could be more popular and therefore more profitable. Remember, the menu is a selection of dishes that you believe customers will want; whether or not you like the dishes yourself is immaterial.

Whatever type of hotel or restaurant you are operating, one objective is clear: you must make sure that you maximise all opportunities for food sales.

Don't assume, for example, that because the restaurant is busy there are no other sales opportunities. Can you serve bar snacks which could encourage a greater drinks turnover? Can you serve morning coffee and afternoon tea? Hotels in busy shopping areas can build up a profitable trade with local shoppers. If you have an unused or undeveloped part of the building (especially with access to the main street) is it worth converting it into a coffee shop, fast food restaurant or a wine bar? With separate access from the street, would it be more worthwhile to use the space as a public bar and so build up a good lunch-time snack and bar trade? Cocktail bars are often grossly under-utilised; turning the area into a public bar may generate extra turnover and additional profits. Staff should also be trained to upsell – to encourage the sale of additional dishes or drinks.

Long-established favourites always sell well so, unless you are pursuing a particular theme, it's important to mix old favourites with new choices; if you offer roast sirloin of beef on a Sunday lunch, 85 per cent of the diners will choose it which can be a frustrating experience for any proprietor who is anxious to introduce more exciting dishes to his menu. On the other hand, his main objective is to give his customers what they want.

There is no point in needlessly seeking to extend the range of a menu if customers don't want this; if all the well established dishes are discarded, the clientele will dine elsewhere. At the same time, however, customers want to feel that the choice is there if they want to try something new. Striking the balance between the old and the new, therefore, is the secret of success. Again, that element of surprise is important. Of course, some restaurants may decide to offer *only* unusual and exciting dishes and in doing so will build up an enthusiastic following, but they are the exception.

How big should the menu be?

To begin with at least, the wise hotelier will seek to offer a small number of high quality dishes rather than create a large à la carte menu that offers a great deal but frequently delivers very little. A choice of five or six starters, eight or ten mains, three or four desserts and some good cheeses would be sufficient for most restaurants and for most occasions. A small menu is beneficial in other ways, too: the menu gives you scope to introduce new dishes on a regular basis.

Shorter menus also prevent customers becoming confused when faced with an extensive choice and they help to cut down mistakes in the production and service of the food and reduce costs in the preparation of the dishes. In the same way, a limited wine list reduces the necessity of holding expensive stocks of little used wine and aids customer choice, particularly if the character of the wine is briefly described on the list. Dishes should be similarly described if their content or make-up is not obvious.

In fact, descriptions are important in promoting sales.

People are more ignorant about food and wine than many hoteliers realise and customers are often worried when ordering from a menu. A restaurant that insists on using French terminology in its menu without the necessary English translation runs the risk of deterring those many customers who will not want to display their ignorance by asking for a translation of a dish. The same problem, but greatly magnified, exists with the wine list. Here, even more mystique exists, often encouraged by proprietors themselves, many of whom foolishly believe it is good business to produce a wine list that is as informative to the layman as a race card to a non-racegoer. The wise restaurateur will also recognise that many diners now prefer to buy wine by the glass.

19

Both the menu and the wine list are sales tools

Their prime aim is to promote sales and to tempt customers to buy. They should not be viewed as an obstacle course which a customer has to overcome. For this reason it is often good practice to suggest wines with particular dishes; many customers find such a recommendation helpful.

Costings

The price of your dishes will be dictated by your market and by your own costs. The major items should give you a gross profit of at least 70 per cent and preferably nearer 75 per cent. There is no point in preparing a dish that you have to sell at £17.50 to find that nobody wants it because it is too expensive. If the market demands dishes priced at £10, then you will have to create dishes at that price.

Many operators now take the view that a rigid approach to gross percentages precludes a restaurant from serving popular but high cost items such as fillet steak or lobster. The price of these items becomes too high if the standard gross profit is imposed, so they are forced off the menu. To prevent this, a much lower gross profit is used - say 50 per cent - in the belief that it is better to make £6 profit on a lobster selling at £16 than nothing on a lobster priced at £20 which does not sell. A similar approach is being taken with wine, when the traditional 300 per cent mark up (i.e. treble the cost price + VAT) is being replaced by a more flexible pricing policy. Behind this thinking lies the belief that it is much easier to increase the volume of trade and level of profit by aggressive pricing than it is to squeeze extra profit out of existing business through ever-tighter cost control.

An important pre-requisite to any system of costing is the introduction of standard recipes so that the ingredients do not vary significantly every time a dish is prepared. This presumes close communication and agreement with the chef who is responsible for the gross profit. It also implies discipline on the part of both the chef and proprietor.

The vast majority of chefs say they understand how to cost dishes, but experience would suggest quite the opposite.

A number of headline chefs have opened their own restaurant only for it to close within a year or so because it was not a financial success. For any new proprietor, it would be time well spent to test his chef by asking him to cost out separate dishes on the menu – particularly checking that the chef removes the VAT element on the dish price before carrying out the exercise.

Do you want to move into a new market?

It is good always to remember that proprietors have three key objectives:

1   **Customers - to provide perceived value for money**
2   **Company – to generate potential profit**
3   **Staff – to motivate and manage them firmly but fairly**.

You must start as you mean to continue.

A restaurant should succeed with the dishes that provide the customer with a satisfying meal and the operator with a reasonable profit. Trading up to a higher standard for promotional purposes only and then reducing quality at some later date is not to be recommended. It goes without saying that the reverse situation is equally dangerous. A hotelier can attempt to achieve a higher gross profit by cutting back on portion sizes or on the quality of the ingredients but it is difficult to think of any action that would more successfully empty a restaurant. Regular customers instinctively recognise quality and value. Those who frequently eat out expect dishes of a quality commensurate with the price. A reduction in quality will be recognised immediately. No restaurant could withstand such an assault on its credibility nor would it be able to pick up new customers lower down the market because they would still regard it as expensive.

If you need to move your restaurant down market it should be well planned and well publicised with a new menu, new dishes and new pricing.

Purchasing food

A small hotel is not big enough to demand a high discount from local traders but travelling long distances to fresh meat and vegetable markets is a costly and time-consuming exercise. Often, therefore, independent hoteliers have to rely on the local cash and carry wholesaler or on local retailers and producers. In fact, this may be no bad thing.

Using local producers will enable you to promote your ingredients as locally produced and many restaurants actually name the farm or producer involved just to give it that extra sense of authenticity. This is excellent salesmanship; it uses the menu as a sales tool.

Good purchasing depends on proper specifications combined with realistic costing. You cannot expect to receive the finest fillet steak when you refuse to pay the price. But if you do pay the price, make sure the meat is precisely what you want in terms of weight and quality. To help your cost control procedures, you can ask your meat supplier to cut your steaks to the required weight – for example, 5oz-6oz steaks. This will give you consistent portion sizes as well as protecting your profit margins. **Experience will show that more upmarket customers may require smaller portions.**

19

You should be able to build up such a relationship with your suppliers that they will let you know if the required quality is not available; the chef, who is responsible for accepting incoming food, should always inspect and weigh it on arrival. A supplier who gets away with goods not up to specification on one occasion will certainly try it again – and again. (Incidentally, and just as important, check incoming wet stocks. Always inspect beer, wine and spirit deliveries because shortages are a common occurrence, particularly close to Christmas!)

Any system of food costing must start with the recipes you have devised as they will enable you to cost each dish accurately . . . ,

. . . although it's essential that the chef understands how variable raw ingredient costs can be; prices rarely go down, they frequently increase. There's little point in devising a food cost per portion at the beginning of the year when, 12 months later, the cost of ingredients has risen by five per cent. So food costs must be kept up-to-date, even on a daily basis, so that you remain in control. In a busy restaurant, with annual food costs of £75,000, a five per cent increase in raw ingredient costs will add £3,750 to the food bill – or, put another way, £3,750 less profit. Individual costing sheets for each dish should be introduced to keep tabs on price rises.

The other major factor that affects gross profit is the level of skill in the kitchen. Chefs vary in their business skills; a chef's cooking skill may be high but he may not be adept with figures. If this is the case, he will need help. Even so, it would be wrong to take from him the responsibility for achieving his gross profit because that is one way to measure his efficiency.

Wastage and pilferage in a hotel or restaurant is endemic and needs to be tightly controlled. A wasteful chef, who allows expensive food to be thrown into the swill, may be doing the pigs a good turn but he is ruining your business. If too much food is going to waste directly from the kitchen, the food is not being prepared carefully enough; if it is going into the swill from the plates of customers, the portions are too big or the quality is too poor. Whatever the cause, it needs investigating.

Chefs sometimes argue that food cost control is not really their job. But whose job can it be? They need to be reminded that a key part of a head or executive chef's job is not just cooking but the economic and people management of the kitchen which includes the control of all kitchen costs. This is what they are paid for.

The debate over buffet-style breakfasts continues

Not all guests like them and some hotels have gone half-way – introducing a buffet table of cold items but preparing hot dishes in the kitchen in the traditional way. Self-service breakfasts, particularly if they are highly priced, poorly supervised and inadequately staffed, with overheated display cabinets containing greasy trays of bacon, congealed scrambled egg, drying sausages and overcooked tomatoes are rarely successful. They do not look or taste appetising. There is still a strong case for a well served, well cooked breakfast prepared in the kitchen by a skilled chef and many smaller hotels now recognise this. But too many larger hotels have currently lost sight of this preferring to go down the route of slimming down the number of breakfast staff in order to cut costs. If the market demands this, well and good. But there remains a market which wants to keep breakfast as a more civilised meal and is willing to pay for it. You need to establish what your market wants.

What state is the kitchen in?

One further area which needs to be examined is the kitchen and restaurant equipment.

Because the hotel you are buying is a going concern, it is not necessarily the case that the kitchen is in a good state of repair and suitable for the menu you are proposing to offer. What new items of equipment will you need? You do not want your chef spending his expensive time and energy in overcoming the problem of an inadequate kitchen.

Yet hotel kitchens vary hugely in size and location. Too often they are tucked away in the back or in the basement, inadequately planned and poorly sited by architects or designers who know nothing about kitchen design. Some may have no natural light; others may have steps that inconveniently have to be negotiated by the waiting staff. Kitchens are also hot places with plenty of steam and fumes; too many hotels have inadequate extraction systems that enable fumes to permeate the rest of the building. In many modern hotels, kitchens usually have adequate air conditioning and are properly sited, sometimes in open view of the restaurant which is helpful in building up an atmosphere of activity and animation and giving reassurance to diners that the food is being freshly prepared.

There is no space here for a treatise on kitchen design and planning but it follows that any kitchen must be designed around the menu that you are intending to offer. However, the kitchen need not necessarily be large and spacious – indeed, a large kitchen, particularly if it is badly designed, will mean that the chefs spend all their time walking about in it; there is some merit in a kitchen being compact but it also needs to be well designed with sufficient preparation areas, the correct tabling and cooking equipment, a non-slip floor and clean extraction fans. In other words, the work flow needs to be carefully thought out.

Other areas are important, too. The Still Room (or Still area) needs adequate hot water for tea- and coffee-making and a coffee machine if Italian coffees are to be offered as most customers now demand.

Not only does the Environmental Health Officer disapprove of washing crockery and cutlery by hand, it is difficult to get anyone to work at a sink all day. Better to invest in reliable dishwashing equipment than unreliable staff, though staff will still be needed to fill and empty the dishwashers. There must also be adequate refrigeration and freezer capacity – there are strict rules about storing raw and cooked meats separately and the temperatures at which these are kept. Depending on the size of

19

the kitchen and the complexity of the menu, separate vegetable preparation and pastry sections, the latter with its own oven and hob, might be needed. .

Don't forget the rules and regulations

There is a growing amount of legislation relating to the provision of food in restaurants and it is thus an area which can easily trap the unwary.

If you are not familiar with the legal requirements, this is one area that cannot be ignored; it is your responsibility to ensure that you and your staff comply with the legislation. Lack of adequate cleanliness is one of the most common reasons why food businesses are prosecuted, and heavy fines are imposed if found guilty, so a cleaning schedule is a pre-requisite in a good kitchen. This will ensure that surfaces and equipment are cleaned when they need to be. You should work out what needs cleaning every day or more than once a day, and what needs cleaning less frequently. In some instances, the cleaning regime should include a disinfectant. In this way, you will instill in the kitchen staff the need for total cleanliness.

What about the restaurant?

There must also be a systematic approach to the restaurant. You can have tables all the same size so that a square table for two can become, if joined together, a table for four and so on. But while this is convenient and efficient it lends a certain degree of uniformity to the room that would be alleviated if you have different sizes and shapes of table. Much will depend on the style of hotel and the menu. A steak restaurant would find the series of square tables to be a highly efficient way of using floor space; a more exclusive hotel, with a higher price menu would probably prefer to look more informal and less regimented.

On taking over, you have to make sure that you have enough cutlery, china and glass for the maximum number the restaurant can accommodate; all these items are easily broken, mislaid, or stolen; tea spoons, in particular, have a high pilferage rate.

The waiters' sideboards or tables need to be properly positioned so that they can take all the *mise en place* that might be needed during service such as spare plates, cutlery and condiments. They must also provide space for waiters to put down trays and dishes before service. Pay attention to worn or frayed carpets – they can be dangerous. If you promote wine, do you have enough ice buckets?

Carving meat from a trolley is now almost always restricted to specialist restaurants, most of them traditional and high priced. Although a great customer attraction, they are extremely expensive to acquire, difficult to manoeuvre around a crowded restaurant (so you will probably have to sacrifice some tables to make space for it); they also demand a skilled chef or waiter to carve the meat in front of the customer. In most restaurants, it is better to serve roast meat plated from the kitchen but there is no doubt that a carving trolley is a beguiling attraction for many and if the market exists (or can be created) it can be a very successful sales tool.

If much equipment does need replacing, the cost may be considerable. The larger kitchen manufacturers might provide a free kitchen planning service but, for a small hotel, it is probably better to plan it yourself with the aid of your chef. If you have yet to hire a chef, the services of a kitchen design consultant may well be worth the cost as he will have experience of the most effective layout and the most efficient pieces of equipment, and their relationship with each other.

Staff relationships

The structure and inter-relationship between the kitchen and restaurant staff will also need your attention. The two teams should work together but all too often they give the impression of being on opposing sides in a battleground. During service, this relationship is under great stress so friction can frequently occur with both chefs and waiters under different but very real pressures. This pressure can never be overcome – it is an inherent part of food service – but it can be alleviated by good management and by the kitchen and restaurant staff having complete confidence in each other.

To ensure this, you have to ask some fundamental questions about the staff. Are they sufficiently well trained and skilled for the standard of operation that you want to run? What other skills do they need? Do they need training in social skills – the ability to communicate and please the customer? Do the kitchen staff have the necessary skills to prepare the food *à la minute* – that is, freshly cooked, on time? Do service staff know the dishes being prepared and have they had the chance to taste them (if not, how can a waiter explain a dish to customers, let alone encourage them to order it?)

There is a strong case for having a briefing session between kitchen and service staff before each meal so that all staff understand what is on the menu and the service staff can describe it accurately. This may last only five-ten minutes but the stronger the communication between the two departments, the better the service and the more efficient will the operation become.

And it is always better to provide staff meals before service than after.

A restaurant's success thus depends on so many factors – and not all of them the same in every restaurant – that it is impossible to lay down a blueprint for success. There is no single factor that dictates whether a restaurant will succeed – even a restaurant serving poor food can be a success providing it has other factors going for it that the customer deems important; contrariwise, a restaurant serving great food can fall flat on its face if it has no ambience and lacks a decent welcome. In all this, price may not be the primary consideration though, for a restaurant to be totally successful and become a repeat destination, customers must always recognise that it gives value.

19

It is not just the food that is important (though it is) but the ambience of the restaurant, the welcome the customers receive, the service they get, the taste and quality of the food, the price they pay and the value they perceive.

In the final analysis, it will depend on you ensuring that every meal experience is of the same quality. This demands total quality control of every aspect of the food and beverage operation.

Legislation

The most important food hygiene legislation that applies specifically to food businesses is:

♦ Regulation (EC) No. 852/2004 on the hygiene of foodstuffs.

♦ The Food Hygiene (England) Regulations 2006 (as amended) and equivalent regulations in Scotland, Wales and Northern Ireland.

These set out the basic hygiene requirements for your premises, its facilities and the personal hygiene of your staff. They also include temperature control requirements, and the requirement to put in place 'food safety management procedures' and keep up-to-date records of these.

Food hygiene – a guide for businesses is an excellent booklet that can be downloaded at www.food.gov.uk/foodhygiene-guide.

General Food Safety Regulations

You must also comply with the General Food Law Regulation (EC) No. 178/2002 and the General Food Regulations 2004.

If food is described as suitable for people with a particular food allergy or intolerance, (such as nut free or gluten free), then you should consider the possible risks for that group. The provision of allergen information is a requirement for any food intended for the final consumer and chefs and restaurants will have to take this regulation very seriously if court cases are to be avoided.

Beware! Ten points to consider about your restaurant

1   The F&B department is the most difficult to control and the easiest in which to lose money.

2   There is no blueprint for restaurant success – each restaurant survives or fails on its own merits.

3   What's the competition – can you beat it?

4   What eating-out market are you in? You must decide – and stick to it.

5   What kind of menu will you offer?

6   Do you have the right skills to develop a restaurant?

7   Remember: customers come for the whole meal experience – not just the food.

8   What state is the kitchen in? Do you need to refurbish it?

9   Do your kitchen and restaurant staff have the necessary skills?

10 Trends in the restaurant sector are fast-moving and continually evolving – can you keep up with them?

19

20 You and your staff

"Employees represent the biggest challenge and greatest opportunity for any hotel. An average hotel with great staff can be a market leader but a top-end hotel with poor staff will never realise its potential.

The most important element to establish from the outset is the culture - what we call 'the way we do things around here'. The leader of the business must make it clear what is expected. Room attendants must always acknowledge and greet a guest they meet on the corridor; maintenance must always deal with a customer-facing issue as a priority over any other task; the kitchen must always be prepared to cook a dish that is not on the menu if they have the ingredients. These standards and values must be hard-wired into the business so that any deviation will be picked up by anyone in the team.

The manager must lead by example. Hosting cannot be an afterthought – it must be a priority. The standards must be delivered by the person at the highest level in the organisation.

Communication is vital but don't expect everyone to listen or always understand. A simple and important message can get lost or ignored in the journey down the organisation, so action points from meetings must always be recorded and reviewed.

Pay and conditions are important but employees also want to have a sense of belonging to something bigger and a pride in the business they work in. Make work rewarding and fun by introducing incentives that encourage the behaviour that is required and celebrate success by thanking and recognising excellent performance.

Allow staff to make decisions and give them authority to act for the benefit of the customer. When Laura remembered that a previous guest had been unhappy that there was no Guinness available during his stay she put four complimentary cans in his room for his next visit. It made a massive difference to his experience and confidence in the hotel.

Your job as the leader is to constantly raise the bar and develop and encourage the asset that will make or break your business: the people who work in it."

Tim Rumney
Proprietor, Castle Green Hotel, Kendal, Cumbria (a Best Western Plus hotel)

This is not a chapter about human relations in the hotel industry – there are plenty of textbooks books on this subject – but any new owner has to take immediate control of his staff and will face problems during the initial period of ownership.

Your staff will be the key element in your ultimate success, but they represent the biggest problem for any hotel owner. Although this is probably true for any business it is particularly so for a hotelier for three main reasons.

1 **A hotel has to rely on its staff to a far greater extent than most other businesses.** A hotel without staff is just a building – it is people who provide the services and who give it life. Few industries are in such face-to-face contact with the customer all the time. It follows that staff need the technical skills to carry out their job but they need something else – the social skills to enable them to engage with the guest. The success of most hospitality businesses depend on them correctly exercising those skills on a daily – even hourly – basis.

2 **The hospitality industry experiences high labour turnover – estimated at over 30 per cent though this varies from region to region and from outlet to outlet and can be much higher with poor management**. But even at 30 per cent, that means you have to recruit one third of your staff every year. The job categories that suffer the worst turnover are kitchen porters, room-maids and waiters though skilled kitchen staff are also very susceptible. The constant recycling of people puts ever greater strains on the business's ability to train new recruits in order to maintain standards.

3 **The hospitality industry continues to have a poor employment record, though this is gradually improving**. However, its image of low wages, anti-social hours and hard work has not yet been thrown off. This affects the recruitment of young people and their willingness to carve out a career for themselves in hospitality. It has also encouraged the employment of migrant labour in jobs that should be able to attract British labour.

There is no single cause of high rate of turnover. Of course, employees leave to take advantage of better – or different – job opportunities and to gain more experience but traditionally the industry has been plagued by the tendency for workers to vote with their feet: frequently, they change jobs for no reason other than to find a different place of work. This is probably more a sign of worker dissatisfaction as a result of poor management; indeed, a University of Surrey report put much of the blame on 'management abrogation':

"too often, staff are left to cope with difficult situations without management support."

This may go some way towards explaining the constant movement of staff from one employer to another even though few of them find substantially higher wages or markedly better working and living conditions. There is no doubt that the hospitality industry workforce is of an itinerant nature and is more mobile than that of many other industries. Many workers are also of foreign descent, who may be in this coun-

20

try as migrants and who find employment in hospitality relatively easy to find, and easy to quit. Another reason may lie in the high number of women workers, many of them working part-time, while the younger women leave to have children. As a result, absenteeism and time off to cope with a crisis at home can be high.

For all these reasons, a hotelier quickly has to learn to operate with a staff at less than full strength.

But not all this turnover is negative. The high incidence of seasonal, part-time work undertaken mainly by students is extremely beneficial as it suits both employer and employee. And the ability to bring in fresh blood when someone leaves can invigorate a business.

No unions

Another particular aspect of the hospitality industry is that union activity is very weak and few small employers will ever have to deal with union demands.

Without union representation, except in some of the largest companies, levels of pay and conditions of work do not typically match those of most unionised industries. This may be yet another cause for the industry's high rate of labour turnover. With no union to help work out a solution to a problem, hospitality staff will think nothing of walking out on their employer in a sudden burst of anger or frustration.

Certainly, employers and many employees have been happy to accept this, safe in the knowledge that many front-of-house staff earn tips or a share of the service charge which can boost their take-home pay well above NMW levels, without putting extra strain on the payroll. Other staff might be offered subsidised living accommodation while all typically receive meals on duty, uniforms and other benefits – all of which have to be costed into the payroll budget. Although HMRC makes great efforts to tax tip income there is little doubt that a proportion escapes the tax authorities' notice.

Whatever the reasons for turnover, having to recruit up to a third or more of your staff every year is a process which is frustrating, time-consuming and expensive.

By far the best solution is to provide working conditions that positively encourage your staff to stay happy and content in your employment. How do you achieve this?

It might be argued that high wages and good working conditions will ensure that staff will stay in satisfied employment but even that will not succeed if the manager does not manage and lead his staff so that they are motivated and encouraged to believe that they are important members of a team. Staff need to be made aware of the fact that on their efforts will depend the ultimate success of the enterprise. This is true of any industry but particularly so in a service industry.

In a report into best practice – *Improving Performance, Boosting Profits* – undertaken for the industry's Best Practice Forum by the University of Surrey, which houses one of the country's major schools of hospitality management – the most important factor to emerge in the success of any business was, unsurprisingly, its leadership.

Here, the owner of a small business has a huge advantage over the group-owned unit. This is because of his constant presence and his ability to set an example; he can introduce the standards he wants to set and maintain. He can develop a relationship that motivates his staff and enables them to identify with the business. If the owner displays an unwavering commitment to the hotel, that commitment will rub off onto his staff; if he does not, how can he expect the staff to be committed?

No-one with any experience of human or industrial relations, however, will deny that employees are unpredictable. They will often let you down, frequently argue and upset each other, cut corners in doing their job and will always need supervising and managing. In the hospitality industry, some will not be able to resist the temptation to fiddle you either in cash or stock in the bar or kitchen.

On the other hand, they will need to keep their cool with an irate customer and be polite to an over-friendly one. They must stay cheerful when events go awry and keep their heads when the hotel is overrun with business. They need to smile when they are on their knees and look happy when they are feeling their glummest. They need to be alert when they are exhausted at the end of the day and be happy at 6.00 am when they first come on duty.

Is it a surprise that hoteliers sometimes expect too much of their staff?

It follows that, as owner or manager, your major objective must be to create the conditions of work that enable staff to believe they are an essential part of the enterprise and are sufficiently empowered to make their own decisions, when necessary.

How you communicate this enthusiasm and commitment depends on your own style of management but, certainly, within the first week of your purchase you must hold an informal interview with each employee to understand their background, the current perception of their job, their attitude to their work and address any problems or grievances which they may have.

Ensuring that they know you mean business and that, at the same time, they are a key player in the future is the first hurdle to overcome in the relationship with your staff. Your ultimate aim must be to ensure that your physical presence is not always essential to maintain standards. If you have to be on the premises every hour of the day and night then there is something amiss. Truly successful leaders ensure that every member of staff is sufficiently well trained and motivated not to need your constant presence.

"When recruiting, remember you can't generally teach people to be friendly and hospitable. So if you have a choice between someone who has all the experience in the world but is socially difficult, and someone who you genuinely like but has limited experience (but in whom you see potential), then go for the latter every time."

Tim Hassell
Proprietor, Ilsington Country House Hotel, Devon

20

Taking over a new hotel is the time where clear vision and unwavering drive is important because it's a natural human reaction to resist change. If staff have worked in a particular way for many years, presumably to the satisfaction of their former boss, it is hard for them to understand why change is necessary. As a result, managing a changing scenario, such as buying a hotel that needs change, demands more people skills than managing the status quo, where change is not so urgent.

Staffing levels

How many employees are you going to need? How many of the existing staff do you want to stay? What skills do they need? What additional skills will *you* need? Is it possible to ask some staff to leave and will this involve redundancy payments?

It is impossible to generalise about how many employees a hotel needs.

Staffing ratios depend on the style of hotel, size of the property, its age and its type of business. An old property will probably need more staff than a modern hotel because the hotel will be less efficiently planned. A room maid can clean up to 12 bedrooms in a six hour shift (30 minutes per bedroom) but the size and state of the rooms are factors to be considered. A hotel with extensive public areas will clearly need more cleaning staff than one with a restricted ground floor; a hotel with extensive gardens will need in-house or contract gardeners. The area that creates the greatest demand for staff is the food and beverage department which, as we have seen, provides the lowest profit percentage. What implications on staff numbers will your plans have?

Working out staff numbers for your hotel will be a matter of experience but, generally speaking, it is better to have too few than too many staff.

This is not only because fewer staff mean lower costs but fewer staff also mean busier staff and staff, within reason, are happier when they are busy and have less time on their hands.

> **Remember, when calculating wages, use the wage departmental percentages that we used in our examples in Chapter 6.**

TUPE

If you want to dismiss existing staff, remember that The Transfer of Undertakings (Protection of Employment) Regulations (TUPE) protects employees' terms and conditions of employment when a business is transferred from one owner to another. Employees of the previous owner when the business changes hands automatically become employees of the new employer on the same terms and conditions. It's as if their employment contracts had originally been made with the new employer. Their continuity of service and any other rights are all preserved and there are very limited grounds for you to change any employee's existing contractual terms.

Once you have taken over the hotel, and met all the staff, do not assume that that is all the positive communication and explanation that you have to undertake.

The University of Surrey's research also revealed the need for good communication.

It is a vital ingredient in almost every aspect of the organisation. This is not only because staff must understand the business's goals and aspirations; you, as the owner, must also understand the needs and concerns of the staff.

Why communicate?

Because staff need:

1 To be properly trained to do the job in hand.

2 To know what standards the business is aiming for

3 To know what is expected of them and how they are to achieve – and maintain – those standards.

4 To have the appropriate authority that allows them to take decisions on their own.

5 To be encouraged to give their views and put forward new ideas.

In any hotel, a well-informed and highly motivated workforce is the difference between success and failure. Why? Because management and staff must share common objectives.

Involving staff in the planning and organisation of the hotel and making sure they understand your aims and aspirations will be the key factor in your success.

There is another advantage: good two-way communication – from the staff up and from the management down – can cost very little. Given the will, it is relatively simple to introduce but its benefits permeate any organisation, giving it strength and purpose. Encouraging staff to give their opinion and their ideas about their job and about the business in general gives them a sense of ownership, creates greater commitment and motivation and builds up a genuine team spirit. These are all important benefits in a service establishment like a hotel. Productivity will also improve because a strong culture is developed in which each member of staff feels involved in the success of the business.

One of the special strengths of managing a small business is that most communications can be informal which generally means face-to-face discussions, but too much unrecorded information can lead to ineffective or misunderstood communication.

20

Let's meet!

Staff meetings are frequently postponed because of pressures of work; they can also be very boring, extremely time-wasting and negative. It's your job to make sure they are relevant, lively, productive and positive.

The difficulty of getting a message out to staff should not be under-estimated We've all heard of Chinese whispers – the simple message that gets so distorted as it is passed around the organisation that by the time it reaches the last person it means the opposite to what was originally intended. Meetings have a role to play in any business but one benefit of regular meetings is that they demonstrate and encourage commitment. And, of course, your own commitment and enthusiasm will shine through and influence decisions.

Because of the 24/7 nature of much of the hotel industry, regular management briefings are essential, the bigger the hotel, the more vital and more regular they are.

But daily meetings should be short and work to an agenda that should be tightly controlled. Their purpose is to keep heads of department up-to-date, to look ahead to the day's (and the week's) events and to reflect on the events of the day just passed. In a small hotel, daily meetings may not be essential but it is important to give key members of staff a voice which they can use on a regular basis; a weekly or even a monthly meeting may be sufficient for this purpose. Alternatively, a meeting with an individual member of staff may be more effective. Whatever the means, the purpose is to keep all staff up-to-speed with the hotel's progress as a business, to absorb guest reactions and to ensure that every member of staff is working as a member of a team.

Remember, the key objective of almost every meeting is to make an informed decision so that the business can move on.

Three key benefits from good communication

1   If staff know what's going on in the business and are involved in decision-making, they will be less inclined to look for a job elsewhere.

2   Good communications help to resolve any possible friction that may be looming. Developing a positive environment where people support one another and work as a closely-knit team is how successful businesses achieve higher sales with the same number of staff, especially at busy times.

3   Perhaps, most important of all, by creating a climate in which staff are involved in decision-making and are frequently asked for their views and opinions, different solutions to problems are obtained. Such a climate can produce amazing new ideas. Young people frequently have a different approach to important issues. They may, for example, appreciate more clearly the need to harness the latest technology for the benefit of the business.

There are other ways of keeping staff informed.

A small hotel would not need to produce a staff newsletter but a one page photocopy is one way to making sure the same message gets out to every staff member; in the same way, the staff notice board can be an effective means of communication but is often used misguidedly. A notice board should not be strewn with notices which have passed their sell-by date. If these continue to be exhibited, staff will take no notice of them; worse, they won't notice the new messages that are being pinned up. Staff can also be encouraged to use the board for their own use but someone should be given the responsibility for keeping it tidy and up-to-date. Often, now, social media is used to keep staff in touch with events and developments.

Providing a positive working environment . . .

. . . . is essential to get the most out of staff and this means a true commitment to their support and development, not forgetting that those in the lowest paid jobs might require the most support and encouragement. Making sure they get the necessary training is a powerful element in staff support and, once trained, they become more productive. At the same time, the true leader develops a concern for the personal well-being of the people who work for him; they not only work for the business but spend a third of their life in it.

Creating a team is a critically important element of hotel management.

Making sure that every member is working together with a sense of common purpose and with an eye on achieving common goals, is, without doubt, the secret of a well run hotel. This common sense of purpose cannot be achieved without you, as the boss, setting the standards and ensuring that they are maintained; you have to generate commitment in the job, praising good work and encouraging and improving poor performers.

One thing is certain: if you don't lead the business, no-one else will.

In all this activity, the ultimate goal is to generate a sense of pride within the hotel so that staff have a sense of belonging to a great team which can achieve great things. Pride is an essential factor in team building and all kinds of benefits flow from it: greater commitment to work, stronger motivation, increased loyalty to the business, better customer service, greater productivity – all of which will act to discourage staff being attracted to another job elsewhere.

But do businesses employ too many staff?

20

This is not such a strange question as those beset by staff shortages might think. In an industry employing over 2m people it's inconceivable that there is not some over-employment, but how much? No-one knows. But even if it is as little as one per cent, that's over 20,000 people who may not be needed because businesses are not sufficiently careful in organising their workforce or staff are not sufficiently productive. The cost of that, assuming an average annual salary of £15,000, is £300m. One international chain discovered, for example, that more effective labour scheduling in its housekeeping department cut the department's payroll costs by 20 per cent.

As about one-third of your total revenue is spent on payroll costs keeping them under control must be your primary aim.

At the same time, your rates of pay must not fall behind the wages of other hotels in the area. Because of its impact on costs and profit, labour usage holds the key to higher productivity; the better the staff are trained, the leaner the business will be. The leaner it is, the more profitable it is.

Productivity

The Best Practice Forum measured labour productivity as the amount of sales revenue produced for every £1 spent on labour but found some big differences. Taking sales revenue, the average across all hospitality businesses was £3.24 in sales for each £1 spent on labour, yet the more successful, and productive, businesses were generating as much as £18.44 - six times as much.

Table 20.1: Sales revenue generated for every £1 spent on labour. Source: Best Practice Forum

	Lowest	Average	Highest
Hotels	£2.14	£4.05	£18.44
Pubs	£2.55	£5.70	£11.11
Restaurants	£1.66	£3.53	£6.10
Conference Venues	£1.45	£2.44	£3.67

There are five drivers that power productivity and, ultimately, profitability.

◆ Increasing customer spend.

◆ Building customer volume.

◆ Controlling material costs.

◆ Improving the way work is organized.

◆ Reducing labour costs.

Best Practice Forum studies concluded that more than a third (about 37 per cent) of working time is wasted. This is mainly a result of:

◆ Doing too much.

◆ Waiting around.

◆ Transporting.

◆ Unnecessary actions.

◆ Dealing with faults.

Three-quarters of that wasted time within hospitality businesses was down to poor planning, a lack of work organisation and inadequate supervision.

The implication of this means that every hotel has to keep its labour requirements on a tight leash. Matching staff numbers to likely demand is clearly the aim of every hotel but forecasting demand is difficult. That, however, only makes it all the more important to make the effort. It cannot be true to say that that no benefit can come from a close look at how staff are organised, how staff rotas are prepared and how methods of work are planned and undertaken.

In good times, it's all too easy to hire more staff to cope with peaks of demand . . . .

. . . but this might not be the right approach; when the troughs appear, payroll costs will surge to an uneconomic level and you will have to lay off or reduce hours.

Hiring additional staff should be a carefully considered option and should only be undertaken after you have analysed individual staff workloads. Can work processes be better organised to avoid hiring more staff? Can existing staff be better trained so that additional skills enable them to cope? Can investment in new equipment help solve the problem?

This highlights the need for simple job descriptions and the preparation of operating manuals that lay down the standards of work expected and how they are to be achieved. In the long-term, the aim might be to introduce a form of bonus or profit-sharing so that staff have a personal interest in the continued success of the business.

Seven points for successful leadership

1   Communicate your aims and ambitions to all your staff. They need to know where you are going.

2   Build the team – then staff will go the extra mile for you.

3   Support your staff – don't let them flounder in difficult circumstances.

4   Make sure your staff are properly trained.

5   Encourage your staff to be proud of what they do by making sure standards are maintained.

6   Thank your staff when they've done well – and positively guide them when standards slip. Recognition is a vital human need.

7   Let your staff share in your success. Reward them fairly and ensure they know the basis of their rewards.

20

Staff turnover

For many businesses, staff recruitment is like filling a bucket with a hole in the bottom; the cost of this exodus is high. But how high? The hotel has to pay to advertise or pay an agency. Then there is the cost involved in recruiting and selecting new members of staff which may take several weeks, during which time the work involved falls on others. This, in turn, puts extra pressure on them, which might encourage them to leave as well; this could affect standards of service and thus lead to guest disappointment. Once appointed, the new staff member has to be inducted and trained with the added burden that he might upset customers through inexperience or incompetence until he finally settles in.

Adding up all these costs can be a salutary experience and almost certainly is higher than most operators believe or want to believe.

Controlling staff turnover is thus a key aspect of hotel management.

How do you measure labour turnover?

Add up all the staff who have left in the last 12 months divide it into the total number you employ and multiply by 100. Thus, if 12 staff have left during the year (including perhaps three kitchen porters who each left the same position consecutively after three months in the job) and you employ an average of 24 staff, then your staff turnover is 12 divided by 24 x 100 – which equals 50 per cent.

It is, however, more accurate to take account of part-time staff so that you have a staff turnover representing full-time equivalent workers but this is not generally necessary in a small establishment.

Let's induct!

Research shows that the majority of new employees, if they are going to leave, will quit within the first few weeks of employment. This tells us something about the importance of induction. Too often, induction is neglected or even omitted. This is a grave mistake because this is the time when new recruits are at their most vulnerable. They know very little about the business, how it works, how their boss works – they know few if any of their work colleagues, do not understand the work culture of the business and are even unfamiliar with the layout of the building. Little wonder they feel insecure and unsure of their place in the business.

Preventing staff departures during these critically important first few weeks must be a top priority . . .

. . . and ignoring adequate time for induction is wasting the time you spent on recruitment and, just as important, the money it has cost to recruit.

When new members of staff join, a proper induction programme is essential. Someone should be put in charge of them – often called a buddy system – to make sure they have someone to turn to and are not left to flounder. Induction can last a day or a few days or as long as a week and it is an investment that can save you money. It is certainly time well spent if the new recruit stays to become a valuable member of your team.

Let's train!

Too often, smaller businesses tend to poach the staff that others have trained.

However, the best way to encourage staff to stay in your employment is to enable them to reach their maximum potential through the training and development that you provide for them. Making sure that there are career development opportunities for staff so that they can see the chance of advancement if they want to, is a powerful motivating factor and encourages them to stay in your employment. This is a key benefit for your business and you gain through greater productivity, better standards and better customer service. The individual gains through greater job satisfaction.

Advancement and promotion is naturally more difficult in a small business where opportunities are limited and where staff may be perfectly happy with their present job responsibilities and are not seeking advancement. Nevertheless, giving staff the opportunity for personal development is good practice and the wise hotelier will recognise the role that training can play not only in upgrading skills but in staff retention.

Not all of this training needs to be outsourced – some of the most valuable can be provided on-the-job if there are sufficient skilled workers in-house. Training can take place in more informal surroundings by gathering relevant staff together and taking them through a training session. Advice on training can be obtained from any local college offering catering and hospitality courses or from national organisations such as People 1st, the industry's Sector Skills Council.

Training sessions also provide an opportunity to encourage staff to introduce new ideas and suggestions.

Staff should be encouraged to make suggestions for improving the way the business is run always with the ultimate aim of maintaining and improving standards. Research has shown that involving staff in decisions about the business can be an important factor in its success.

What about multi-skilling?

Not all employees crave such variety in their work. But there are examples of hotels that have introduced multi-skilling in the front of house areas, particularly in the bar and lounge areas and ground floor activities such as food service. This enables staff to be switched from one section to another during times of peak demand. Of course, multi-skilling can only be undertaken by staff who want to take on more than one job and it demands good training, but it can be very effective – with an

20

added bonus: it encourages staff to gain an insight into the work of other departments so that they work better, are better motivated and are more willing to help when the pressure builds.

Switching staff from one job to another at peak periods of service pressure can contain payroll costs but some financial incentive is usually necessary to encourage staff to undertake a range of different job training, the cost of this being offset by higher productivity.

If multi-tasking is to succeed, it has to be introduced carefully. Over a period of 18 months, you could aim to train or develop up to half your full-time staff in one other department's set of skills – for example, training half your waiting staff as bar staff, or vice versa.

What about standards?

When you take over you will be faced with one of three challenges: you will have to establish standards, maintain them or improve them.

Only in exceptional cases would you want to reduce them. But standards can be established only if you know exactly what you want to do. Staff cannot be expected to work well if nobody has told them what is required of them. The sooner you tell them, the better will be the changeover to your ownership.

In every area, you will have to work through people. If you are seeking to improve standards, do all the staff understand what you want and are they capable of achieving those standards? If not, why not? Do they need retraining or replacing?

Raising standards may not, however, just be a question of staff attitudes and competence. One hotelier took over a hotel where the staff were already demoralised and could hardly care less. The first thing that he did was to shut some of the rooms, get in the decorators and plumbers, renovate the bathrooms and buy in new carpets, linen and curtains. New vacuum cleaners were purchased and more efficient cleaning materials were obtained.

Staff reaction was positive as the action showed that the new owner was serious. In the early weeks, the owner accompanied staff explaining exactly how he wanted changes to be made in the cleaning routine – and why (reasons are important because staff resent changes in their working routine). A new work scheme meant that staff were able to clean the rooms more quickly. He took the same approach in the kitchen.

By these actions, the new owner demonstrated his positive intentions far more effectively than any words could achieve.

An owner's drive, his leadership skills, his personality, together with his ability to communicate with his team will dictate the success of the new enterprise. But it will be people – your staff – who provide the means by which this success is achieved.

What to read?

The employment area has become a legal minefield for employers so an owner must quickly understand the main provisions of the most important employment laws, and have the facility for keeping up to date with new legislation.

The Pink Book: Legislation for tourist accommodation produced by VisitEngland (www. vistengland.com).

Employment Law for Hotels, Pubs and Restaurants by Julian Yew, Pennington Manches (www.penningston.co.uk) gives information on the legal issues of employing staff.

Human Resource Management in the Hospitality Industry: A Guide to Best Practice, by Michael Boella and Stephen Goss-Turner (9th edition 2013 Routledge,) is a standard textbook on human relations in the industry and covers all aspects of managing and developing staff.

Staff will always be your biggest challenge

1   Staff costs, on average, amount to 30 per of total turnover but can be much more. They are your biggest single cost.

2   Managing and motivating your staff will be the key element in your success. Or the reason for your failure.

3   Communicating with your staff is your most important task; if you don't tell them what's going on, why should they care?

4   The hospitality industry's poor image makes recruitment difficult.

5   Create favourable conditions of work that enable staff to believe they are an essential part of the enterprise . . .

6   . . . because they alone provide the means by which your success will be achieved.

7   High staff turnover (over 30 per cent) is damaging and costly. It's usually caused by poor management.

8   Not all turnover is negative – some turnover brings in fresh blood.

9   Recruitment or retention – both pose major challenges.

10 What skills do your staff need? How best to ensure they have them?

"People are the lifeblood of the hospitality industry. To ensure employees are engaged, fully committed and buy into the vision and mission of the business you should create an environment and a culture whereby they enjoy their jobs. Your business plan should include a human resources strategy to ensure continuous improvements through training and development."

Harry Murray MBE
Chairman, Lucknam Park Hotel and Spa, Wiltshire

20

21 Keeping up the investment

No hotel or restaurant takes care of itself. It needs to be kept up-to-date to ensure that it is able to continue to attract the market it aims at. So you need to have a Repairs and Renewals budget that allows you to invest in the property in order to keep it up to standard.

In December 2013, the Lanesborough Hotel, the five star luxury property at London's Hyde Park Corner, closed for a nine month refurbishment (although it was actually closed for more than 15 months) selling off all its furniture and furnishings at auction. With new designs, it wanted to start all over again. In the words of the hotel's general manager, Geoffrey Gelardi, "The renovations are part of the hotel's commitment to providing guests with an incomparable experience and will incorporate the latest in contemporary luxuries and technology."

The interesting fact about this closure is that the hotel only opened in 1991. With just over 22 years of operation and with the constant care and attention lavished on such a luxury property you would have thought that a complete refurbishment was low down on the list of the hotel's priorities. In fact, such refurbishments are now commonplace, though not many lead to such a lengthy closure. Hotels which have opened only in the last couple of decades are having their rooms and public areas upgraded, restyled and revamped. At a time of intense competition in the marketplace the requirement to keep pace with modern trends is overwhelming. The need to introduce new styles of comfort and to incorporate more up-to-date facilities, including new technology such as internet access and wi fi in rooms, is ever more pressing – hence The Lanesborough's multi-million pound revamp.

Refurbishment programmes are costing millions of pounds every year

– in London, the cost of upgrading the Savoy Hotel in 2008, which originally opened in 1889, was initially costed at £100m and eventually came in at £220m (at least, that was what was admitted). Other major hotels have had similar upgrades. It is significant that most of them are company or group owned but independent operators must take note of what's going on in the industry. **Without constant reinvestment, they are in danger of being left behind.**

A hotel, once built and furnished, is not set in stone. It has to be kept up-to-date; it must recognise changing trends in fashion and style and be aware of evolving customer demands. Most guests expect a hotel room to be at least as good as their own at home; in expensive properties they expect the room to be much better. So no hotel can rest on its laurels.

In today's intensely competitive environment, hotels must innovate, refresh and refurbish if they are to keep alive their attraction to their regular clientele and attract new markets at the same time.

One reason for this is that it is a common assumption by many people coming into the hotel industry that guests will take as much care of hotel property as they will of their own. Sadly, nothing is further from the truth. Except in a few isolated instances, there is little intentional damage in a well-run hotel but customers will unintentionally damage property in minor but irritating ways. They will accidentally tear curtains or drop keys or other heavy objects in the wash basin or floor tiles. They will scratch or mark lift doors and pilfer spoons and other pieces of cutlery to say nothing of more valuable ornaments or pieces of equipment.

All this is over and above the normal wear and tear that a hotel bedroom or busy restaurant can realistically expect: even with regular upkeep, many a hotel, looking ultra smart when it opened 20 years ago, is now looking faded and care worn – hence The Lanesborough's revamp.

Of course, the heavier the usage the greater is the need for refurbishment. It's commonly accepted that hotels with 80 per cent average occupancy need to upgrade their bedrooms every three years; hotels averaging 75 per cent occupancy need to upgrade every four years and those with 70 per cent occupancy need to upgrade every five years.

Carpets need regular cleaning and wear with heavy traffic; bed and table linen need replacing in direct proportion to the number of times they are laundered, wallpaper and paintwork fade with age, chairs give way with constant use, styles of furniture and décor that were modern can rapidly become dated.

The hotelier must take all this in his stride but the consequence is clear: in any hotel there is a normal cycle of repairs and renewals which is quite separate from any plans you might have to extend the property by adding new bedrooms or other facilities. Constant re-investment in the fabric of the building and the facilities offered – called Repairs and Renewals – is critically important and a hotel's maintenance programme needs to be realistically and carefully planned, and budgeted.

There is little point in spending money and time on winning new customers through your expensive marketing efforts, only to throw them all away when your hard-to-win guests actually arrive at your hotel.

21

Unfortunately, in times of recession or in a severe downturn in business, this budget is frequently the first to be cut back (followed, typically, by the marketing budget). In hard times, it is natural to think that the chairs that should have been renewed this year can probably last another year; guests probably won't notice the tired paintwork that needs renewing; the bathrooms are clean – even if the grouting needs attention and the cracked tiles need replacing.

What the hotelier is in danger of forgetting is that his guests will notice the property's shortcomings more quickly than he does; they bring a fresh eye to the scene while most hoteliers are too close to the front line to see objectively.

How much to re-invest?

How much should a hotel re-invest every year to ensure that the property is kept up-to-date and up-to-scratch?

This depends on the type and scale of the property but a minimum of five per cent of turnover is a realistic figure for most hotels. If it is a modern hotel, the need to spend large sums of money on R&R is unlikely to be as great as it would be in an older property where the key electric, plumbing and gas systems may need regular attention and where some of the facilities are wearing out. On the other hand, some buildings constructed in the Victorian age may be in better structural shape than those built since the last war – indeed, their solid construction may present problems if you want to knock walls down to enlarge rooms; as a result, Victorian buildings can be more expensive to convert. The advantage of a modern building is that the service pipes and cables will have access chambers; pipes will also be lagged so that they are more energy efficient, while air conditioning and telecommunications systems will have been integrated into the initial design of the building not built in later, as is the case with older structures.

Repairs and renewals should be budgeted out of revenue

In a small hotel, there is much to be said for putting aside a certain amount each month into the R&R account so that the money is there if needed. Apart from the intended and expected items to be replaced or repaired, there are bound to be times when there are unexpected emergencies which need immediate attention and financial outlay. Planning for the unexpected puts you in a better position to cope with it when it arrives, as it inevitably will.

Planning your maintenance programme

The best course of action in planning your maintenance programme is to draw up a list of essential tasks giving them an order of priority. It is unlikely that you will be able to afford everything that needs doing but, unless the premises and its furnishings are in such a poor shape that they act as a positive deterrent to any guest, you will have to prioritise and concentrate on the most important areas at the beginning.

It may not only be front-of-house, of course, that needs attention – the kitchen and the back-of house are equally important. Behind the scenes, you need to give attention to the kitchen equipment, boilers and the cleaning of trunking, canopies and drains.

Regular maintenance contracts on these essential pieces of equipment are important if they are not to break down at some inconvenient moment or need to be replaced before the end of their expected life.

Ensure that you enter into contracts which provide an out-of-hours service without swingeing surcharges, as equipment failures have a nasty habit of occurring when the hotel is at its busiest – at the height of service, for example.

At the outset of your purchase, you will have already identified those areas that need immediate attention.

One approach in any maintenance programme is to assume that the priority areas should be those that yield the greatest revenues but this cannot always be the main consideration. You might have to put in a new boiler or re-install the toilets, neither of which will generate any revenue but without which the hotel can hardly operate. However, if the hotel's bedrooms are in poor shape and its target market is mainly corporate business, then it would be sensible to bring the rooms up to standard before you begin work on the public areas. An overnight businessman, for example, may not even enter the lounge area during his stay.

On the other hand, if a large proportion of your revenue comes from the restaurant and bars then those areas might be given priority and the bedrooms left until later. But remember, out-of date rooms will be a deterrent to building up the most profitable side of the business.

Whatever decisions you make, plan the programme carefully because it is important that you keep operating while the refurbishment is in progress; the more rooms you have off the less revenue you will be earning to pay for the work. This is why in many hotels, maintenance programmes are scheduled over a period of several years so that rooms can be taken off-stream during the quietest times causing the least disruption to guests and revenues.

One aspect that is frequently forgotten in any R&R programme is the need to make staff more productive; investing capital in plant and machinery enables you to reduce staff numbers.

More efficient catering equipment in the kitchen and food service areas might mean fewer staff but would also give your staff greater satisfaction and better working conditions. Good design is a particularly important consideration in any kitchen upgrade. The introduction of appropriate computer equipment will enable front-office staff to perform more efficiently; on-line booking, for example, needs little human interface whereas a telephone booking could take up ten minutes of a receptionist's time. This is not to say that the hotel should discourage potential guests from personally telephoning the hotel – indeed, the more direct contact there is, the better – but many guests are happy just to book the room without having to pick up the phone. From the hotel's point of view this saves staff time and cuts back on mistakes.

Similarly, the poor design of bedrooms and bathrooms can result in additional

21

work for room maids. Cleaning will be made easier if you dispense with corners and crevices in favour of rounded edges; fitted furniture is more efficient than free standing items. Bathroom floors should be tiled or have a sealed plastic floor so that they are easily washed and a drain hole in the floor is useful for those guests who inadvertently leave the bath water running (they do). If the baths are old fashioned and very large, it would probably be more economic to replace them with smaller baths which use less water; alternatively, high quality walk-in showers are becoming increasingly popular if space is limited. Shower curtains over the bath are generally detested by guests; much better to fit a glass or plastic screen which is more hygienic and more easily cleaned. **Sufficient shelves in the bathroom for toiletries are often noticeable by their absence**. If you are refurbishing a bedroom, make sure there are enough power points at the right height for all the in-room facilities such as the electric kettle, mini bar, computer terminals, hair dryer (not forgetting that the plug should be near a mirror) and for the room maids who need to clean the room. Lighting and lighting levels should also be checked and there should be appropriate mirrors for make-up as well as one full length mirror.

Don't forget to test all the mattresses to check that they do not need renewing. As the new owner, you would be wise to stay overnight in every room in the hotel to check their comfort and facilities.

When re-equipping bedrooms and public areas, purchase the most appropriate fittings. A heavy duty carpet will appear ruinously expensive but, in the long term, it will be cheaper than one of a poor quality that needs to be replaced within a few years. Resist the temptation to drive to the nearest retail store to purchase the goods immediately because this will be an expensive way of buying new capital items. There are buying organisations which specialise in hotel and catering equipment – see end of chapter.

Some couples who buy a hotel believe that they will be able to do their own redecoration and refurbishment. A do-it-yourself approach may be feasible in a resort property that closes during the winter season but this is not a very practical solution for a hotel that is open all-year-round; besides, you are diverting yourself from other and even more important activities. Only the largest hotels can employ their own handymen so most hoteliers have to engage outside workmen. Here, again, the cheapest quote may not be the best.

The critical consideration is not the cost but the time spent in completing the job.

You are losing potential revenue every day the room is out of commission so accepting a quote that is cheap simply because the decorator intends to work on the room on an 'as and when' basis, using workmen as they become available from other projects, is not in your best interests. The loss of room revenue incurred would mean that the cheapest quote could turn out to be the most expensive.

In all your maintenance work, try to build up a reliable and dependable team of tradesmen including a plumber, electrician, jobbing builder and carpenter who you can call on in emergencies.

Cost benefit exercises

Begin any maintenance and redecoration scheme or extension assessing its cost benefit. Although it can be difficult to estimate in precise financial terms what benefit will accrue by spending money on refurbishing a bedroom, the primary consideration must be the certain knowledge that if the rooms are not brought up to standard there will be a certain disbenefit: you will begin to lose trade. In the short-term this may not be particularly noticeable but in the long-term the dip in occupancy will be clear. You will lose out to rival hotels which do keep up-to-date.

The same difficulty arises when considering upgrading other areas; there will be no directly attributable additional revenue if you upgrade the public areas but how much trade will you lose by leaving them in a sub-standard state? It's easy to forget that public areas make an immediate impact and are the ones which create the first impression.

Except in the most basic guest house or hotel, a bath/shower room en suite is now universally expected and any rooms that you may have that do not have this facility should certainly be an immediate target for conversion even if this means that you lose some bedrooms. Holiday Inn, which built its first hotel in 1952, ensured all its bedrooms were en suite from the very beginning.

Part of any cost benefit exercise is to calculate the loss of income from the bedrooms against the additional revenue you gain from being able to sell en suite rooms at a higher price. You have a similar consideration when converting single rooms into doubles, or introducing a bath/shower into a room.

The five major considerations in any scheme are:

1 How many bedrooms do you lose to make room for the bath/shower room or to create larger suites?

2 What income do you lose from the lost bedrooms?

3 How much extra occupancy will be generated by the new rooms?

4 How much extra can you charge for the rooms with private facilities and over what period of time will the investment be recouped?

5 How much revenue will you lose while the rooms are out of commission?

The answers will dictate how much you need to budget and the payback timescale.

The need for planning is important as conversion costs can be high – anything up to £25,000 per room depending on the structure of the building, the run of the plumbing pipes and the extravagance of the bathroom fittings. Even refitting an existing bathroom with new tiling, flooring and new facilities can be well over £10,000. A similar exercise needs to be undertaken with any extension you are considering. A new bedroom block added to an existing hotel in the provinces would cost between

21

£40,000-£100,000 per room depending on the style of hotel, the difficulties of the site and the facilities installed; in London, the cost would be higher. A project of this nature, however, demands a separate budget as it would not be funded from the R&R budget but from a separate development budget which may require the raising of additional finance.

Buying Organisations

Best Western Hotels, www.bestwestern.co.uk

Beacon, www.beaconpurchasing.co.uk

Pelican, www.pelicanbuying.co.uk

Beacon is affiliated to Best Western Hotels, the marketing consortium.

Buying organisations enable individual businesses to fulfill all their purchasing needs at rates that would normally be unavailable to individual, independent operators. They can also provide services that include price comparisons, price guarantees and tender management as well as web based services from e-billing to full e-procurement solutions.

Five pieces of advice

1   A hotel is not set in stone: it has to be kept up to date . . .

2   ... regular investment is needed to innovate, refresh and refurbish.

3   Yes, guests can be careless . . . but they will notice poor standards of upkeep quicker than you.

4   The R&R annual budget should be in the region of five per cent of total turnover. Plan it over several years to avoid too much disruption.

5   Prioritise the key revenue-earning areas first.

– and five key questions to answer

1   Can you develop new markets if you introduce new facilities?

2   Will the cost of new facilities yield worthwhile profit?

3   Can you introduce new equipment to reduce the need for staff or to add to staff skills?

4   Have you slept in every room to check them all out?

5   Are you using a buying organisation to obtain furnishings, furniture and equipment? It will save you money.

22 What of the future?

No-one can predict the negative impact of wars, acts of terrorism, climate changes and other factors that deter domestic and world travel. But it is worth noting that tourism is a hardy beast.

In the last decade, while wars have raged in the Middle East and Afghanistan as well as in other parts of the world, international tourism has been on the increase. People's memories are short. The Twin Towers attack, the London and Madrid bombings and more recent outrages do not remain in the public memory for long, hideous though they are and horrific as they remain for those involved. **New York and London are experiencing record levels of visitor demand, along with many other parts of the world. This trend is likely to continue unless there is some catastrophic upheaval in world affairs.**

The UK will benefit from this as will its hotel industry. Of course, there will be changes. The march of the franchise chains will continue, threatening the independent hotelier with their brand names, sophisticated reservation systems and standardised facilities even more than they have in the past. The growth of the budget chains will also influence the independent hotelier, making life more difficult for him and providing yet more competition as they emerge on established doorsteps. At the other end of the scale, five star luxury will become six star and then seven star as hotels attempt to outgun each other by enhancing guest comfort and seeking to attract the wealthiest of the global travellers. **And that's another point – the number of wealthy individuals has grown hugely in the last decade and will continue to do so, leading to ever-increasing demands for luxury accommodation and food. The need to upgrade becomes relentless.**

Social media will continue to play an ever more important part in sales and marketing activities – and who knows how that will develop in the future? Tomorrow's hoteliers will have to understand ever more comprehensively the role that technology plays in what is, basically, a traditional service industry.

How this will play out in the future is anyone's guess. Amenity creep in every hotel sector – whereby an ever greater number of additional facilities is provided in existing hotel properties (which includes the budget sector) – will gather pace. This is good from the guest's perspective as hotel upgrades, hotel improvements, refurbishments and extensions will continue; standards will thus rise. And so will prices. The impact of this on the independent hotelier will be significant. The pressure will be on him to invest further in his property the longer he retains ownership. But if the future demands ever greater levels of investment on the part of every hotelier his prices, also, will have to rise to keep pace. This will challenge his existing market.

Of course, there will be some moves towards automation. Many budget hotels, for example, already have automatic check-in and check-out though how far this can go remains unclear. Unless in the cheapest hotel, people will still expect some personal service and not be served by a machine. How efficiently service is provided will be the key to success and the wage bill is likely to remain the highest cost item in any hotel operation. Using contracted labour, which can rein in costs, might be one route to a more efficient operation; many major hotel groups and the largest hotels now employ contracted cleaning and housekeeping staff in favour of recruiting and directly employing their own people.

Some hotels have also contracted out their staff feeding arrangements and others have leased out their restaurant to a celebrity chef, thereby reducing – indeed, eliminating – the cost of their notoriously difficult food and beverage operation. There is scope, too, for reducing the number of staff backstage through the use of machines – automatic glass and dishwashers are only two examples – and through good design. Good kitchen equipment saves much time and frustration. In front-of-house, carpets need constant upkeep but wooden floors are almost upkeep-free. Nevertheless, the need to provide the kind of service that guests expect remains paramount. Sacrificing service staff for automation or for self-service (for example at breakfast) are certainly options but they must be most carefully considered and constantly monitored.

Because of its high percentage cost, the wage bill must be kept under constant review and this will become ever more important, particularly if the National Minimum Wage moves nearer to the level of the London Living Wage. With additional pension costs being imposed on employers by the government, operators will find their wage ratio under increasing pressure. Even so, recruiting and retaining the right staff will remain the most difficult of all management responsibilities and its cost will rise particularly if the UK economy strengthens. Energy and food prices, too, will remain volatile. Can tariffs rise to keep pace? As it is, migration has kept wages (and wage percentages) down in the last decade as foreign workers take up jobs in the UK industry that could be performed by unwilling British born youngsters – but at a higher cost; unfortunately, as an industry, hospitality does not attract them in sufficient numbers. The challenge for the future will be to encourage more British people into hospitality which is something that it has failed to achieve in the past.

The trend toward short holidays in the UK (and more of them) will continue; so will the eagerness of British people to travel abroad on holiday. This is largely driven by their wish to enjoy guaranteed sunshine which the UK can never provide. The impact of the recent economic recession has been noticeable but the number of those holidaying abroad will inevitably rise again. They are, anyway, of sufficient magnitude to be of lasting concern to the hotel industry in the UK as more British people travel abroad than overseas visitors arrive in Britain – though the latter numbers are rising, also. This is a situation that will endure so hoteliers will need to be mindful where their custom comes from and be very aware of their markets and how they reach them. London can more or less take care of itself – it will remain one of the world's greatest business and leisure cities – but hotels in the provinces must be wary. Without greater demand and compensating increases in tariffs, ever higher costs will gnaw into profitability and endanger survival.

In all this, what role does government have to play? Successive governments have largely ignored tourism – a curious situation when it employs well over 2m people and has an annual turnover in excess of £100bn. A string of tourism ministers has not encouraged the industry to believe that government is wildly supportive and adverse legislation, such as air passenger duty and visa restrictions actively deter visitor numbers.

The rate of VAT, at 20 per cent, is one of the highest in Europe, and makes the UK less attractive than France, Germany or other competitor countries in Europe which have a lower rate. It's doubtful if the current campaign to lower VAT for the hospitality industry alone will succeed given London's extraordinary success as a tourism destination; in any case, the government doubts the industry's figures of the gain the Treasury would make if VAT was to be reduced to five per cent for hotel accommodation and there is no guarantee that any reduction in VAT would be passed on.

Support for VisitBritain and other national promotional agencies is somewhat niggardly and there is some doubt about their long-term future while the introduction of Local Enterprise Partnerships, which succeeded Regional Development Agencies and which were hailed as the saviours of local businesses, including those in hospitality, has had little impact. This type of local agency is always subject to political whims. Nor is there much money for local tourism promotion – something that is unlikely to change.

So the message is clear: the hotel industry remains largely on its own as has always been the case. It will survive, prosper even, only by its own innovations, by its own commitment and by its own endeavours. No-one purchasing a hotel or guest house should think otherwise.

Being an independent hotelier is what it says – being independent. Only by an owner's own efforts will he (or she) ever prosper.

22

Index